The RHETORIC of SOCIAL INTERVENTION

To William R. Brown
Friend, Scholar, Intervener
and
In memory of Lee Snyder
Friend, Colleague, Contributor

The RHETORIC of SOCIAL INTERVENTION

AN INTRODUCTION

SUSAN K. OPT
Salem College

MARK A. GRING
Texas Tech University

SAGE

Los Angeles • London • New Delhi • Singapore

Copyright © 2009 by SAGE Publications, Inc.

Illustrations: Gregory S. Opt, The Graphic Image, Dayton, OH.
http://thegraphicimage.com Photograph: Preston C. Opt

For information:

SAGE Publications, Inc.
2455 Teller Road
Thousand Oaks,
    California 91320
E-mail: order@sagepub.com

SAGE Publications India Pvt. Ltd.
B 1/I 1 Mohan Cooperative
    Industrial Area
Mathura Road, New Delhi 110 044
India

SAGE Publications Ltd.
1 Oliver's Yard
55 City Road
London EC1Y 1SP
United Kingdom

SAGE Publications Asia-Pacific
    Pte. Ltd.
33 Pekin Street #02-01
Far East Square
Singapore 048763

Printed in the United States of America

Library of Congress Cataloging-in-Publication Data

Opt, Susan K.
The rhetoric of social intervention: an introduction/Susan K. Opt, Mark Gring.
    p. cm.
Includes bibliographical references and index.
ISBN 978-1-4129-5689-5 (cloth)
ISBN 978-1-4129-5690-1 (pbk.)
    1. Social change. 2. Social problems. 3. Rhetoric. I. Gring, Mark. II. Title.

HM831.O78 2009
303.401—dc22   2008017671

This book is printed on acid-free paper.

08   09   10   11   12   10   9   8   7   6   5   4   3   2   1

Acquisitions Editor:	Todd R. Armstrong
Editorial Assistant:	Aja Baker
Production Editor:	Astrid Virding
Copy Editor:	Alison Hope
Typesetter:	C&M Digitals (P) Ltd.
Proofreader:	Gail Naron Chalew
Cover Designer:	Candice Harman
Marketing Manager:	Carmel Schrire

Contents

SECTION II: RSI CRITICISM ESSAYS   165

List of Figures and Tables

Foreword

One index to our hard-work-and-perseverance culture is how often we are reminded of Einstein's wondering what would appear if one could ride a light beam. That playfulness is recited with a tone of wonder in a culture that touts head-on, hard-headed, practical attacks on problems.

The writers of this book, when studying the model they explicate, came to their study in a spirit of play, asking "What If," which of course entailed, "Let's Pretend." The joy of inquiry that they and many others experienced made my last years of graduate teaching an exhilarating time. I hope that users of this book will find in themselves a spirit of inquiry enlivened by the free air of intrinsically motivated scholarship, described powerfully by another of my colleague-students, Professor Lee Snyder, in Chapter 6 "Under the Lens." (In a spirit of play with time, the reader may want to read the chapters in reverse order.)

In that spirit, readers will know, recognizing that while tools of the model need to be practiced, the pleasure of inquiry lies not in their rehearsal, but rather in what they help the scholar see in the case being investigated.

In that spirit, readers will not be tempted to practice factionalism in relation to other models of rhetorical inquiry. Each promises to let us see and understand something about a communication event that others may not.

In that spirit, the Rhetoric of Social Intervention (RSI) model is seen as feedforward, not as destination.

What if the model laid open for someone the dynamics operating in a blended family?

What if the model allowed someone to "see" what happens over time in work environments, including what is afoot in development of norms in mixed-gender, ethnically diverse work forces?

What if the model helped us to "see" how the public converges on an interpretation of public affairs?

What if the model helped us depict ideology carried as a side effect to globalization? Would such insight help Westerners empathize with followers of Islam who say that they are under attack from the West?

What if to someone—given advances in sampling public opinion—poll results gave "communication indicators" prompting interventions premised on a communication model: interventions that would be analogous to those now based on models of economics? Would these then be complementary to legal and economic starting points for communication-policy studies? Could such communication-based interventions promote social change but spare people the paroxysm of revolution?

And what of the individual level of appreciating the popular and fine arts? What if the RSI model opened up reasons *I Love Lucy* is in perpetual reruns? Why concrete art speaks to us in this day of the disposable? Why music concerts function as religious experience?

Closer to home, perhaps, what if the model helped you "see" how you as intervener might promote innovations at home, school, or work?

Further, as side effect of such studies, what if one's experience of reality were marked by an increasing perception or conception of the universe and all beings in it as being holistic? Of the sense that, in a happening, all the universe is there, all the time? Of the cognition that category systems are based neither on "either-or" nor "both-and," but rather on *both* "either-or" *and* "both-and?" What if you find yourself adopting a consistently reflective attitude toward what is said? That is, you consistently were aware of symbolically constructed reality?

Such possibilities, multiplied and selected from for your own study give energy for scholarly mountain climbing—not in order to be King or Queen of the Mountain, but because the view is better up there.

Happy climbing!

William R. Brown
Worthington, Ohio

Preface

Although this book is geared primarily to upper-level undergraduate and beginning graduate students in courses such as rhetorical criticism, rhetorical theory, public address, social movements, and persuasion, its approach to social change can be applied in other communication areas, such as organizational, family, health, and public relations. It presents a basic model of communication that builds students' abilities to reflect on their symbolic nature and to act as critics and initiators of social interventions.

This book, which introduces the Rhetoric of Social Intervention (RSI) model, conceived by William R. Brown (1978, 1982, 1986, 1987), can serve as the primary text or as a supplement for a course. The ideal classroom environment for it is one in which the RSI concepts are actively discussed, giving students the opportunity to respond to and challenge the model's premises. In addition, the discussion lends itself to in-class group work in which students talk through the intellectual challenges that the RSI model might pose.

The RSI model directs students' attention to communication as the basic driver of social change, an approach compatible with perspectives of other fields of study. Such compatibility promotes interdisciplinary insights into communication and social change and, at the same time, establishes the communication field as a full partner. In addition, the RSI perspective complements other critical approaches advocated within the field, such as Neo-Aristotelian, Narrative, Dramatistic, Fantasy-Theme, Feminist, Cultural, and Ideographic analysis.

Besides encouraging students to focus on communication as the catalyst of social change, the RSI approach

- develops students' awareness of the communication patterns that drive social change,

- enables students to contemplate the holistic nature of social change as interventional side effects,
- allows students to critique systemic levels of the communication process ranging from the intrapersonal to the cultural,
- offers students an easily accessible framework for critically analyzing rhetorical intervention within a social system, and
- provides a systemic methodology for guiding students' actions as social change agents.

In all, the RSI model offers a means by which students can develop both as critics and as mediators of social change.

Until now, no convenient, accessible, single resource for teaching the RSI model was available. Instructors had to create classroom materials drawn from Brown's published articles and handouts of his unpublished work. This book integrates both the published and unpublished pieces to explore the RSI model's foundations, assumptions, and use in analyzing and promoting social change.

Section I of the book introduces the RSI concepts and describes the process and practice of critiquing and enacting social interventions. Section II presents student and scholar essays that demonstrate the model's critical application and offer opportunities to critique scholarly expectations associated with critical writing.

This book develops students' skills as critics and change agents and assists instructors' teaching of the material through the following features:

- A chapter devoted to the process of conducting and writing rhetorical criticism
- A chapter dedicated to the process of creating and enacting social interventions
- A service-learning activity throughout Section I that unites the RSI concepts and provides students with a real-world application opportunity
- An "Under the Lens" featurette in each chapter that supports students by sharing others' experiences with the RSI model and encourages reflectivity on their own experiences
- End-of-chapter exercises that promote individual and group critical thinking about symbol-generated experience and intervention processes

- End-of-chapter review questions that highlight key RSI concepts
- An Additional Readings list that provides a convenient resource for further study of RSI concepts

The book is written in a clear, engaging manner that includes student-relevant examples. Several undergraduate rhetoric and persuasion classes provided frank and insightful criticism on manuscript drafts, thus enhancing the book's student-friendly style.

Overall, the book is designed to promote an interactive classroom environment that encourages students' self-discovery of their symbolic nature. It prompts their self-discovery by reminding students of their "forgetfulness." Brown often said that we make life both miserable and good by simply "forgetting" that much of our common sense reality is our *interpretation* of that reality, which we have lost sight of as interpretation. In envisioning the RSI model, he tried to remind us of what we have forgotten to enable us to find ways to live together more peacefully and cooperatively. This book, by introducing students to the RSI model, directs their attention to their "forgetfulness." It increases their awareness of the symbolic, interpretative nature of their reality so that they might come to know what it means to be the "naming creature."

❖ ACKNOWLEDGEMENTS

This book is an outcome and tribute to the many people who supported our efforts. We appreciate the assistance of Todd Armstrong, Aja Baker, and Katie Grim of SAGE, who saw possibilities in the manuscript. We also thank reviewers Benjamin J. Cline (Culver-Stockton College), Steven R. Goldzwig (Marquette University), Tricia S. Jones (Temple University), John Makay (Bowling Green State University), Scott W. Marshall (University of St. Francis), Lee Snyder (University of Nebraska at Kearney), and Patricia A. Sullivan (State University of New York at New Paltz), whose insights expanded our thinking.

We are deeply grateful to Salem College students LaShea Agnew, Delia Dunphy, Samantha Eaton, Mreedu Gyawali, Kathy May, Caroline McLaughlin, Omolara Oyelakin, Emily Peterson, Toni Skidmore, Susan Smith, Lenora Speech, and Christina Weatherman, and Texas Tech University students Kelsey Adams, Tara Alvarado, Avery Burns, Seth Burt, Abbi Covalt, Erin Dickey, Lee Elliott, Jonathan Fox, Chad Hasty, Jacob Jones, Katie Loveall, Shannon McLaughlin,

John Means, Nathan Miller, Michael Mitchell, Shaun Neidigh, Travis Odom, Joseph Pratt, Stephen Schuh, Paul Slaughter, Matthew Tickle, Chris Wanner, Todd Wise, and Kayla Yorton, whose critiques greatly enhanced the book.

We thank Texas Tech University graduate students Jennifer Eshleman-Thomas, Marisa Harrison, Shereé Keith, Seth Phillips, and Mary Walker, who taught us by using this method for their theses, and other students who expressed interest in this model.

We also express gratitude to Salem College student Dianne Willard for her assistance and "Under the Lens" inspiration. In addition, we thank colleague Lee Snyder for his contributions, and Vicki Snyder and Alison Hope for proofreading and critiquing the evolving book.

A special thanks to our family members—Norm, Dana, Corinne, Evan, Nathan, and Dorothea—whose support enabled us to complete the book, and to Gregory Opt and Preston Opt for providing graphics and photographs.

Finally, we express our deep gratitude for the work and friendship of William R. Brown, whose ideas made this book possible. We hope that our book will help promote and enact his dream of making the world a better place.

SECTION I

The Rhetoric of
Social Intervention Model

CHAPTER 1

Rhetoric as Social Intervention

One afternoon you relax in front of the television and channel surf to catch up on world events. A reporter is interviewing not-for-profit organization leaders at an international AIDS conference about responses to the spread of HIV. A talk show host is attempting to help a young man confront his fear of clowns. A prominent senator is explaining how the president's domestic policy, offered as a way to solve serious problems, will actually create more problems. A sales person is demonstrating a portable video system that can be attached to a treadmill.

You turn off the television and skim the day's newspaper. A front-page article describes disagreements over the legality of a proposed wind turbine farm to generate electricity for a local community. An editorial column applauds the school board's decision to fund a remedial reading program. You set the newspaper aside and pop open your laptop to cruise the Internet. You peruse photos of adoptable animals posted on the Humane Society's Web site. You glance at the new videos uploaded on a popular Web site. You read an email from a friend who complains about current politics. You put the computer to sleep and phone your parents. Your mother chats about a recent stock investment she has made. After you hang up, you reflect on your afternoon.

You realize that, despite the variety of people, media, and messages you encountered, one underlying commonality unites them all: Each has the potentiality to shape the meaning you give to the world around you. Regardless of whether the communicators are informative or persuasive, entertaining or serious, they all in some way attempt to intervene in how you interpret experience. They offer choices for making sense of the people, objects, and events of daily life. After interacting with these communicators, you might alter your interpretation of the president's domestic policy from *good* to *poor*, or of treadmill exercise from *boring* to *tolerable*. You might become aware of a need to learn more about wind power or stock investments.

All of these potential interventions arise out of the rhetorical nature of the human being: in our talk or discourse, we interact in ways that attempt to influence others who, at the same time, attempt to influence us. In our symbolizing activity, we seem to practice a **rhetoric of social intervention**:

- *rhetorical* because it involves communication,
- *social* because our rhetorical acts occur in interaction with other people, and
- *interventional* because these acts potentially shift the way in which we (and others) interpret and respond to experience.

This book is about our lives as rhetorical creatures who create, maintain, and change the symbolically constituted world around us through our ability to symbolize. It examines how each of us acts as a social intervener, constantly interacting with others to shape interpretations of needs, relationships, and experience. To see the process by which we do this, we present a model for interpreting the rhetoric of social intervention. This model highlights the communication patterns that underlie our social interventions and provides a way for us to analyze and enact interventional activities. It empowers us to reflect on our own participation in the rhetoric of social intervention. In learning this model, you add to the choices that you have for making sense of and giving meaning to your own social interactions.

To communicate about the rhetoric of social intervention, we must agree on the meaning of some symbols—words—used in this book. These words will be important when we discuss the model, so we, the authors, need to explain how we use them. Take a moment to write down your definitions for these terms: *intervention*, *systems*, and *rhetoric*. Then, as you read this chapter, compare your way of *naming* these experiences to ours. Notice how we, the authors, define and give examples of *intervention*, *systems*, and *rhetoric* to illustrate our way of **naming** or symbolically categorizing these experiences—how we make these concepts "real." Consider how we attempt to intervene in your interpretation of the symbols *intervention*, *systems*, and *rhetoric!*

After presenting some key vocabulary, we preview the Rhetoric of Social Intervention (RSI) model, which is the focus of this book. We describe its development and briefly compare it to several rhetorical criticism approaches. We also examine reasons for conducting rhetorical criticism and analyzing the rhetoric of social intervention. We close this chapter with an overview of the book's objectives and structure— a glimpse of the exploration ahead. Let's begin this journey by talking about intervention.

❖ INTERVENTION

Intervention is a symbol, or word, that frequently is used in conjunction with words such as *drug, alcohol, suicide, crisis, addiction*, and *family*. In popular and professional literature, *intervention* often means an intentional intercession or act to bring about change. The act might be designed to promote or encourage certain types of behavior (e.g., living alcohol free, solving a problem) as well as to prevent or impede certain kinds of behavior (e.g., killing oneself, falling behind in school). For example, a *drug intervention* might involve a health educator working with teenagers to promote intentionally a behavioral change—from taking cocaine to avoiding cocaine. A *family intervention* might entail a therapist counseling a family on how to shift intentionally its dynamics from dysfunctional to functional.

We also use the word *intervention* to refer to an act to promote or prevent change. More specifically, we define **intervention** as a communication act that attempts to encourage or discourage change. Our definition highlights *communication* because we assume that interventions are based on symbols. Through **symbolizing activity**, such as speaking, writing, or signing, we communicate our interventions. Suppose you have a sibling who smokes. You want to intervene in how your sibling interprets the experience of smoking—to shift the interpretation from *fun and relaxing* to *risky and dangerous*. Your intervention will involve some form of communication such as talking to your sibling about the health risks, showing your sibling a Web site with quitting strategies, or giving your sibling an antismoking brochure to read.

Multiple Outcomes and Interveners

Our definition of *intervention* emphasizes that our communicative acts are *attempts*. Although an intervention might be well planned and executed, the outcome might not be as we had hoped or anticipated.

Despite your various appeals, your sibling might continue to smoke, avoid you rather than listen to your nonsmoking reasoning, or smoke more to irritate you. Your interventional *attempt* might not have the desired outcome of changing your sibling's interpretation of cigarettes, and your sibling's actions might intervene in your interpretation of the smoking experience. Maybe now you interpret it as *hopeless*!

Our interventional acts are always attempts because all interventions involve multiple **interveners**, which we define as people and groups enacting and responding to interventions. At the same time as you encourage your sibling to rename the act of smoking, other interveners—friends who smoke and cigarette companies—might communicate messages that emphasize maintaining the current interpretation of smoking. Interveners, then, both promote and impede change.

Intervention Intent

Our definition of intervention lacks mention of *intention*, although throughout the book we discuss the goals and purposes of intervention and give examples of intended interventions. Also, when we analyze social interventions, we typically focus on ones we consider intentional so that we can compare an intervention's outcome and side effects to its purpose or intention. However, naming only communication acts that have been clearly defined as intentional as interventions might limit our knowledge and understanding of the rhetoric of social intervention. Besides, what an intervener names as *intentional* and what others around the intervener interpret as *intentional* may differ. Ultimately, all interventions can encourage and result in unintended change. Regardless of whether the intervener intended the effect, the influence is still there. Thus, the question of intent is relevant only when we attempt to measure what the intervener tried to accomplish and what actually took place.

Finally, our definition of intervention assumes that interventions take place within *systems*. Because system will be a recurring term, let's consider a few features of systems.

❖ SYSTEMS

To characterize a system, we must consider the meaning of the word *system*. Economist Kenneth Boulding (1985) defines a **system** as "any structure that exhibits order and pattern" (p. 9). We can identify ordered and patterned structures and processes all around us. A house is heated and cooled by a *system* of interconnected ducts and machinery. We drive across the country on an organized structure of roadways called the interstate *system*. System theorists suggest that a system includes several key features along with order and pattern. Besides system characteristics, we will also examine two types of systems—social and ideological—and catalysts that prompt system change.

System Characteristics

One important characteristic of a systemic structure is the interrelatedness or interconnectedness of its components (Boulding, 1985). A system's components are the parts that we identify as constituting the system. The house's heating and cooling system consists of components such as a heat pump, vents, ducts, thermostat, and forced air. The human circulatory system includes components such as the heart, blood vessels, and the blood itself. These systems are organized around a goal or purpose—to heat the house or to feed and oxygenate the body. All systems have a minimum of two parts (Hanson, 1995). These interrelated parts form an integrated whole (Laszlo, 1972).

Interdependence. A system's components are interdependent. **Interdependence,** in terms of a system, means that each system component interacts with and affects the other system components. Any shift or change in one component of the system alters or influences all parts of the system (Hanson, 1995). When the room temperature reaches a selected point, it *alters* the thermostat and the air conditioning unit *changes* and switches on or off. Environmentalists often discuss how an increase in one component of the ecosystem—such as carbon dioxide—interconnects to changes in all ecosystem parts—such as global temperature and glacier size.

Causality. Another characteristic related to systemic interconnectedness is that system change is not based on a single cause-and-effect relationship among the parts. Sociologist Barbara Hanson (1995) explains, "Any action or inaction will reverberate through the entire system leading to unpredictable effects and sometimes effects that are precisely the inverse of the intended effect" (p. 27). She compares intervention in a system to pushing down on a waterbed: "Pushing on one corner leads to disruption in all areas, and possibly ultimately back onto the first corner we push" (p. 29). Thus, *causality* means that a change in one part of the system has side effects for change in all system parts.

Open or Closed. Systems can also be described as open or closed. An open system is one that is open to various inputs, which it processes in various ways. An *open* system is a dynamic system, and can adapt to changes within the system and within its environment. A company that alters its product line in response to changed customer demand exemplifies an *open* system.

A *closed* system is one that processes limited inputs in one patterned way. A company that refuses to listen to customer input and adapt to changes in customers' needs would be a *closed* system. Closed systems tend to run down over time. An unchanging company (closed system) will probably fail (Laszlo, 1972).

Endurance. Systems vary in terms of how long they endure. Systems theorist Ervin Laszlo (1972) explains that some systems, such as political systems or live oak trees, are long lived. Other systems, such as butterflies or soccer games, are short lived. Laszlo notes that maintaining relationships among a system's components is the key to its continued existence. Although a system's components might change, a system *endures* as long as its relationships continue. For example, the U.S. government system continues to exist even though a new president is elected every few years.

Subsystems. Finally, a system can itself be composed of systems. For example, the human body system consists of components such as the circulatory, digestive, endocrine, nervous, musculoskeletal, respiratory, and reproductive systems. Systems within a system are **subsystems** of a greater or superordinate system. Laszlo (1972) explains, "A system in one perspective is a subsystem in another" (p. 14). We can identify components that construct each subsystem, such as the heart, blood, and vessels of the circulatory system. Each subsystem influences the other and the state of the superordinate human body system. For example, a heart that beats too fast (circulatory system) can lead to changes in the lungs (respiratory system).

Social Systems

In this book, we primarily study the interaction of two types of systems—social systems and ideological systems—although other systems, such as interpersonal systems, will be mentioned. A **social system** is made up of a network of human interconnections. Human beings in a social system influence and affect each other.

Composition. Social system components are composed of individuals and groups. At the individual level are *intrapersonal* systems, which we identify as a single person, and *interpersonal* systems, which we identify as connections that develop between two intrapersonal systems, such as between a parent and a child or between two friends. Networks of interpersonal systems create larger social systems, such as a family. A family consists of interdependent components, such as mother, father, stepparent, sister, stepbrother, and grandmother. A medical practice system includes individuals such as doctor, nurse, technician, and patient.

Social systems are also composed of groups. For example, the social system known as a university is composed of groups such as students, faculty, staff, administration, and alumni. The university, in turn, is part of the social system known as the state educational system. The university and other universities and colleges within the state form this social system.

Constitution. In discussing systems and social systems, we have acted as if they are real and have existence in the physical world. However, systems theorist Lars Skyttner (1996) points out that the word *system* "does not refer to existing things in the real world but rather to a way of organizing our thoughts about the real world" (p. 35). Social systems arise out of our ability to name experience, thereby organizing it. That is, social systems are symbolic constructions. They have been created or *constituted* through symbols.

In interactions with others, we identify the components and define the relationships among those components that comprise the social system. We choose, for example, the qualities and behaviors that constitute the social system we call *family*. Consequently, we might not always agree on the components that make up a social system. For example, can a system of interconnections that includes two men who act as *mother and father* be named as *family?* To analyze interventions within a social system, then, we have to define what we consider to be the components of that system.

Purpose. We assume that social systems develop around a *purpose* or goal (Skyttner, 1996), in the sense that they meet some human need. For example, a family system meets the needs of infants and children to grow and survive. School systems satisfy learning and knowledge needs. Political systems meet the need for social order. Examining purposes and goals can help us identify the components of a social system that seem to be key to achieving those goals.

Ideological Systems

Our discussion of social systems suggests that they consist of relationships that are organized around meeting needs. In the process of symbolically constituting social systems, we also constitute ideological systems. An **ideological system** is a comprehensive way of interpreting and giving meaning to all of our experiences. We considered it a system because it is composed of the interpretations that we give to our needs, relationships, and daily experiences. It is organized around meeting the innate human need to construe an ordered and meaningful world. We create, maintain, and change an ideological system in communication with others. Participants in social systems symbolically construct and are constructed by ideological systems that influence how participants symbolically constitute social systems. We will talk more about ideological systems later in this chapter.

When we intervene, we attempt to shift or prevent a shift in an ideological system, or how a social system interprets its needs, relationships, and experience. A change in the ideological system influences the social system's growth and development. A shift in your sibling's interpretation of cigarettes can alter his interdependencies with the social systems in which he participates. Your sibling might interpret himself as having less interdependency with smokers and cigarette vendors and increased interdependency with nonsmokers and nicotine gum vendors. If your sibling continues to name smoking as *fun* and *relaxing*, then relationships with smoking friends and cigarette vendors will likely stay the same. The upcoming chapters detail how our rhetorical interventions to promote or impede ideological system change influence social system dynamics.

System Change Catalysts

What scholars view as the catalyst of social system change, or the force that drives social system change, varies with their field of study and expertise (Brown, 1978). For example, a psychologist might focus on the family as a system and consider a shift in attitudes among family members as the catalyst of change. An economist might focus on buyers, sellers, and suppliers as a system and point to a shift in marketplace forces as the driver of change. An ecologist might focus on the earth as a system and view a shift in environmental forces as the spark of change.

As our definition of intervention indicates, we emphasize *communication* as the generator of social system change. Fields of study such as psychology, economics, history, biology, and—for that matter—communication, exist only because we communicate about them. These fields arise out of our ability to symbolize and talk about experience that we define as *psychology* or *economics* and so forth. As rhetorical scholars, we identify *our ability to symbolize* as the driver of social system change. Social systems change as a result of our naming and renaming of needs, relationships, and experience. We build on this idea throughout the book as we examine how we symbolically create social systems and intervene to maintain and change those constructions.

Overall, we use the word *intervention* to remind us that we interact with, rather than act on others. We *intervene* into, rather than control, the development of ideological systems, and, by extension, we intervene into the social systems in which we participate (Brown, 1978). Our interventions introduce choices about directions for possible development. However, the choices that each of us offers are not the only ones available. When we intervene to move a person or group toward change, other communicators may attempt to forestall change. When we intervene to prevent change, others may encourage change. We have no buttons to push to ensure that our interventions will result in the social system selecting the choice we are advocating. Rather, intervention is a rhetorical act that *attempts* to nudge people and groups toward an interpretation of needs, relationships, and experience that we hope leads toward a particular social outcome (Brown, 1987). The emphasis on rhetorical action points to another symbol important to our discussion of social intervention—*rhetoric*.

❖ RHETORIC

Rhetoric is a word that circulates in popular media, often in a less than positive way. Think about the times you have heard phrases such as "that's mere rhetoric" or "she was not impressed by his rhetoric." How does the use of the word *rhetoric* in this manner shape your interpretation of the situation? Does it suggest that what you are hearing is trustworthy? Untrustworthy? Objective? Biased?

The word *rhetoric* also circulates in the academic media. Rhetorical scholars often debate how to characterize the word. Definitions range from Aristotle's well-known statement that rhetoric is "an ability in each [particular] case, to see the available means of persuasion" (Aristotle, 2007, p. 37) to rhetorical theorist Barry Brummett's (2006) claim that rhetoric is "the ways in which signs influence people" (p. 4). Rhetoricians Richard Cherwitz and James Hikins (1986) suggest that rhetoric is "the art of describing reality through language" (p. 62).

Symbolic Foundations of Rhetoric

Such a range of definitions for rhetoric is a reminder that our symbolizing ability enables us to construct and communicate concepts such as *rhetoric*. We are the ones who conceive the idea of *rhetoric* and make *rhetoric* "real" in our talk and interactions. In our conversations and writings with each other, we negotiate the characteristics and attributes of *rhetoric*. We decide which experiences constitute *rhetoric* and which experiences do not constitute *rhetoric*. The word *rhetoric* itself is a **symbol**. A symbol is a word that stands for or represents a particular behavior or experience.

The definition of rhetoric we use highlights the symbolic foundations of the word. We define **rhetoric** as the creation and study of meaningful symbols that symbolically constitute reality. By *symbols*, we mean words that people agree shall represent and communicate particular experiences. So far, we have given meaning to the symbols *intervention, system,* and *rhetoric* by defining and giving examples of experiences that these symbols name. In defining and explaining these symbols, we also symbolically constitute reality. We make *intervention, system,* and *rhetoric* "real." We can talk about and act as if *intervention, system,* and *rhetoric* exist in our daily experience.

Symbol-based Reality

Our definition of rhetoric assumes that much of what we experience as *reality* is based on symbols. Consider, for example, your response to these questions that rhetorical scholar Lee Snyder shared in an email to the authors.

- How far back do your personal experiences extend? That is, what is your earliest memory? How do you know about dinosaurs, the Pilgrims, or World War I?
- How many famous people do you know? How do you know they are famous? How do you know about these people?
- How much of the world have you traveled? What countries or states have you been in? How do you know about Antarctica, Mt. Everest, or Easter Island?
- How much of your past exists in actual artifacts—pictures, videos, and audio files? How much exists only in your memory? Are your memories made of actual objects or symbols?

- What is your greatest ambition? What is your greatest fear? Are your dreams and fears physical and literal, or are they symbolic?

As you reflect on your responses to these questions, think about how much of your reality is based on words and mediated images or, in other words, is *symbolic*. Much of what you "know" does not come from your own direct experience with people, objects, and events. Rather, much of your knowledge of the world is symbolically constructed from interactions with other people's interpretations of experience, such as the stories they tell, the reports they share, the photos they broadcast, the blogs they post, and the documentaries they create.

The field of rhetoric is one in which scholars investigate the process by which human beings create symbolic interpretations of experience that they consider reality. When we assume a rhetorical perspective, we study how, in our symbolizing activity, we construct, maintain, and change our symbolic reality. As rhetorical theorist Sonja Foss (2004) observes, "What we count as real or as knowledge about the world depends on how we choose to label and talk about things" (p. 6). We explore this labeling or naming behavior in depth in the next chapter.

Part of our definition of **rhetoric** includes the *study* of meaningful symbols that symbolically constitute reality. When we conduct such studies, we become rhetorical critics.

❖ RHETORICAL CRITICISM

As students of rhetoric, we often engage in **rhetorical criticism**. We seek in an organized manner to interpret, analyze, and critique the symbolizing activity that underlies the growth, maintenance, and decline of our ideological and social systems. Foss (2004) describes rhetorical criticism as "an everyday activity we can use to understand our responses to symbols of all kinds and to create symbols of our own that generate the kinds of responses we intend" (p. xi).

Each time we interact with others we have an opportunity to observe and reflect on how we create meaningful symbols that symbolically constitute reality. We can study the rhetorical strategies, tactics, and maneuvers that underlie the rhetoric of social intervention. The knowledge gained from our observations can enhance our ability to act as interveners and to create symbols that *attempt* to generate the responses we desire.

Components of Rhetorical Criticism

Foss (2004) suggests that the execution of rhetorical criticism involves three components:

- systematic analysis as the act of criticism,
- acts and artifacts as the objects of analysis in criticism, and
- understanding rhetorical processes as the purpose of criticism. (p. 6)

First, rhetorical criticism requires an organized way of studying human symbolizing activity. Typically, a rhetorical critic adopts a methodology or framework as a lens through which the critic interprets and critiques symbolic interactions. Second, rhetorical criticism involves the analysis of some type of symbolizing activity, such as a conversation, speech, book, movie, email, or Web site. The rhetorical critic identifies the discourse to investigate, and draws on the methodology as a pattern to guide the analysis. Finally, the primary reason we employ rhetorical criticism is to expand our knowledge of the symbolic nature of human beings.

Brummett (2006) adds a fourth component to the execution of rhetorical criticism—the critic's findings must be shared with others to complete the criticism process. By sharing our analyses with others, we contribute to the knowledge base of all rhetorical critics. We also reinforce the need for rhetorical criticism. Foss (2004) explains that the results of rhetorical criticism can lead to greater knowledge about the nature of rhetoric, expansion of rhetorical theory, improvement in our communication practices, and our own growth as critical receivers of messages. Communication theorists Malcolm Sillars and Bruce Gronbeck (2001) comment that understanding communication processes is key to understanding how societies function. Brummett sees the outcome of rhetorical criticism as providing ways for others "to see and experience the world differently" (p. 102). In all, rhetorical criticism is an intervention that potentially shifts how scholars interpret and explain human communication processes.

Rhetorical Criticism of Social Intervention

This book emphasizes the rhetorical criticism of social intervention. A critique of the rhetoric of social intervention can make numerous scholarly and social contributions by increasing our insight into the following:

- the symbolic processes underlying social system dynamics of continuity and change
- the rhetorical strategies, tactics, and maneuvers used to create, maintain, and change interpretations of experience
- the direction and outcome of our own rhetorical interventions
- the kinds of *futures* being created and promoted in our symbolizing activity

For example, in the 1960s, women began to attend to the *future* being created for them in gender-specific symbols such as *firemen* and *policemen* and advocate an alternative future using gender-neutral symbols such as *fire fighters* and *police officers.*

The rhetorical criticism of social intervention foregrounds the *process* by which we enact interventions. It focuses attention on *how* we construct symbolic interpretations of reality rather than on the *correctness* of those interpretations or the critic's own personal feelings about the interpretations. As social intervention critics, we seek to observe the patterns of communication that generate the content of communication. We attempt to expand our knowledge of how interveners rhetorically promote particular symbolic realities and how social system components react to and enact responding interventions. Understanding the *how* enables us to reflect on our role in intervention and to develop strategies that guide our own interventions.

As Foss (2004) notes, the act of rhetorical criticism requires *systematic analysis* or a *methodology* for investigating symbolizing activity. We need a framework that provides a pattern that we can use to interpret and critique the rhetoric of social intervention. Thus, this book introduces the RSI model as a methodology.

❖ RSI MODEL

The RSI model was conceptualized in the thinking and writing of rhetorical theorist William R. Brown (1978, 1982, 1986, 1987).

RSI Model Beginnings

The model's beginnings can be traced to Brown's graduate school interest in Will Rogers, an Oklahoma cowboy and vaudeville actor who became a well-known U.S. humorist and social commentator. In the 1920s and 1930s, until his death in a plane crash in 1935, Rogers traveled around the country, giving speeches and writing newspaper columns that offered respected insights on society and politics. Today, the Will Rogers Memorial Museums in Oklahoma (www.willrogers .com) commemorate Rogers's activities and influence. Brown, a native Oklahoman, was curious about the source of Rogers's social persuasiveness and authority.

In research published in the book *Imagemaker: Will Rogers and the American Dream*, Brown (1970) attributes Rogers's popularity with and influence on the U.S. public to his embodiment of characteristics associated with American dream ideology. Brown maps the rise and structure of the American dream ideology and explores how Rogers symbolically identified with it. Brown was frustrated by his explorations, though, because, although he believed he had painted an interesting portrait of Rogers's rhetoric, he perceived that the picture was static (personal communication, September 29, 2006).

This frustration led Brown to investigate the rhetorical processes by which the U.S. social system constitutes the ideology known as the **American dream**, which had shaped Rogers's communicative interactions. In his research on Rogers, Brown describes the components of the American dream, such as *freedom, equality, individualism,* and *pursuit of happiness.* "But I wanted to find a way to put it into motion—a way for the content of ideology to become background and the process of ideology to become foreground" (personal communication, September 29, 2006). In his search to understand *how* human beings symbolically construct ideology, he turned to books and articles on language, linguistics, and philosophy as well as conversations with communication colleagues.

From these idea generators, Brown synthesized a model to explain the rhetorical process by which we create, maintain, and change ideological and social systems. He published three articles that describe the model's concepts (Brown, 1978, 1982, 1986). Brown's RSI model provides the framework used in this book for understanding the rhetoric of social intervention and the processes of social change and continuity.

RSI Model Foundations

The RSI model is built on the assumption that *naming* is the fundamental activity of human beings (Brown, 1978). That is, we *name* or symbolically categorize both physical, sensed experience and conceptual, non-sensed experiences to communicate and share these experiences with others. In essence, we transform all experience into symbols (Langer, 1980). For example, words such as *book, desk,* and *pen* name physical, sensed experience. Earlier in this chapter, we *named* the conceptual, non-sensed experiences *intervention, system,* and *rhetoric* as we described the characteristics of those symbolic categories. As we learn language, or learn symbols and their definitions, we learn to name and constitute symbolic reality.

To symbolically categorize experience, we abstract from experience. For example, to name an object a *book,* we pay attention to the object's use as a source of information and knowledge. Because names for experience are abstractions, they categorize only some aspects of experience but not others. In the case of the experience known as *book,* naming the experience *book* directs attention away from the object's use as a source of fuel, piece of art, or as weapon. Our symbolic reality labels only a portion of all experience, although we often act as if our names capture the whole of experience (Leach, 1976). We act as if a *book* is a *book* and nothing more. Chapter 2 discusses symbolic abstraction in more depth.

How we name experience influences how we interpret and respond to that experience, for names create expectancies about experience. Of course, each of us can name the same experience differently depending on what we pay attention to in experience. For example, you might name a military attack on another country *justified* while your friend names it *unjustified,* depending on what each of you abstracts from experience to create the name *justified* or *unjustified* military attack.

Brown (1978) takes the idea of naming and builds it into a model that describes the process by which we create overarching names to explain all of experience. In addition, the model provides a way to analyze interventions to influence the symbolic process.

RSI Model Overview

The RSI model focuses attention on the process by which we create *superordinate* names in our symbolizing activity to make sense of the world around us. Brown (1978) calls these superordinate names *ideology.* We can view the *American dream* as an example of a superordinate name, or ideology, that influences how participants in the U.S. social system communicate, interpret, organize, and share their experiences.

Brown (1970) describes the main attributes of the **American dream** as "the belief in the dignity and worth of the individual, the anticipation of enjoying freedom and equality in a democracy, the hoped-for opportunity for success, and the vision of progress" (p. 33). In essence, the American dream is "the dream of Paradise to be regained" (p. 33).

This superordinate name, then, both constitutes and is constituted by our daily symbolizing activity. For example, a television commercial that suggests that a newly introduced computer can be *individually* tailored and offers the *freedom* to work at home is organizing experience in line with American dream ideology. The commercial implies that consumers can come closer to achieving the American dream by purchasing this computer.

The RSI model assumes ideology emerges from and constitutes three components of human symbolizing activity—how we name needs, how we name relationships with others, and how we name the events and actions of experience. Brown (1978) calls these components *need*, *power*, and *attention* subsystems. Together they form a system of ideology, or an ideological system.

RSI Model Subsystems

Briefly, the RSI model assumes we have growth-and-survival needs, such as food and water, which we express with communication. We also symbolically create needs, such as *freedom* and *progress*, which we attribute to each other through communication. At the same time that we symbolically construct or name needs, we also constitute relationships or interdependencies to meet those needs. We symbolically create social systems in the form of social roles and hierarchy.

In naming needs and relationships, we also simultaneously constitute interpretations of the events and actions of daily experience by what we pay attention to in experience. These interpretations influence how we understand and organize symbolic reality. These three subsystems of ideology—need, power, and attention—form the basic building blocks of the RSI model. Figure 1.1 provides a visual representation of the RSI model components.

The RSI model assumes that human beings have an inherent need to create an ordered and meaningful world (Brown, 1978). Our attempts to make sense of and give meaning to our experiences result in social interventions that maintain and change our ideological system. Interventions occur as we attempt to shift or to prevent a shift in how we name needs, relationships, and the events and actions of experience, resulting in what Brown (1978) calls *need, power,* and *attention interventions.*

RSI Subsystem Interconnection

The RSI model assumes that the ideological subsystems are interconnected. A change in one subsystem results in simultaneous changes

Figure 1.1   The RSI Model Components

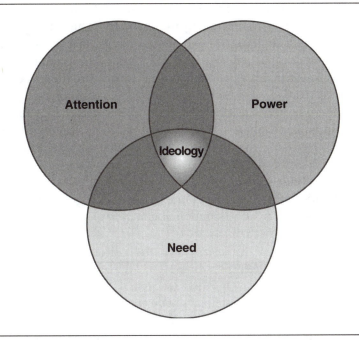

in the other two subsystems. A shift in interpretation of needs, for example, will also alter power and attention. Shifts in the ideological system will be reflected in shifts in the social system.

Suppose you watch a television report about the lack of medical personnel in sub-Saharan Africa that are trained to deal with AIDS. Prior to watching the show, you named the AIDS in Africa experience as *not affecting my life*. But the show made you aware of problems in that symbolic interpretation of experience. Perhaps the television report mentioned how the spread of AIDS might destabilize national governments, resulting in conflicts requiring international attention and resources to resolve. The program directs your attention to aspects of experience that your name for the event had de-emphasized. The way you had been symbolizing the AIDS in Africa experience no longer seems to make sense of experience. Thus, when you rename the AIDS in Africa experience as *affecting my life* you regain a consistent and meaningful world. The show has intervened in your symbolic reality—how you name and interpret experience—via an attention intervention.

A shift in attention has consequences for the other two subsystems of ideology. Needs shift as you become more attentive to the physical suffering of human beings in another part of the world. Power shifts as you become increasingly interdependent with AIDS organizations that can meet the need to relieve AIDS patients' suffering by providing medical care that is connected to the alternative meaning you now attribute to the AIDS in Africa experience. Notice that the situation in Africa did not change: just your way of naming the situation changed. Your renaming can bring about changes in the situation because of your altered relationships with the social system components. Overall, the RSI model provides a way to examine how social change arises out of our symbolizing ability. It assumes that rhetorical interventions underlie the growth, maintenance, and decline of our symbolically constructed social systems.

The RSI model is the approach that we take in this book to conduct rhetorical criticism. It joins a long line of methodologies that rhetorical critics have used to critique symbolizing activity.

❖ RHETORICAL LENSES

Since the time of Aristotle, scholars have employed rhetorical criticism to increase our understanding and improve the practice of communication. In your studies, perhaps you have encountered rhetorical criticism methodologies with names such as Aristotelian, Narrative Paradigm, Fantasy Theme Analysis, Dramatism, Feminist Criticism, and Cultural Studies. Like these other approaches, the RSI model offers a lens through which we can examine our symbolizing activity.

Method Commonalities

Communication scholar David Swanson (1977a) notes that all rhetorical criticism methods share two key commonalities. First, all rhetorical criticism must be carried out in what he calls the *natural attitude*. Swanson explains that the natural attitude means that a critic must assume that "the world is real or objective" and that investigating the world "can yield factual knowledge" (p. 210). To conduct rhetorical criticism, then, we take for granted that persons, objects, and events around us exist. We also believe that the world is knowable and presents itself in similar fashion to all persons. Finally, we presume that we can gain information from our observations.

Second, Swanson (1977b) points out that all rhetorical critics use *interpretive* or *representational schema* to analyze symbolizing activity. He defines these interpretive or representational schema as "systems used by critics to interpret and create meaning for rhetorical phenomena"

(p. 306). Thus, to do rhetorical criticism, we assume a point of view or a way of looking at the world. The approach we use is influenced by our assumptions about what is "real" in the world. We apply our framework or methodology to critique the symbolizing activity under study. Our approach shapes how we interpret the people, objects, and events that we are analyzing. In essence, all rhetorical criticism involves putting on a set of lenses to explore the everyday common-sense world we assume exists and assume is common to everyone.

Method Differences

Swanson (1977b) also highlights two key differences among the various rhetorical criticism methodologies. Rhetorical criticism approaches differ in their assumptions about the source of meaning in the symbolizing activity and the purpose of criticism. First, although all rhetorical critics use frameworks to interpret and give meaning to symbolizing activity they are analyzing, critics adopt different types of representational schema and stances toward the schema (Swanson). Consequently, rhetorical critics make different assumptions about the creation of meaning in symbolizing activity.

Some rhetorical criticism methods place the critic in the role of constituting the meaning of the symbolizing activity being studied (Swanson, 1977b). For example, neo-Aristotelian critics might give meaning to a rhetorical event they have observed by applying externally created concepts such as *ethos*, *pathos*, and *logos* to the symbolizing activity. Genre critics might give meaning to their observations by comparing symbolizing activity to categories or types of rhetoric that they assume exist independently of the rhetorical event.

Other rhetorical criticism methods view meaning as arising out of human interactions (Swanson, 1977b). They assume that meaning is participant generated. Dramatistic critics might analyze the relationships among act, scene, agent, agency, and purpose within the context of a symbolic act to understand how its participants create meaning. Critical studies scholars might attend to the class struggle they interpret as going on within a cultural phenomenon to understand the meanings created by participants within that event. The RSI model leads critics to search for interventions occurring within symbolically constructed social systems, with particular attention to how the system's participants generate, maintain, and change meaning within those interventions.

Second, critical approaches differ in their assumptions about the purpose or outcome of the rhetorical criticism (Swanson, 1977b). For example, neo-Aristotelian critics might link the speaker's use of *ethos*, *pathos,* and *logos* to the resulting effect on an audience. An outcome of the analysis might be to learn how to increase a message's persuasiveness. Dramatistic critics might examine our identity as rhetorical actors within a particular historical experience. An outcome of such a critique might be an increased understanding of a communicator's motives and how those motives reflect and affect the cultural assumptions.

Critical studies scholars might expose the included and excluded parties in messages, thereby creating awareness of hidden power within a social system. Their identification of rhetorical struggles within a symbolic experience might result in the empowerment of an excluded people and a power shift within the social system. RSI critics might search for patterns of symbolizing activity involved in the birth, growth, and decline of a social system. The resulting RSI critique might lead to an improved understanding of the rhetorical processes associated with ideology creation.

No matter which methodology a rhetorical critic adopts, that critic contributes to a greater appreciation of our lives as symbolizing creatures. Each approach offers a way to examine symbolizing activity and highlights aspects of experience that might be *hidden* in another approach. We, the authors, as students of William R. Brown, grew up academically with the RSI model, hence our preference for that method. We have found its concepts useful in our professional and personal lives. We have also observed that our students find the model's ideas compelling and applicable to their own experiences. Thus, in this book, we share the RSI model so you might evaluate its relevance to your own critiques of symbolic reality. So let's talk about how we envision our intervention.

❖ BOOK OVERVIEW

We intend our presentation of the RSI model to spark your curiosity about the symbolic nature of human beings. More specifically, this book provides a critical framework for analyzing social continuity and change from a rhetorical perspective that enables you to

- identify attempted social interventions,
- critique the rhetorical strategies, tactics, and maneuvers of interventions,
- contemplate side effects of interventions,
- reflect on the apparent outcome of interventions, and
- enact and critique your own social interventions.

We use a variety of techniques throughout the book to enable you to achieve these goals.

Section I: The RSI Model

The first section of the book explains and illustrates the RSI model's assumptions and concepts. Chapter 2 lays the foundation for the RSI model by presenting concepts related to the naming process. We examine how and why we name, and the rhetorical functions and strategies of naming.

Chapter 3 introduces the assumptions of the RSI model, which are built on the naming foundation. We take a closer look at how ideology emerges from the three subsystems of need, power, and attention.

Chapter 4 lays the groundwork for using the RSI model as a representational schema for rhetorical criticism and intervention. It describes the nature of attention, power, and need interventions and highlights the rhetorical strategies, tactics, and maneuvers related to each starting point for intervention.

Chapter 5 discusses how to use the RSI model as a method of rhetorical criticism. It provides questions for analyzing the intervention discourse and a guide to writing a rhetorical criticism essay.

Chapter 6 concludes by showing how the RSI model can be used as a framework to guide the development of a social intervention. We also consider how the RSI model relates to other areas of communication and other fields. Finally, we ask you to reflect on this book as an attempted intervention.

Section II: RSI Criticism Essays

The second section of the book consists of student and scholar essays that illustrate the RSI model's application. A brief author reflection and questions accompany each essay.

In Essay 1, Shannon DeBord, through the lens of the RSI model, analyzes the symbolic construction of Down syndrome and the interventional attempts of two young men with Down syndrome to shift the social expectancies related to the syndrome.

In Essay 2, Seth Phillips and Mark A. Gring use the RSI model to examine how Margaret Thatcher, via an address to the Conservative Party Conference, attempted to shift how the British populace named its role in the country's economic development.

In Essay 3, Omolara Oyelakin adopts the RSI perspective to trace the patterns of communication enacted by the Mirabel sisters in their intervention to challenge Dominican Republic social hierarchy to bring about a reordering of that society.

Finally, in Essay 4, Lee Snyder uses the RSI model to highlight the rhetorical patterns of a white supremacist organization, the Posse Comitatus, to understand how a group with a worldview repugnant to many U.S. Americans was able to attract followers.

❖ CHAPTER SUMMARY

This chapter has provided an overview of the rhetoric of social intervention by introducing some of the key vocabulary and concepts to be presented in greater detail in the upcoming chapters. We defined and described the characteristics of terms such as *intervention, systems,* and *rhetoric*. We examined the characteristics of systems, social systems, and ideological systems. We considered reasons for engaging in rhetorical criticism of symbolizing activity, and reviewed the components of the act of rhetorical criticism. We also described the scholarly and social contributions that result from critiquing the rhetoric of social intervention.

Next, this chapter has provided a brief introduction to the RSI model, the main focus of this book. We summarized its conceptualization and highlighted its key assumptions. We previewed concepts related to the model, such as *naming, ideology, need, power,* and *attention*. In addition, we considered the RSI model's similarities and differences to other rhetorical criticism approaches. Finally, we previewed upcoming chapters. We highlighted key ideas you will encounter on your exploration of the rhetoric of social intervention.

In all, we intend this book to be a rhetorical intervention—one that shifts how you name and construct your symbolic interpretations of experience. Although the RSI model is basic in its concepts, through its lens you will discover and explore the complexity of the human symbolizing process. We hope that one day soon when you are media surfing, as exemplified at the beginning of this chapter, you will attend to the ongoing symbolic process of social continuity and change underlying the various discourses that you encounter.

By learning about the rhetoric of social intervention, you will be better equipped to develop your own interpretation of the human being as symbolizing creature. You will see that all of us are rhetorical interveners in some form or fashion, whether we are parents attempting to shift how our child names homework or politicians attempting to alter how a social system interprets climate change. All of us, when

we interact with others, have the potentiality to intervene in constructing ideological and social systems.

❖ REVIEW QUESTIONS

1. What is intervention? How do we intervene into each other as systems?

2. What constitutes a system? How are systems and people interdependent?

3. What is meant by the symbolic construction of social systems and ideological systems?

4. How does communication generate social change?

5. How do the authors attempt to shape your naming of *intervention*, *system*, and *rhetoric?*

6. What is the purpose of rhetorical criticism?

7. What are the three RSI model components?

8. How do Brown's attributes for the American dream compare to characteristics you associate with the American dream?

9. According to the RSI model, is there any time when a person uses symbols that she or he is not trying to intervene into a social system? Is there a time when a person is not overtly or covertly, intentionally or unintentionally, intervening into a social system?

10. How is the RSI approach similar to or different from other communication or rhetorical approaches that you have studied?

❖ CHAPTER EXERCISES

1. Create a chart and track your own symbolizing activity for one day. Respond to the following questions as you record information for the day: With whom did I talk? What did we talk about? Were the events we talked about ones that I personally experienced or witnessed? How about the other person? If the events were not something I or the other person had personally experienced, how did I or the other person gain knowledge of the events? In what way is my knowledge of these events symbolically constructed?

2. Keep a one-day journal of your communication interactions with people or media (e.g., conversations, email, television). Which of these interactions would you classify as attempted interventions? What characteristics of an intervention did these interactions demonstrate? In what ways did these interactions try to shape your interpretation of needs, relationships, or experience?

3. In a small group, brainstorm and outline the components and connections of a system in which you participate (e.g., economic, educational, ecological, family, political). Around what needs is the system organized? In what ways are the system's components interdependent? What shifts might occur in one component that could influence all other components?

4. Review the advertisements in a popular magazine. How do the advertisements communicate the American dream? What appear to be the characteristics of the American dream as suggested in the advertisements? What words, objects, and images used in the advertisements represent ideas associated with the American dream? Write a short paper about your findings and share your findings with your class. What commonalities and differences appeared in the analyses of the American dream?

5. Write a brief paper that discusses how you would classify the RSI approach in the spectrum of communication theories and methods. Is it quantitative, qualitative, critical, ethnomethodological, some combination of these, or something new? Does it fit within a laws, rules, systems, or other metatheoretical category?

❖ SERVICE LEARNING EXERCISE

Select a not-for-profit organization whose interventional activities you can observe and critique throughout the semester. Its members should be willing to grant interviews and allow you access to organizational materials and meetings. In exchange, at the end of the semester, you will provide a rhetorical critique of the organization's interventions so that the organization might enhance its communication with its publics. In addition, you might suggest alternative interventional strategies for it to consider.

Begin collecting information about the organization to use as you progress through the chapters of this book.

Under the Lens: Sharing Students' Insights

As we developed the manuscript for this book, our students read the drafts and wrote critiques about their experience of learning the RSI model. We share some of their remarks for the insights they provide on your journey to acquire the concepts of the RSI model. As you read the remarks, consider how the students *name* their experience.

- Learning the RSI model was interesting, informative, and difficult at times, but it became easier to understand once I got into the main points of each chapter.
- After reading this book, I found myself asking, "What is reality?"
- Understanding the concepts of the RSI model can help us make sense of our day-to-day experiences and reactions to those experiences, both good and bad, in a way that promotes continuous learning.
- As I began to form an understanding of the model, I could see it applied to a number of things going on in my life. Interestingly enough, the model has affected the way I watch television!
- The RSI model has made me aware of interventions in my life and how I affect and am affected by them.
- Learning about the model has changed the way I look at life. It has changed the way I act toward others and the way I interpret the actions of others.
- The RSI model has helped me to become a better critic, instead of just going with the flow. I am gradually developing the habit of standing back and analyzing the systems around me.
- When you are using the model to write an essay, don't lose sight of the overall ideology surrounding the intervention you are examining.
- Be creative in the ways you choose to examine or use the RSI model. Don't be afraid to make it a challenge.
- To get the most out of this experience, allow yourself time to study the material, do research, and really think about how you are using and applying the RSI approach. Also, when an idea pops into your head when talking about this model, write it down immediately. It might be useful for your paper!

CHAPTER 2

Naming as Social Intervention

In the early 1970s, eight sane persons checked into psychiatric facilities around the United States. These pseudopatients claimed they heard voices. Doctors diagnosed them as schizophrenic even though, on hospitalization, the voices disappeared (Rosenhan, 1984). A review of hospital records revealed that after the diagnosis, doctors interpreted the pseudopatients' remarks, behavior, and history to fit expected schizophrenic patterns. The disappearance of their schizophrenic symptoms was explained as the schizophrenia being in remission. David Rosenhan, professor of psychology and law who headed the experiment, writes, "Once a person is designated abnormal, all of his other behaviors and characteristics are colored by that label" (p. 125). All of the pseudopatients' past and current communication and actions were interpreted to fit the label *schizophrenic*. Rosenhan adds, "The tag profoundly colors others' perceptions of him and his behavior. Again, in a very real sense, a specific 'reality' is thus constructed" (p. 125).

Rosenhan's study points to a starting place for investigating the **rhetoric of social intervention**—how we use language to rhetorically create, maintain, and change symbolic reality. His study illustrates how names give meaning to experience. At the same time, names shape how we interpret experience—what we pay attention to, or **foreground**, and what we ignore, or **background**, in experience. To label the pseudopatients as *schizophrenic*, medical personnel foregrounded behaviors that fit characteristics associated with schizophrenia and backgrounded behaviors that fit characteristics ascribed to *normal*. The foregrounded behaviors **reified**, or made real, the patients' schizophrenia.

The name *schizophrenia* altered how doctors interpreted events in the pseudopatients' family histories. Events that might have been named *normal* family experiences were now viewed as contributing to the pseudopatients' mental illness. Names influence how we behave toward people, objects, and events. The label *schizophrenic* conveys the expectancy that a person is abnormal, acts in an odd way, and needs treatment. We might avoid a person named *schizophrenic* unless we are medical professionals or loving family members. We are unable to do without names. If the pseudopatients had not been named *schizophrenic*, then they might have been labeled *normal*.

This chapter begins our investigation of the rhetoric of social intervention by focusing on *naming*. Naming forms the structure on which the Rhetoric of Social Intervention (RSI) model is built. We start with an overview of naming. Next, we examine the sensory categorization and symbolic categorization aspects of the naming process. We look at how we learn names and how names function to shape symbolic reality. Then, we review the rhetorical functions of naming, including how names clarify ambiguous experience, suggest approach and avoidance values, and create blindering or transcending effects. Finally, we turn to the rhetorical strategies involved in proposing, generating, enacting, changing, and maintaining names.

❖   NAMING OVERVIEW

To begin the naming discussion, we must agree on how we are using the symbol *name*. What experiences do you associate with the word *name*? The story in the Bible of Adam naming the animals? The process of creating a name for a school group or business? A toddler who pesters you by repeatedly asking, "What's that?" Regardless of the association, common to these examples is the activity of *naming*.

Defining Naming

To talk about experiencing animals, groups, and toddlers, we must convert that experience into symbols to communicate and share it with others. **Naming** is the process by which we transform experience into symbols. It is the most fundamental human activity (Brown, 1978). Our ability to name defines our humanness and allows us to build relationships with others and the world.

When we name, we **symbolically categorize** experience. We compare experience to the symbolic categories that our language community has created to communicate about experience. We select the category into which the experience seems to fit. Then we use the symbol associated with that category to talk about the experience.

Suppose you encounter a four-legged being with a tail. To communicate this experience to others, you transform it into a symbol. You name the experience. You compare the experience to symbolic categories you have learned, such as *cat*, *dog*, *cow*, or *horse*. You review its characteristics, such as its size, color, sounds, behaviors, and habitat. If its features match the characteristics that your language community attributes to members of the symbolic category *cat*, then you say to other people, "There's a cat."

Psycholinguist Roger Brown (1958) notes that words do not name the specific item itself. Rather words indicate the symbolic category to which the item belongs. When you say *cat*, you are indicating that the experience you have encountered belongs to the category of experience for which your language community uses the symbol *cat*. Using the community's agreed-on categories and symbols enables other community members to comprehend your symbolic transformations.

Negotiating Names

This leads to a key aspect of naming: we must use a language system to communicate with each other. A language system consists of shared symbols and rules for combining and organizing those symbols for sensed and non-sensed experience. In our communicative interactions, we **negotiate** names for experience—that is, we discuss and agree on how to organize experience into groups and what symbols to use to represent those groupings. For example, English speakers use the shared symbol *cat* to represent a category of fur-covered, four-legged experiences that make the sound "meow." Other language communities have negotiated alternative symbols, such as *Katze*, *gato*, and *paka*. When encountering such an experience, we probably would have little disagreement with other English speakers about how to categorize it—we would all agree on *cat* to distinguish it from fur-covered, four-legged experiences that make the sounds "woof," "moo," or "neigh."

Some experiences are more difficult to categorize and may require many communicators and conversations to negotiate the name to be ascribed. For instance, psychology professor Steven Pinker (2007) describes the problem of categorizing experience associated with September 11, 2001. The difficulty revolved around this question: "Exactly how many events took place in New York on that morning in September?" (p. 1). Insurance company lawyers argued that one event—a plot masterminded by one person—occurred when the twin towers were hit in New York. World Trade Center leaseholder lawyers claimed that two events occurred when each building collapsed. The difference in the symbolic categorization of *event* meant the difference between a $3.5 billion insurance payout for one event and $7 billion for two events (Pinker).

We negotiate the name to ascribe to experience—*one event* or *two events*—in **symbolizing activity**, such as newspaper editorials, speeches before Congress, and courtroom testimony. We often turn to people we name *experts* for guidance on how to categorize experience (Keil, 2005). We might agree to a state department official's symbolic categorization of the experience as *one event*. Lawyers in the World Trade Center case brought in legal experts to support their version of symbolic categorizing. Overall, in our communication interactions we negotiate the attributes for creating symbolic categories. These negotiations become social interventions.

Selecting Attributes and Criterial Attributes

Our use of attributes and criterial attributes to create symbolic categories forms another key aspect of naming. An **attribute** is a feature or characteristic of experience that we interpret as varying from experience to experience (Bruner, Goodnow, & Austin, 1965). For example, you could use the features of hair color, eye color, gender, or age to distinguish yourself from a classmate. These attributes are ways that you interpret the experience of *you* as differing from the experience you name *classmate*. An attribute must have variations that we can distinguish (Bruner et al.). If we all had black hair or if we could not distinguish differences in hair color, then hair color would no longer be an attribute because it would no longer vary.

Although attributes are differences that we can notice, they do not always alter how we name an experience. You include yourself and the other people in class in the symbolic categories *classmates* and *human beings,* despite the physical differences. You background the differences and act *as if* you and the others are the same and all fit into the symbolic categories *classmates* and *human beings.* A **category**, then, is a range of different experiences that we treat *as if* they were the same (Bruner et al., 1965).

Some attributes, however, make a difference in how we symbolically categorize people, objects, and events. Psychologists Jerome Bruner, Jacqueline Goodnow, and George Austin (1965) use the name **criterial attribute** for this type of attribute. A change in the value of a criterial attribute alters how we categorize an experience. A criterial attribute is a "difference that makes a difference" in how we name experience (Makay & Brown, 1972, p. 378). The symbolic categorization of the World Trade Center experience hinged on whether the criterial attribute emphasized was "the change in a state of an object, such as the collapse of a building" or "the goal of a human actor, such as a plot being executed" (Pinker, 2007, p. 4).

Consider this list of object names—*stocking, cuff link, shoelace* (Makay & Brown, 1972). Suppose you are asked to select the object that does not belong on the list. Which will you choose? You could name the objects as *things-to-be-worn-on-the-foot* and say cuff link does not belong. You could categorize the list as *things-to-hold-things-together* so that stocking does not belong.

What you interpret as *same* or *different* in experience varies according to the criterial attribute you have selected to create the relationship among the items (Makay & Brown, 1972). If you select *location of use* as the criterial attribute, then cuff link does not fit because it is not worn on the foot. If you select *type of use* as the criterial attribute, then stocking does not fit the category *things-used-to-hold-things-together*. What if you symbolically categorized the objects as *things-to-wear-to-a formal*? What does not fit then?

Your choice of criterial attribute shapes your interpretation of the similarities and differences among experiences. You and a friend might disagree on how to categorize the objects because each of you pays attention to different criterial attributes. Maybe you foreground *location* of use, and your friend emphasizes *type* of use. At the same time, each of you backgrounds aspects of experience—in your case, *type* of use. Despite encountering the same experience—the list—each of you "sees" it differently. The name you ascribe to the objects might also alter your behavior toward them. If you categorize shoelace as *thing-to-be-worn-on-the-foot*, you might have more difficulty viewing it as something to tie back your hair than if you name it *thing-to-hold-things-together*.

Creating Complex Names

The list of objects example illustrates another aspect of naming. A name can be as simple as a single word that refers to a specific category of experience, such as *shoelace*. But a name can also refer to a complex of symbolic categories. These symbolic categories name relationships among categories. For example, we relate attributes from the symbolic category *shoelace* to attributes from the symbolic category *stocking* and constitute the name *things-to-be-worn-on-the-foot* or *foot apparel*. We create a **complex name** by relating together several symbolic categories to form an interpretation of experience (Makay & Brown, 1972).

When the U.S. president presents the State of the Union Address, the president offers a complex name for the current experience of the United States. Suppose the president advocates this complex name: *Weapons of mass destruction threaten the quality of life in the United States.* The president's speech relates a series of symbolic categories to create this complex name. The U.S. public's acceptance of the complex name shapes how it interprets the U.S. government's behavior toward other countries. The opposition might advocate an alternative complex name: *Lack of medical care threatens the quality of life in the United States.* Adoption of this complex name would lead to a different set of expectancies and behaviors.

In summary, *naming* is the transformation of experience into symbols. To communicate with others, we share common symbols for naming and a common way of categorizing experience. We *negotiate* the criterial attributes that form our symbolic categories. We also create *complex names* by relating together symbolic categories. Now let's look more specifically at the process of naming.

❖ THE NAMING PROCESS

As human beings, we exist in a world of ongoing, complex sensory and symbolic experience. The range of our sensory perceptions is impressive. For example, researchers estimate that if we have optimal vision, we can differentiate seven million colors (Nickerson & Newhall, 1943). Furthermore, we can extend our physical senses with mechanical aids, such as telescopes and stethoscopes.

If we paid attention to all of the differences and unique qualities that we are capable of perceiving, the complexity of experience would overwhelm us (Bruner et al., 1965). Imagine what your vocabulary and memory would be like if you tried to name the seven million colors that you can perceive (Scheidel, 1976). Consider what life would be like if you were aware of all the sights, sounds, and smells around you. You would be "stuck" in the here and now. The overwhelming nature of sensory and symbolic experience has led sociologist Niklas Luhmann (1979) to argue that *the* problem facing humankind is complexity. Thus, we have to find ways to simplify and manage the profusion of experience so that we can, as rhetorical theorist William R. Brown often said in class lectures, "get the universe between our ears."

We deal with this apparent abundance of experience through sensory and symbolic categorization. Our ability to categorize appears to be one of the most fundamental ways that we adjust to and cope with our apparently complex experience (Bruner et al., 1965). It enables us to escape being completely caught up in here-and-now experience. The adjustment and coping process begins with sensory categorization.

Sensory Categorizing

In our daily lives, we experience a world of sensation that is accessible to our five senses—sight, hearing, touch, smell, and taste. Our senses detect stimuli in the environment and respond to those stimuli. Communication scholar Thomas Scheidel (1976) explains, "We experience sensation as a change in the environment. Basically sensation is a response to *energy change*" (p. 77; emphasis in original). If we paid attention to all sensations, we would be overwhelmed by the sensory input and would be "stuck" in sensation. Thus, our senses constantly **abstract** or select from environmental stimuli (Langer, 1980).

Our senses abstract by registering only some sensations and ignoring others. They abstract by foregrounding and backgrounding aspects of experience. Think about the last time you were in a grocery store. How many cracks in the walls did you see? Do you remember them, or did your visual senses abstract from experience, that is, *foreground* the walls and *background* the cracks? A veterinary assistant was surprised one day when a client asked her how she tolerated the noise of the barking dogs. The assistant realized that she had not noticed the sound. Her senses abstracted relevant qualities of the animals, but backgrounded the irrelevant barking.

Our senses organize abstracted experience into forms (Langer, 1980). That is, we perceive more than just random dots of light or bits of noise. Our senses and brain organize sensory data into shapes and objects. Your ability to read this page depends on your brain and senses organizing the sensory data of light and dark into shapes or categories we call *letters*. Those letters must be organized in relation to other letters to form categories we call *words*. Our ability to abstract from sensory data allows us to interpret experience as *things*, such as letters and words (Langer).

Overall, the **sensory categorization** process involves attending to and selecting sensory inputs from experience and organizing that sensory data into shape and form categories. When you see a car or smell a pecan pie, no actual car or pie is in your brain. No light or smells are inside your head, only cells turned on and off in response to environmental stimuli, creating experience that we interpret as shapes and forms. What we see, hear, feel, taste, and touch is an abstraction of what our sense organs can detect and what we attend to in our environment.

Sensory categorization helps us deal with the complexity of sensory experience by filtering and simplifying experience. We give meaning to that abstracted sensory experience through symbolic categorization.

Symbolic Categorizing

All creatures share the ability to collect sensory data about their environment, although they differ on the types of experience their sensory organs can register. For instance, dogs smell odors undetectable by human noses and hear frequencies outside the range of human ears. All beings must select from and organize sensory data from their complex daily experience so they can react to that experience. Linguist Zoltán Kövecses (2006) explains, "Categorization is necessary for action, and it is essential for survival" (p. 17). A deer survives by detecting and responding to shapes and forms that it categorizes as predators.

Human beings seem unique in their ability to go beyond sensory categorization to the step of **symbolic categorization**. We abstract details from our sensory categorizations of experience and transform those details into symbolic categories. Our ability to name—that is, to transform experience into symbols—appears to be the fundamental ability that marks us as human—the criterial attribute by which we might be defined. Rhetorical theorist Sonja Foss (2004) comments, "As far as we know, humans are the only animals who create a substantial part of their reality through the use of symbols" (p. 4).

Like sensory abstraction, symbolic abstraction provides a way for us to deal with the quantity of experience. Symbolic categorization enables us to cope with the apparent complexity of our environment in four main ways: It reduces the number of symbols used and constant learning. It reduces the strangeness of experience. It creates predictable experience. It enables us to give meaning to experience.

Reducing symbols. Naming reduces the number of symbols we have to use to communicate about experience (Bruner et al., 1965). We symbolically categorize a multitude of different and unique experiences as being the same and give them the same name. We abstract similarities among discrete experiences, group these experiences together, and use one symbol to describe them.

Suppose you have two objects in your pocket that you name *pennies*. A numismatist might note that one object was manufactured in 1995 in Denver and has a hairline die crack on the obverse above the ear. The person might point out that the other object was created in 1975 in Philadelphia and has an acid mark from a fingerprint on the reverse. Despite the differences, we abstract the similarities, such as color and size, and use one symbol to represent both experiences—*penny*. Imagine if you had to give each *penny* you encountered a unique symbol. It would be like trying to name the seven million colors we can perceive!

Our ability to abstract and symbolically categorize experience means that we avoid constantly learning new names for each experience we encounter (Bruner et al., 1965). Once we learn the criterial attributes of a category, we can recognize new instances of it. However, that is not to say that the uniqueness of each person, object, or event should go unnoticed. If we fail to recognize the differences of experience, we might fall into the error of assuming that all experiences named *Muslims, Swedes, doctors, tax cuts,* or *wars* are exactly alike.

Reducing strangeness. Our ability to name enables us to cope with the apparent complexity of experience by reducing the strangeness of it (Bruner et al., 1965). We make sense of or give meaning to the various persons, objects, and events in experience by naming them. When we lack names for an experience, we often feel bothered by uncertainty. "We experience terror in the face of the uncanny" (Bruner et al., p. 12) when we lack a name for experience.

If an airplane crashes on landing, we feel uneasy until we can symbolically categorize the experience—*act of terrorism, mechanical failure, pilot error*. We cope with new or unknown experience not simply by fighting with it or fleeing from it, "but initially by symbolizing it, thereby transforming it into some recurring form or concept" (Brown, 1978, p. 127). Once we name the crash as *mechanical failure*, we reduce uncertainty about the experience, create an interpretation of it, and know how to respond to it.

Creating predictability. Our ability to categorize symbolically reduces the apparent complexity of experience by enabling us to make predictions about experience. Our predictions are based on how we have named experience (Bruner et al., 1965). We associate certain attributes with specific symbolic categories. When we name experience, we create the expectancy that those attributes will be present in the experience.

Naming an upcoming event *birthday party* creates expectancies. You will probably bring a gift, eat cake, and sing "Happy Birthday to You." You gain a sense of control over or certainty about the experience. Think about times you have felt ill. Perhaps you felt anxious until you could name the sickness. Once you were able to categorize the illness symbolically, it was no longer strange. The name created expectancies about treatment and outcomes. You probably felt better even though you physically still felt ill!

Categorizing also makes experience repeatable (Brown, 1958). Although the particulars of specific events are not repeated, the *kinds* of events are. For example, your second experience with an illness that you name *the flu* will not be exactly like your first experience with an illness that you also named *the flu*. But the *kind* of event—being sick with the flu—repeats because we give it a familiar name. We abstract the similarities between our first and second experience of being ill to create the complex name *being sick with the flu*.

Creating meaning. Finally, our ability to categorize symbolically reduces the apparent complexity of experience by enabling us to relate and order categories. We give meaning to experience by connecting and organizing categories (Bruner et al., 1965). Suppose you observe a woman feeding an infant and name the event *breastfeeding*. You can relate this symbolic category to another symbolic category, perhaps *caregiver*, and form a more abstract symbolic category called *nurturing*. By relating categories, you create meaning for the woman's actions.

In addition, we create value by ordering and relating symbolic categories. We can categorize a person who has more money as ranking *higher* than a person who has only a small amount of money. We might ascribe more value to the higher person and say that means the person has achieved success. We can categorize a person who has an office with a window as *more important* than a person who has a windowless office. We can categorize a person wearing a business suit as *more credible* than a person wearing ripped jeans. Naming gives us a sense of being able to organize and order our complex experiences, thereby creating meaning and value.

Capturing experience. Symbolic categories—like human sensory receptors—capture only portions of experience. General semanticist Wendell Johnson (1946) offers this example: "A statement about direct experience can never be a duplicate of, or a full substitute for, the experience. Bite your tongue—not too hard. Now, try to *say* the feeling!" (p. 109; emphasis in original). We can *say* what we feel, but the words are not the feeling.

Our names, as abstractions, never embody the whole of experience. Pinker (2007) compares symbolic abstracting to digitizing analog information. To digitize music, a computer samples from the continuous, analog experience of a band playing and converts the sample into numbers (zeroes and ones) to be stored in an online music file. The digitized version of the music captures only a portion of the whole sound experience. In a similar manner, our names digitize experience. "[B]y digitizing the world, language is a 'lossy' medium, discarding information about the smooth multidimensional texture of experience" (Pinker, p. 276).

Transforming experience into symbols is not enough to ensure communication with others. Suppose a person transforms experience into the word *sinreveliagee*. What is the person attempting to convey? To communicate, we must learn the names negotiated by our language community and the criterial attributes that our language community has agreed should constitute those symbolic categorizations of experience. Pinker (2007) notes that "words are owned by a community rather than an individual" (p. 15). He adds, "If a word isn't known to everyone around you, you might as well not use it, because no one will know what you're talking about" (p. 15). That is not to say that you cannot introduce a new name into your language community's symbolic system—but language communities do not adopt every symbolic categorization of experience that individuals propose. Thus, we spend time learning our language community's agreed-on names.

Learning Names

Throughout our lives, we rely on and act as **language tutors**. Psycholinguist Roger Brown (1958) explains that a language tutor is anyone who teaches us the symbols and categories of our language community. Parents, peers, professors, and the media, among others, act as language tutors.

A language tutor teaches us by naming experience according to our language community's conventions. Language development theorists note that to begin acquiring names a child must come to recognize that another person's utterances or signs are an attempt to encourage him to attend to some aspect of experience (Tomasello, 2003). The child follows the language tutor's gaze or pointing finger to determine the experience to be linked with the name that the tutor is saying or signing (Tomasello; Woodward, 2004).

We indicate our learning of the name by attempting to apply it to new experiences (Brown, 1958). When we make mistakes, the tutor corrects us. When we successfully name experience in the agreed-on convention of our language community, we show that we have paid attention to the appropriate criterial attributes (Brown).

We learn both the symbols—words—that our language community uses to name experience, and our community's way of symbolically categorizing experience. Language tutors teach us the "difference that makes a difference" to distinguish *male* from *female, war* from *peace,* and *justice* from *injustice.* Think about vocabulary words you have had to define on examinations to demonstrate to educators that you have learned your language community's conventions for naming.

Suppose you encounter a child who uses the word *cow* to categorize experience that your language community names *horse.* How could you act as a language tutor to teach the child the "difference that makes a difference" between *horse* and *cow*? Both creatures have four legs, two eyes, a tail, and eat grass, so a child could categorize them as the same. As an adult, you might reason that genetic differences exist between a *horse* and a *cow.* But your language community had to agree on *genes* as a criterial attribute. You could also interpret *cow* and *horse* to be the same because they both have genes!

As we acquire names, we learn how to categorize both the external, sensed experience (e.g., *dog, cat, cow*) and internal, non-sensed experience (e.g., *freedom, marriage, transportation*) of our language community (Leach, 1976). Some symbolic categories name experience that we can detect with our senses. Other symbolic categories name experience that has no tangible existence.

To teach us names for external, sensed experience, language tutors typically show us objects in our environment to which these names are applied. The tutor points to a horse and says "horse" or picks up a cat and says "cat." These symbolic categories name experience that we can see, hear, taste, touch, and smell.

To teach us names for internal, non-sensed experience, tutors often point to groups of objects or actions and behaviors that are examples of the symbolic category. A tutor explains the name *transportation* by listing a group of objects contained within that symbolic category, such as car, train, and plane. The tutor describes the objects' similarities that form the criterial attributes of *transportation.* A tutor teaches us the symbolic category *marriage* by listing behaviors, such as exchanging rings, saying vows, and living together, that constitute the criterial attributes of that name.

Although we have acted as if language tutors teach us names directly or one on one, Pinker (2007) points out that we rarely learn a name "by looking it up or asking someone to define it," but instead learn "by hearing it in context" (p. 9). We learn indirectly by observing how those around us name experience. We learn by being immersed in a language community.

Language communities construct social systems in the form of institutions that sustain their ways of symbolically categorizing experience and teach the next generation (Berger & Luckmann, 1966). These institutions include governments, schools, religious organizations, not-for-profit organizations, prisons, and families. These institutions arise out of how we have symbolically categorized experience. In turn, they shape how we name experience. As we learn our language community's symbolic categories, we acquire our community's way of interpreting experience—its symbolic reality.

Constituting Symbolic Reality

When we name experience, we give life to our symbolic categories. We construct a **symbolic reality** alongside physical reality. Symbolic categories—such as *goat*, *snake*, *peace*, and *equality*—become *real* in the external objects, events, behaviors, and actions that we say embody the attributes we associate with these symbols. When we communicate, we exchange symbols with each other, rather than the physical experience. We share symbolic categorizations of experience—a symbolic reality—not the experience itself.

Anthropologist Edmund Leach (1976) explains how we constitute symbolic reality. He says that we create all symbolic categories internally, or *in the mind*. Some categories symbolize our external experiences (e.g., *cat, dog*); others reflect internal concepts that we relate to external experience (e.g., *transportation, marriage*). We construct symbolic reality and meaning for experience by "forgetting" that we created the connection between the internal symbolic category and external experience. We act *as if* our symbolic categories have physical existence and are real. Leach calls this symbolic-to-reality transformation **"code switching"** (p. 22).

Suppose you attend a lecture about the impact of technology on society. Symbolic categories such as *technology* and *society* are internal, in the mind. They have no existence in external experience or in nature. We create the symbolic reality of *technology* by ascribing the symbol to specific objects, actions, and events in our external experience that we say are examples of *technology*.

The lecturer might describe the criterial attributes that constitute *technology* to give meaning to the word *technology*. *Technology* becomes reified, or made real, in objects such as computers, cell phones, and the Internet, or in actions such as measuring keystrokes or the speed of instant messaging. We code switch—we "forget" the internal, in-the-mind origin of the symbolic category *technology* and act as if *technology* has external existence. As a result, the lecturer can talk about technology as if it were a force that drives society. The lecturer creates meaning for the name *technology*.

Leach (1976) also believes we take external experience and transform it into symbolic experience. Suppose the key-and-lock system of securing doors in your office building is replaced by a swipe-card system. You and your coworkers might name this experience *progress*. You transform an external sensed experience into non-sensed symbolic experience. You and your coworkers "forget" that replacing the lock system is simply an external experience and act *as if* the event is an example of the symbolic category *progress*. You create meaning for the experience.

Leach (1976) suggests we constitute symbolic reality and meaning through the intertwined actions of storytelling and of creating objects to which our symbolic categories can be attributed. The symbolic category *freedom* becomes real and meaningful in the stories we tell in conversations, movies, articles, blogs, and so forth, about events such as protests and wars. We reify *freedom* in the actions and behaviors we point to as representing criterial attributes of *freedom*. We also create objects, such as flags, and give them meaning by saying they represent symbolic categories, such as *freedom*, *country*, or *United States*. In the process, we "forget" that we have symbolically transformed experience and act *as if* the name for the experience *is* the experience. We act *as if* the flag *is* the United States and should be treated with the same respect as the country. We interpret harm to the flag *as if* it were injury to the country.

In summary, in our symbolic transformations of experience, we constitute symbolic reality. Psychologist Paul Watzlawick (1990) notes, "Real *is*, after all, what is *called* real by a sufficiently large number of people" (p. 19; emphasis in original). By code switching between internally created symbolic categories and external experience, we give meaning to our symbolic transformations. Leach (1976) emphasizes that the relationship between our symbolic categories and experience is conventional—we create the relationship and we can change it. We may disagree over the name to give an experience and the meaning to be associated with that name. To one person a flag may be simply *a piece of material* that can be worn as clothing. To another person, a flag may mean *freedom from oppression*.

Regardless of how we symbolically categorize experience, our names shape how we interpret and respond to experience. Thus, we use names to attempt to influence how others interpret and act toward experience.

❖ THE RHETORICAL FUNCTIONS OF NAMING

Suppose as you walk across campus with a friend, she says, "Look at that cat over there." What do you expect to see? A small, fur-covered, four-legged, tailed being that meows, purrs, and chases birds? You expect an experience that embodies the attributes you associate with the symbolic category *cat*. Your expectancies might be violated if you see experience that you symbolically categorize as *tiger*. Although a tiger can be named *cat*, where do you usually expect to see tigers? What if your friend gestures toward another person as she says the word *cat*? What expectancy does she create about experience?

The expectancies that we associate with symbolic categories make possible the rhetorical functioning of names. How we name experience shapes other people's expectations about that experience. Names create interpretations by what they foreground and background in experience. Makay and Brown (1972) summarize the three main ways names function rhetorically: they clarify apparently ambiguous experience, suggest approach and avoidance value, and create "blindering" and "transcending" effects (p. 372).

Clarifying Ambiguous Experience

Consider the ambiguity of this event. Conflict breaks out in a foreign country. Both the government and the people fighting against the government claim to represent the citizens. Which group do you support? How does naming the experience clarify the ambiguity of experience?

You might abstract from experience to name the current government *a dictatorship* and the people fighting against the government *liberators*. The symbolic category *dictatorship* creates expectancies of a threat to democratic practices valued in the United States. Likewise, naming the opposing forces *liberators* suggests attributes akin to soldiers battling an oppressive government. This naming of experience functions rhetorically by clarifying the ambiguity of which group you should support—the liberators.

Consider how the expectancies associated with the event change when the names shift. You might abstract from experience in ways to name the current government *socialist*. Socialism, although different from democracy, does not create the expectancy of threat. The opposing forces, then, become categorized as *terrorists*. Now, the people fighting the government are interpreted to be a threat to U.S. interests. In this instance, the names clarify ambiguity by suggesting support for the in-place government.

How you name the event depends on the criterial attribute you use to categorize the experience. The names give order and meaning to otherwise apparently ambiguous experience and suggest ways to act toward that experience. A shift in names creates different expectancies about and meanings for the experience (Makay & Brown, 1972).

Suggesting Approach/Avoidance Value

Names also function rhetorically by suggesting approach and avoidance values. A car advertisement might emphasize how driving an SUV reflects criterial attributes that constitute the symbolic category *freedom*. In the United States, *freedom* is a name associated with approach value. On the other hand, an environmental group might link the purchase of an SUV with the criterial attributes of the symbolic category *terrorism*. *Terrorism* is a name that has avoidance value in U.S. culture.

Suppose two people are walking down a street one night and spot a disheveled man sitting in a darkened doorway. One says, "Look at the crackhead." The other says, "Look at the homeless person." How do these diverse names invite approach or avoidance responses? Consider the approach and avoidance value associated with these pairs of names: *office manager* versus *secretary*, *juvenile delinquent* versus *child at risk*, or *bombing an airport* versus *denying the enemy a runway*.

Our symbolic categories function rhetorically by directing our attention to certain attributes in experience and by suggesting responses to experience. Psychology professor Steven Pinker (2007) remarks, "[W]ords don't just point to things but are saturated with feelings, which can endow the words with a sense of magic, taboo, and sin" (p. 3). Linguist Zoltán Kövecses (2006) agrees, noting, "How we categorize entities may determine how we feel, and conversely, the feelings we have toward entities may influence how we categorize them" (p. 87). Consider, then, how the emotions might we associate with a name relate to the approach/avoidance value suggested by the name's expectancies.

Creating Blindering/Transcending Effects

Finally, names function rhetorically by creating expectancies that encourage us to pay more attention to *differences* or more attention to *similarities* among experiences. Naming one experience *dog* and another *person*, or naming one group of persons *liberators* and another *terrorists*, may *blind* us to the similarities between the two categories of experience and direct our attention to differences.

Names also rhetorically function to transcend. The experiences we name *dog* and *person* could be recategorized as *mammal*, a symbolic category that transcends difference and emphasizes similarity. *Liberators* and *terrorists* could be renamed as *people who fight for a cause* or as *human beings*. We create transcendent names by emphasizing the attributes that experiences share. Transcendence shifts our attention from that which divides us to that which unites us (Makay & Brown, 1972).

In a speech about social issues facing the United States, cultural critic Michael Eric Dyson (2005) concluded by using names rhetorically to foreground the similarities among various groups of U.S. Americans. He created a complex name for all U.S. Americans that transcends their economic differences:

> And as I end, that's why you and I are on the same ship. In fact, we travel in the same plane. You might be in first class eating filet mignon; I'm eating peanuts back in row 55. . . . And if you're on the plane, being in first class ain't going to stop you from going down with the rest of us. When there is turbulence, there is turbulence everywhere. Everybody be shaking. And if that plane goes down, you might die first in first class. Yes, some of us are in first class, but the plane is in trouble!

Names can simultaneously blind and transcend. Consider a person who renames the experience of artificial insemination as *reproductive prostitution*. This alternative name blinds attention to the *procreative* aspects of artificial insemination (Pondozzi, 1988). At the same time, by symbolically categorizing the experience as *prostitution*, the person invites others to unite in the condemnation of the practice (Pondozzi). Overall, names create expectancies about what is the same (transcending) and different (blindering) about experience.

Because the relationship between our symbolic categories and experience is arbitrary and because people pay attention to different aspects of experience, we often must negotiate the name to be ascribed to an experience. The final part of this chapter examines the rhetorical strategies we use to promote our naming of experience.

❖ THE RHETORICAL STRATEGIES OF NAMING

Together with others, we create, maintain, and change the attributes that our community says constitute our symbolic categories for organizing experience. However, because naming always involves abstracting from experience, each of us can abstract differently and create different names and expectancies for the same experience. As a result, much of our daily symbolizing activity reflects attempts to reach social consensus about the appropriate name to ascribe to experience (Makay & Brown, 1972).

Proposing Names

Our daily written, oral, and visual symbolizing about people, objects, and events is the place to find the rhetorical strategies we use to argue for our names for experience. To advocate our name, typically we must go beyond just stating the name. Suppose you say to a group of friends, "Speechmaking is not scary; it's an opportunity." Are they likely to categorize the speechmaking event as an *opportunity* just because you say so? Often, we must explain the criterial attributes that lead us to reason that the experience fits the symbolic category that we have proposed. We *rhetorically reason* with others to argue for our symbolic categorizations (Makay & Brown, 1972).

Makay and Brown (1972) summarize the three attributes of the **rhetorical reasoning** process. First, you propose a name that reflects your symbolic categorizing of experience. You propose the name *opportunity* for the event of speechmaking by saying, "Speechmaking is an opportunity." Second, you explain how the experience embodies the criterial attributes that constitute the proposed name. You offer examples of how speechmaking fulfills the expectancies associated with the symbolic category *opportunity*. You say, "Like an opportunity, speechmaking gives you these advantages—a chance to have your voice heard and a chance to develop skills that open up exciting career paths." Finally, you indicate the expected response to the proposed name or list additional reasons that your name fits the experience. You suggest this response: "Because speechmaking is an opportunity, we need to make as many speeches as possible during our college years." Rhetorical reasoning, then, constitutes a process by which we advocate the appropriateness of our names for experience.

Underlying the structure of rhetorical reasoning is a broader pattern of discourse, which Makay and Brown (1972) refer to as "the difference that makes a difference" (p. 379). They call this pattern the "one major name generator" (p. 379) or universal topic of message invention.

Generating Names

The one major name generator forms the basis of what Makay and Brown (1972) identify as the two main strategies of rhetorical reasoning—"this-is-the-same-as-that" and "this-is-different-from-that" (p. 380). Suppose you propose the name *just war* to create meaning for a current international conflict. You foreground aspects of the present experience that match the criterial attributes that your language community agrees constitute the symbolic category *just war*. You reason that this current event is *the same as* or shares the same attributes as past experience that has been named *just war* (this-is-the-same-as-that). You also emphasize how the current event is *different from* past experience that has been categorized as *unjust* (this-is-different-from-that).

At the same time you advocate your name, your friend might reason that the name *unjust war* makes more sense of the international conflict. She foregrounds the similarities between the current event and the criterial attributes that constitute the symbolic category *unjust war* (this-is-the-same-as-that). She highlights the differences between the present event and past experience that has been named *just war* (this-is-different-from-that). You and your friend use the two rhetorical strategies to generate and promote the appropriateness of your ways of symbolically categorizing experience.

Enacting Naming Maneuvers

To enact the rhetorical reasoning strategies, we employ a variety of rhetorical **maneuvers**, such as arguments by sign, example, and comparison, to generate the difference that makes a difference. As you read the following scenario, notice the rhetorical maneuvers that underlie each communicator's rhetorical reasoning strategy as each attempts to affect the other within this interpersonal system.

Your friend invites you to watch a movie that she recently downloaded from the Internet. The movie has just been released in theaters and is not yet available for rent or for download from an online video retailer. She explains that she downloaded it from a file-sharing site, without having to pay. You reflect for a moment and then propose this symbolic categorization of her actions: "Do you know you're a criminal?"

You rhetorically reason for the appropriateness of your name by stating that the act of downloading a copyrighted movie is the *same* as *stealing* from the movie studios. Her actions are the same as *robbing* the movie theater operators because they lose money on ticket and concession sales.

In addition, you equate downloading pirated movies off the Internet with *shoplifting*. You describe her actions as the same as walking out of a video store with a stolen video or hacking into an online video retailer Web site. By comparing the current experience of downloading to already named past experience (*stealing, robbing, shoplifting*), you demonstrate how her actions fulfill the criterial attributes of *criminal behavior*. Your rhetorical maneuvers invoke the strategy "this-is-the-same-as-that" in the attempt to shift how your friend names experience.

Your friend is shocked, offended that you would label her a *criminal*. "I am a law-abiding citizen with rights," she says, proposing her name for experience. She states how her actions *differ* from the expectancies associated with the symbolic category *criminal*. Criminals steal to *make money*, and she is not making money on the movie download. She downloaded the movie for *personal use* only and does not sell copies. Furthermore, thieves steal things of *value*, but the movie studios will not lose anything of value from her one download because they make so much money. In fact, she suggests that the movie studios' actions are criminal because they earn large profits and get rich by charging high tickets and rental fees. Her actions do not hurt the movie studios; the movie studios' actions, like criminals' actions, hurt the public. Finally, she reasons that if the information is freely available on the Internet, then she has a *right* to that information, no matter how the source of the information acquired it. The source might be a criminal, but she is not. Overall, her rhetorical maneuvers invoke the strategy "this-is-different-from-that" to maintain her name for experience.

You respond that criminals might also personally use what they steal, so personal use is not a difference that makes a difference. Also, if someone offered to give her a stolen car, would she take it? Availability is also not a difference that makes a difference. She counters with examples that emphasize differences between experience and your proposed name to reason that your advocated name does not fit. The conversation continues with each of you attending to different aspects of experience to constitute alternative names and meanings for the event.

As the two of you negotiate the name to be given to the experience, each of you may alter how the other names the event. Consider the side effects of a naming shift. How would adopting your friend's symbolic categorization change your actions and behaviors? What differences might you notice in her actions and behaviors if she agrees to your naming of experience? Of course, the interventions may result in no shift, and you and your friend walk away without consensus on how to name the experience.

Changing and Maintaining Names

Interventions occur when we attempt to change or maintain how others name experience. To *promote* a symbolic recategorization of experience, we emphasize how experience no longer fits the expectancies associated with the current way of naming it. We highlight how our proposed symbolic category makes more sense of experience. In downgrading Pluto from planetary status, scientists reasoned that it did not fit the expectancies associated with the symbolic category *planet*. The criterial attribute *size* became a difference that made a difference.

To *maintain* the current way of naming experience, we redefine the criterial attributes or expectancies that constitute the symbolic category so that the name continues to fit experience. We also emphasize how the experience does not fit the criterial attributes of the proposed name. Some scientists advocated a shift in the criterial attributes constituting the symbolic category *planet* to continue naming Pluto a *planet*. Size would no longer be a difference that made a difference.

Overall, much of our daily conversation is spent negotiating the appropriate name to give experience. The name generator "difference that makes a difference" provides a starting point for understanding the dynamics that generate continuity and change in our ideological systems and social systems. As we will see in the next chapter, the rhetorical patterns that underlie the naming process also underlie the RSI model.

❖ CHAPTER SUMMARY

This chapter has introduced the naming process of the RSI model. We assume that naming, or the symbolic transformation of experience, is the fundamental activity of human beings. We construct symbolic categories by abstracting from experience. Sensory and symbolic abstracting help us cope with the abundance of experience. Naming enables us to simplify and organize our complex sensory and symbolic environments.

We learn how to categorize experience symbolically from language tutors and immersion in a language community. Tutors teach us the criterial attributes for constituting the simple and complex names we ascribe to sensed and non-sensed experience. By code switching, we constitute meaning for our internal and external experiences.

As we learn names, we acquire the expectancies associated with specific symbolic categorizations. This enables us to use names rhetorically to create expectancies about experience. Naming seems to clarify ambiguous experience, suggest approach and avoidance value, and serve to blind and transcend.

Because we abstract from experience to name, we can create alternative names for the same experience. Often we negotiate with others about the appropriate name to give to an experience. We rhetorically reason for our names by employing the name generator "difference that makes a difference" and the strategies "this-is-the-same-as-that" and "this-is-different-from-that." We enact these strategies by using rhetorical maneuvers to promote our names and to prevent shifts to names advocated by others.

As you review this chapter, reflect on how we, the authors, have attempted to transform experience into symbolic categories and act as language tutors to introduce you to the naming process. Consider some of the names we introduced—*category, criterial attribute, code switching, complex name*—and how we reified these non-sensed experiences. How have we attempted to intervene in your interpretation of naming? How have we named naming in the way in which we wrote about naming?

❖ REVIEW QUESTIONS

1. What examples or words could be used to define *foregrounding* and *backgrounding*?

2. How does this chapter name *naming*? What criterial attributes does it use to constitute *naming*?

3. How might *criterial attribute* be defined in terms of code switching?

4. How are sensory categorization and symbolic categorization similar and different? How do the categorization processes enable us to cope with the complexity of experience?

5. What are language tutors? What do they teach us?

6. How do names create expectancies about experience?

7. Why might a group protest naming a U.S. nuclear submarine the *Corpus Christi*? (Note: This Latin name translates to "Body of Christ," and a city in Texas shares this name.) How might the name *Corpus Christi* function rhetorically?

8. What are the steps in rhetorical reasoning? How is *rhetorical reasoning* a symbolic category?

9. Semiotician and philosopher Umberto Eco talks about how symbols *re-present* (make present again) ideas, people, and things. How is code switching similar to and different from making experience present again?

10. What are the potential ethical implications of *code switching, reifying, foregrounding, backgrounding,* and *naming,* in general?

❖ CHAPTER EXERCISES

1. Identify a person you name as *friend* and a person you name as *best friend.* Write down five expectancies that you associate with each category. Then list the criterial attributes that distinguish the *friend* experience from the *best friend* experience. Compare your list to a classmate's list. How are the lists similar and how are they different?

2. Choose an experience that you and another person have shared. Record what you experienced and abstracted from the event. Then interview the other person about the event and note the similarities and differences between your sensory and symbolic categorization of the event and the other person's categorizations. How did your categorizations of the event reduce strangeness, create predictability, and provide meaning?

3. Find two newspaper, magazine, or Internet articles reporting on the same event. In what ways are the two accounts similar in the story they tell? How do the two accounts differ? Overall, what complex name for the event does each article create? How might the complex names influence your interpretation of and response to the event?

4. With another classmate, role-play this exercise: Student 1 and Student 2 are classmates. One day, Student 1 finds a copy of an exam for the class left behind in a photocopier. Student 2 sees Student 1 make a copy of the exam to keep. How might Student 1 rhetorically reason copying the exam? How might Student 2 rhetorically reason to intervene?

5. Research the naming of hurricanes. What was foregrounded and backgrounded in 1979 as the list of hurricane names was expanded from only female names to include male, Spanish, and French names? How do hurricane names function rhetorically? What are the potential side effects of reifying hurricanes by giving them human names?

6. Research the Narrative Paradigm theory, conceived by rhetorical theorist Walter Fisher. Fisher assumes that human beings are *homo narrans*—storytelling beings. What criterial attributes does Fisher use to construct his name for human beings? Next, develop a name for human beings based on the RSI model. How do the criterial attributes you used to create your name compare to those of Fisher's?

❖ SERVICE LEARNING EXERCISE

Examine documents and web pages produced by the not-for-profit organization you selected in Chapter 1. How does the name of the organization function rhetorically to create expectancies about experience? How does the organization constitute a name for itself in its symbolizing activities? How does it rhetorically reason to support the way it names itself? Search for media reports about the organization. How do the media name the organization? How do the media support their rhetorical reasoning?

Draft a brief report of your analysis of the naming activity related to the organization. Consider how the names function rhetorically and how this might influence the organization's growth and development.

Under the Lens: Making Sense of Experience

Take a moment to examine the photograph in Figure 2.1. Does it communicate anything to you if you cannot put a name to it? How do you make sense of this experience? What names come to mind as you attempt to interpret and organize this experience? Write down the names that you consider that give meaning to what you see.

To which attributes of the experience do you pay attention to symbolically categorize this experience? Which ones do you ignore? Make a list of these attributes.

How do the names you have listed function rhetorically to clarify ambiguous experience, suggest approach/avoid value, and create blindering/transcending effects? Again, note your responses.

Finally, how does the name *photograph* shape your expectancies of this experience? Answer these questions and make your lists before you read on to learn the name conventionally ascribed to this experience.

Figure 2.1   In What Symbolic Category Would You Place This Experience?

If you have lived in the southern part of the United States, you might have recognized this experience as an exemplar of the symbolic category *antlion pits* or *doodlebug pits*. Antlions are insects that dig pits to trap ants and other insects for food. If this is your first encounter with this symbolic category, what does the name *antlion* or *doodlebug* suggest about the experience? You can learn the socially agreed-on criterial attributes that constitute the symbolic category *antlion* or *Myrmeleontidae* by searching the Internet.

CHAPTER 3

Systemic Naming as Social Intervention

During election season, political candidates bombard the media with claims that our lives will be more nearly perfect only if we vote for them instead of their rivals. Contenders link their proposed policies to U.S. cultural values such as progress, success, freedom, equality, and individualism to argue that their proposals are the same as *pro-American*. Candidates advocate the need for people to vote for them to enact these values. They often symbolically categorize their opponents' policies as *ill conceived*, *old-fashioned*, or *unfair* to name their proposals as *anti-American*. In press releases, press conferences, and leaks, candidates use the naming strategy *I-am-different-from-them* to distance themselves from their rivals. Aspirants appeal to voters with whom they are interdependent to achieve their goal of winning the election. Together, contenders and voters share power in choosing a future in which they recategorize some *candidates* as *office holders*.

Despite variations in the candidates' messages, a comprehensive naming pattern tends to unite them—that the world in which we live can be made more nearly perfect or ideal, that we can achieve the American dream (Bormann, 1985; Brown, 1970; Kochan, 2006; Nimmo & Combs, 1980; Obama, 2006; Robertson, 1980). This pattern shapes how candidates develop their campaign messages. A candidate might reason that his educational proposal will enact *equality*, an attribute needed for achieving the American dream.

Chapter 2 examined the naming process by which we symbolically categorize specific experience, such as *dog, cat, marriage,* and *war.* This chapter investigates the ideological system that arises out of the naming process and comprehensively names all of experience. It also shapes how we name specific experience. The Rhetoric of Social Intervention (RSI) model depicts the ideological system as composed of three subsystems of symbolic categorizing—need, power, and attention.

The chapter opens with an overview of ideology and key terms related to it. Then we discuss the need, power, and attention subsystems of ideology. We examine each subsystem's attributes, expectancies, and link to social intervention. The RSI model's subsystems highlight the symbolic creation of ideology. We close by considering the subsystems' holographic nature.

❖ IDEOLOGY

How do you construct the symbolic category *ideology*? What expectancies does the word create for you? Your meaning for *ideology* relates to the criterial attributes you have learned from language tutors. Because we are inducting you into the language community of RSI scholars, we will act as language tutors to explain the criterial attributes and expectancies that the RSI model associates with the name *ideology*.

Defining Ideology

RSI theorist William R. Brown (1978) defines **ideology** as "any symbolic construction of the world in whose superordinate 'name' human beings can comprehensively order their experience and subsume their specific activities" (p. 124). Let's examine the attributes that constitute *ideology*:

- "any symbolic construction": We create the category of *ideology* in our symbolizing activity.
- "of the world": The world is all experience, sensed and non-sensed, external and internal.
- "in whose superordinate name": **Superordinate** name means a more abstract symbolic category that encompasses less abstract names (e.g., *transportation* is superordinate to *car; car* is superordinate to *Toyota*).

- "human beings can comprehensively order their experience": *Ideology* is an interpretive system that enables us to organize and give meaning to our world.
- "and subsume their specific activities": As a superordinate name, *ideology* includes and encompasses the names we use to make sense of daily experience (e.g., *American dream* subsumes and gives meaning to events named *success* and *education*).

In essence, *ideology* is a comprehensive, complex name that we create out of symbols. In our social interactions, we negotiate a "theory" of life that names and interprets all our experiences.

Throughout this book, we use the *American dream* as an example of ideology. We employ this example because we, the authors, participate in the U.S. social system, which symbolically constructs and is shaped by the American dream ideology. Participants in U.S. counterculture social systems and members of social systems outside the United States may have alternative ideological systems. For example, a social system might be shaped by an ideology that emphasizes the goal of overcoming the cycle of birth, death, and rebirth.

Chapter 1 described some attributes that create the American dream ideology, such as *freedom, individualism, equality, success,* and *progress.* Notice how these attributes are themselves names for experience. U.S. society has abstracted these categories of experience to constitute the superordinate name *American dream.* To see how we have abstracted, think about categories of experience not usually considered attributes of the American dream, such as *slavery, sickness, failure,* and *collectivism.* Thus, we construct ideology by paying attention to some aspects of experience and de-emphasizing others.

Creating Expectancies

Like specific names for experience, ideology creates expectancies. For example, the American dream generates the expectancy that we can achieve a more perfect life (Brown, 1970). This expectancy guides our interactions and reduces the complexity of overall experience.

Unlike specific names, ideology creates an overarching, or all-encompassing, expectancy about experience. Brown (1978) identifies this criterial attribute of ideology as *ultimacy.* Ideology provides an *ultimate* or fundamental sense of order, meaning, and comprehensive explanation for all of experience. Ideology is "that category of experience on which one is willing to bet the meaning of one's life"

(Brown, p. 126). We might be willing to go to war or work long hours because the American dream creates the fundamental expectancy that we can build a more perfect life.

The naming process and ideological system interact and interconnect. They are **holographic**. Each encodes and contains information about the other. For example, names for specific experience, such as *freedom, success,* and *individualism,* construct the American dream. The specific behaviors that we enact to constitute the names *freedom, success,* and *individualism* reify the American dream. In turn, the American dream expectancy of creating a more perfect world influences our definitions of *freedom, success,* and *individualism.* When we foreground attention to the ideological system, the naming process is still there but backgrounded, and vice versa.

Construing a World

Chapter 2 discussed how naming satisfies the need to cope with the complexity of experience. As a superordinate name, ideology satisfies an ultimate human need—the need to make comprehensive sense of all experience. It "fulfills a unique growth-and-survival requirement of the human being: to construe a world of connected entities" (Brown, 1978, p. 128). It gives us an ultimate sense of being able to explain and predict experience. It enables us to cope with life by masking the strange, chaotic aspects of experience.

The RSI model assumes ideology emerges from our symbolic categorizing of needs, relationships, and experience, or what the model calls *need, power,* and *attention* (Brown, 1978, 1982, 1986, 1987). The RSI model assumes these three subsystems interact and interrelate to form a comprehensive system of ideology. At the same time, the need, power, and attention subsystems are themselves systems for interpreting and enacting social interventions. Let's look at each subsystem in more detail, beginning with the *need subsystem,* followed by the *power subsystem,* and then the *attention subsystem.*

❖ NEED SUBSYSTEM: INTRAPERSONAL CATEGORIZING

The RSI model assumes that each of us has an inherent *intrapersonal* need to construe order within what we call *self* (Brown, 1978). We construct ideology in interaction with others to satisfy this need. Ideology tells us who we are, our place in the social hierarchy, and who and what around us are important. Suppose you wake up early on a day you have a final exam. You have an infinite number of choices before you, such as boating, sleeping in, or joining the National Guard! Going to class is just one option you could choose. Ideology provides order and reduces the complexity of choices by suggesting what you *need* to do: you *need* to go to class and pass the exam to enact success and achieve the American dream.

The inherent need to construe order and meaning within *self* is not the only type of need we experience. We also symbolically create needs, such as the need for *success*. These needs become attributes that construct ideology, such as the American dream. The RSI model's needs subsystem gives insight into this aspect of constituting ideology.

Constituting Needs

Human beings have needs that must be fulfilled for each person to grow and survive, such as biological needs for food, water, and shelter, and social needs for participation in and acceptance by a society (Brown, 1978, 1987; Maslow, 1998). These **biosocial needs** appear to be innate—apart from our symbolic categorizing of experience—though we *express* them through communication (Brown, 1987).

Communication of biosocial needs begins with a baby's cry that it is hungry, thirsty, lonely, tired, or wet. As we acquire verbal and non-verbal skills, we learn to transform our biosocial needs into symbols. Language tutors teach us our language community's symbols that name these needs so that we can communicate them. A child speaks or signs, "I'm hungry," "Ich habe Hunger," or "Tengo hambre."

Language tutors also teach us our social system's expectancies for communicating and satisfying our needs. A child is taught that banging a spoon on a table is an inappropriate way to communicate his need for food. The action violates expectancies his family social system associates with *good behavior.* He is also taught that the appropriate way to satisfy the hunger he feels in the morning is to eat cereal (or rice or fish). Language tutors instruct us in how to express and fulfill biosocial needs.

As language tutors teach us to name biosocial needs, they also attribute to us symbolically constructed needs. **Symbolically created needs** are needs that we *create* in communication (Brown, 1987). We constitute non-biosocial needs, such as the need for *prosperity* or *convenience*, when we talk and act as if *prosperity* and *convenience* exist. By code switching, we "forget" that we have symbolically constructed these needs and act as if they are as real as rocks and trees (Leach, 1976). We take these needs for granted: we assume they exist and should be acted on. Communication scholar Jeannine Pondozzi (1988) remarks,

"[W]e act as though love, motherhood, justice—and need—are actual *things* because we have observed experiences of love, motherhood, justice, and need, and we have *named* these experiences" (p. 198). Through naming, we populate the world with needs.

We constantly have needs, ranging from the innate need to make sense of the world to ideologically connected needs such as *success* and *individualism*. At any given time, certain needs seem to stand out more than others (Brown, 1987). Right now, you may be more aware of a *need to study* than the *need to relax*. This does not mean you lack the *need for relaxation*. Rather, you background that need as you attend to the *need to study*. Later, as you complete the homework, your attention to *the need to study* diminishes, and your attention to other needs, such as the *need to relax*, increases. As one need is satisfied, other needs become foregrounded.

Attributing Needs

Our attention to specific needs is heightened or diminished in our social interactions. We tell each other what we need and do not need. The RSI model calls this communication behavior **attribution**: we *attribute* needs (Brown, 1987). We say to each other, "You need this." We can accept the attribution and act as if the need were real. Perhaps you enrolled in college because you accepted someone's attribution: "You need to be educated to become successful."

We can also reject or *deny* need attributions. We say to each other, "You don't need this." We can accept the denial and act as if the need is nonexistent. A not-for-profit group might attribute to the community the need for a halfway house and request a permit to build it. The city council might deny the attribution and vote against the permit. Instead, it might listen to the local residents' need attributions to maintain property values by preventing construction of a halfway house. Thus, our attributions and denials of need occur in interaction with others.

Need attributions often involve shifts in interpretations of needs— between what the RSI model calls **individuality-stressing needs** and **collectivity-stressing needs** (Brown, 1987). For instance, your friends might attribute to you the group-based need to join them in volunteering at the local soup kitchen to improve society. However, your professor might attribute to you the individual-based need to keep up with your homework to pass the class and get a diploma.

Although we talk as if individuality-stressing needs and collectivity-stressing needs are opposites, they entail each other. For example, in meeting the group-based need of volunteering to improve society, you also meet an individual need to spend time with your friends. In meeting the individual-based need to do homework, you also fulfill the group-based need for educated social system participants. In addition, the same time that we attribute one need, we simultaneously deny a different need. By attributing to you the need to volunteer, your friends are also encouraging you to deny the need to do homework. Overall, the rhetorical attribution and denial of individual- and group-based needs create social interventions.

Advocating Needs

Whether the needs are biosocial or symbolically created, we are interdependent with others to satisfy those needs. In our symbolizing activity, we make others aware of our need attributions and denials. The RSI model calls this communication behavior **advocacy** (Brown, 1978, 1987).

An environmental group might attribute to U.S. consumers the need for alternatives to gas-guzzling vehicles to reduce global warming. The group advocates this need through channels such as editorials, public service announcements, and protests. A government official, however, might deny this need. The official advocates the denial through press conferences and news stories that suggest that global warming results from natural global cycles, not fossil fuel emissions.

As we learn to name needs, we also learn our language community's expectancies for appropriate advocacy of needs. A community might require the environmental group to acquire a permit to advocate needs via protesting. You could advocate your need for a higher term paper grade by shouting out your need as your professor is lecturing. However, such an action is unlikely to result in the needs-meeting response you desire! Overall, the advocacy of attributed or denied need creates social interventions.

Meeting Needs

When we advocate needs, we become more attentive to persons and groups we think are potentially able to meet our needs. We open channels of communication with them, hoping they will respond to our advocacy. The RSI model calls this attention to others **open-channel behavior**. The persons and groups potentially able to satisfy our needs are **needs-meeters** (Brown, 1978, 1987). Naming them *needs-meeters* does not mean that they can or will respond to our needs, only that we believe they can, so we advocate to them.

Open-channel communication involves two types of behavior: (1) The person or group advocating the need *seeks out* or becomes *open to* a needs-meeting response from potential needs-meeters, and (2) the potential needs-meeters become *open to* giving a needs-meeting response to the advocate (Brown, 1987). An environmental group might seek out a state senator to whom it advocates the need for gas-efficient vehicles. The senator demonstrates openness by listening to the group's concerns and sponsoring a bill to regulate vehicle design. In turn, the senator expects that the group members will be open to remembering her need for votes during election time. However, the senator could also choose to ignore or not respond to the group's advocacy, thus demonstrating **closed-channel behavior**.

Suppose a classmate seeks you out and asks questions about an upcoming exam. He advocates a need for information to improve his grade. He names you as a possible needs-meeter because of your high course grades. You might be open to responding to his need by sharing information. In turn, you expect him to attend to your need for volunteers for a class service project. On the other hand, you could name him as a competitor and avoid sharing information, thereby closing the channels of responsiveness. Thus, engaging in open- and closed-channel communication creates social interventions.

Summarizing the Need Subsystem

We symbolically create needs that shape and are shaped by ideology. The need subsystem highlights communication patterns related to intrapersonal categorizing. In our symbolizing activity,

- we attribute and deny individual- and group-stressing needs,
- we advocate need attributions and denials, and
- we open and close communication channels in response to need advocacy.

The need subsystem interacts with the power subsystem: we form social interdependencies to meet biosocial and symbolic needs.

❖ POWER SUBSYSTEM: INTERPERSONAL CATEGORIZING

As we symbolically construct ideology, we symbolically create and reify interpersonal roles, hierarchy, and relational expectancies (Brown, 1978). We *interpersonally* categorize to fulfill our inherent need to construe an ordered world between self and others—to interpret our role and place in relation to other people.

The RSI model names this aspect of symbolic categorizing as **power**. Power is the degree to which we feel interdependent with another person or group in satisfying our needs and in choosing futures (Brown, 1986). A **power share** is the responsibility that individuals or groups have in selecting futures in a social system (Boulding, 1978; Brown). Power-sharing social systems form around meeting biosocial and symbolic needs.

For example, U.S. society has constructed a power-sharing system to satisfy a couple's symbolic need for marriage. The system components include people who enact the roles of potential spouses, a state licensing official, a minister or magistrate, and perhaps a wedding planner. Power involves agreed-on formal and informal rules for interaction among the system components. The engaged couple pays money to the state licensing official. In exchange, the official provides a license to marry. Each of these power shareholders shapes how the others in the marriage system choose futures. If the two individuals wish to be socially recognized as married, they will choose to acquire a license and say vows before a state-recognized official who will name them as *married*. A person to be married feels increased interdependency or attributes a larger power share to the state licensing official and the minister than a person who is already married. The power subsystem of the RSI model provides insight into the interconnections that constitute social systems.

Constituting Relational Names

To constitute power-sharing systems, we symbolically categorize similarities and differences among people to create the relationships that connect the people and groups of a system. We begin by learning to name *self* and *other*. This fundamental difference between the experience of *self* and *other* enables us to create the symbolic category of *interpersonal relationship*, another name for an interpersonal system (Brown, 1978). Language tutors teach us our language community's names for the components of our social systems and the interpersonal relationships that connect those components. For example, you learn to name a particular system component *mother* and another one *father* and yourself *their child* and the relationship among the components as *parent/child*. Your later life becomes filled with relational names such as *friend, employee, manager, grandparent*, and *political ally*, and relationships such as *friend/enemy*, and *employee/employer*.

Our relational names are symbolically created and have no external existence (Leach, 1976). We make real these symbolic categories by pointing to particular people in external experience who exemplify the criterial attributes we associate with the relational names. We typically give the name *mother* to a person who fulfills the criterial attribute of birthing or adopting a child or who enacts the care-giving attributes associated with the symbolic category *mother*. What happens, though, when a woman who is fifty-six remarries, and the couple desires a child? The woman decides to use another woman's eggs, fertilized by her husband and implanted in her womb. What if the eggs come from her adult daughter from her previous marriage? Who do we name as the *mother, sister,* and *grandmother* when the woman gives birth (Kövecses, 2006)?

We also reify relational names by the use of objects. A diploma reifies a person's status as a *graduate*. Stripes on a person's shirt make real the symbolic category *master sergeant*. What objects reify relational names attributed to you, such as student, employee, or Christian? Through our talk, behaviors, and objects, we highlight the difference that makes a difference among people to constitute relational names.

Our relational names create expectancies about how system participants will behave. Suppose you interact occasionally with a person you name *coworker*. One day, the coworker suggests you go out for coffee together. As expected in the workplace system, you chat about work. A week later, the coworker invites you again for coffee. This time, you discuss movies and hobbies. This pattern of behavior continues; each week you and the coworker get coffee and talk about a widening array of topics. After a while, you wonder whether the behaviors fit the expectancies you have learned to associate with the relational name *coworker*. Maybe they fit the expectancies associated with *friend*. One day the coworker invites you to dinner and a movie. Does the name *friend* still apply, or should this person be renamed as *more-than-a-friend*? How can you decide?

You might seek out people you trust to help determine the criterial attributes for naming the relationship. Your friends might ask, "Did she pay for dinner?" "Did he kiss you?" "Is she married?" to see if the person's actions fit the expectancies they associate with *more-than-a-friend*. In the end, though, you and the coworker must negotiate the relational name. You as an individual cannot decide how to name your connection to the other person without that person agreeing to enact the expectancies of that relational name, and vice versa. Our social interactions to negotiate relational names and expectancies create social interventions.

You alone cannot name your place in the social system without others in the system agreeing to **ratify** or recognize and consent to that name (Brown, 1978). Your relationship with your coworker cannot be *more-than-a-friend* unless both of you agree to enact the behaviors expected of *more-than-a-friend*. Suppose one day a classmate announces, "I'm the professor today. No class." Are you likely to ratify how she has named her place in the classroom system and leave? Although she might say she is the professor, the name will be meaningless unless other system participants agree to attribute that name to her and act as if she can enact the role expectancies of *professor*. Unless people agree to enact the role *students*, she alone cannot constitute the *professor/student* relationship. Thus, in our interactions, we negotiate names for self and other and act together to reify the names. In the process, we symbolically constitute social hierarchy.

Constituting Social Hierarchy

In our naming of self and other, we create what the RSI model calls **reciprocal** and **complementary** relations (Brown, 1986). When we emphasize the *shared* social identity between self and other, we constitute *reciprocal* or peer relationships (Brown). For example, *friends*, *coworkers*, *partners*, and *allies* are names for relationships that we treat as being on the *same* level in the social hierarchy. Reciprocal relational names convey the expectancy of *equality*.

When we emphasize *differences* in social identity between self and other, we constitute *complementary* relationships, or relational names that we act as if they complete each other (Brown, 1986). For example, *employer/employee, coach/player, parent/child, allies/enemies, winners/losers*, and *in-group/out-group* are names we give to relationships we treat as complementary. The names complete each other in that we act as if employers could not be employers without employees, and so forth. Our ability to construct complementary relational names enables us to act as if some social hierarchy roles are *superior* and others are *subordinate* (Brown). Complementary relational names convey the expectancy of *inequality*.

We symbolically construct social system hierarchy by interpreting some relationships as reciprocal and others as complementary. Consider the system of interdependencies constructed to meet your educational needs. One interpersonal system within the educational power-sharing system is the reciprocal *student-student*. Students interact with each other as if they have a shared social identity—learners with similar goals who complete similar tasks to achieve those goals.

Students reify the *equality* of the relationship in language, behaviors, and objects. They call each other by first names, wear similar types of clothing, sit in the same types of desks, and complete the same types of assignments. Each student expects to interact with other students as an *equal*. Students also expect the professor to treat all students alike.

Professor and *student* are names given to an interpersonal system of complementary power shareholders. Students act as if the *professor* holds a superior position in the social hierarchy, and the professor acts as if *students* are subordinate. Professors and students foreground *differences* in social identify through language, behavior, and objects. The professor calls students by their first names; students address the professor by title and last name. The professor stands; students sit. The professor gives assignments; students complete assignments. The professor has an office; students have backpacks. Professors and students expect to interact *unequally*.

Maintaining and Challenging Social Hierarchy

We maintain and change symbolically constructed social hierarchy through shifts in **cooperation** and **competition** (Brown, 1978, 1986). When we *cooperate* to recognize and enact the expectancies of recipro-cal and complementary relationships, we maintain the social hierar-chy's status quo. Professors and students *cooperate* to recognize each other's role and hierarchical place by agreeing to enact the expectancies associated with the relational name.

We can also challenge the social hierarchy by offering *competing* names and expectancies for relationships. You, as student, could choose not to ratify the *professor/student* relationship by refusing to complete course assignments. *Competition* ensues in that you offer a *competing* name or expectancy for the relationship. Perhaps you attempt to rename the relationship from *professor/student* to *dictator/rebel*. You could also attempt to constitute an alternative expectancy—from one of *inequality* to one of *equality* between *professor/student*. The professor might respond by attempting to maintain the current complementary name *professor/student* by giving failing grades if you persist in offering a competing relational name.

Although we talk as if competition and cooperation are exclusive cat-egories, each can entail the other. The relational strategies can be **mixed.** For example, two rival basketball teams must cooperate to compete to enact the game. Politicians must cooperate to compete to enact debates. All systems require cooperative components to exist as a system, although the components might simultaneously compete with each other.

In a different setting, the social system hierarchy among the same persons can change. How do relational names and expectancies shift when the professor takes his car in for repairs and discovers that the mechanic is his student? What happens if the professor attempts to maintain the expectancies of the *professor/student* relationship in this experience and refuses to ratify the *mechanic/customer* complementary name? Could the relationship also be interpreted as reciprocal—*professor/mechanic*—emphasizing the advanced training of each person?

Overall, social interventions occur as we rhetorically shift emphases from (1) cooperating to maintain the roles and rules of hierarchy, to (2) offering competing versions of relational names and expectancies.

Motivating Interdependencies

We assume that people and groups have motivations for cooperating and competing in the formation of systems. The RSI model draws on economist Kenneth Boulding's (1978) concept of social organizers to describe the motivations that we might attribute to system relationships (Brown, 1986). Boulding suggests that the motives of *exchange*, *threat*, and *integry* organize system interdependencies (Brown).

For example, we can interpret the *professor/student* relationship as being organized by *exchange*. Students enroll in the professor's classes and meet the professor's need for a job and financial security. In **exchange**, students expect that the professor will provide useful knowledge at a level they understand to meet their need for education and career potentialities. The relationship is motivated by the *exchange* of needs-meeting behavior.

The *professor/student* interdependency could also be motivated by the *threat* of non-needs-meeting behavior. Students attend class and meet assignment deadlines because they expect the **threat** of failing grades. The professor prepares information-rich and interesting lectures because students could *threaten* to drop the class and influence future enrollments. The relationship is motivated by the expectancy of *threat*.

Finally, we can interpret the *professor/student* system as organized by **integry**, or "based on a shared meaning dependent on the *identity* of [the] parties" (Brown, 1986, p. 194). Students complete assignments because they expect the professor to be an ally in their desire to learn and make the world a better place. The professor develops creative learning projects because she expects students to share in the desire for knowledge as a way for all parties to achieve the American dream. The relationship is motivated by *integry*, or an interpretation of a collective identity as human beings in the meeting of needs.

Overall, as we symbolically create relationships, we constitute expectancies about the motivations underlying the connection between system components. Although we have talked as if one social organizer is primary in motivating a relationship, all organizers can motivate a relationship. The *student/professor* interdependency can entail exchange, threat, and integry at the same time. However, we tend to emphasize one organizer more than the other two when we interpret system interconnections. Shifts in our interpretations of the motivations that generate the interdependencies also result in social interventions.

Choosing Futures

As we symbolically constitute the relationships that form social systems, we create *power* by constituting formal and informal rules for how to interact as part of reifying the system relationship. These rules form what sociologist Niklas Luhmann (1979) names **power codes.** When we interact with others, we face unlimited choices about how to talk and behave. We limit our behavior and actions by agreeing to enact the relationship's expectancies—to follow the relationship's *power code.* In essence, a *power code* is a language that communicates choices (Brown, 1986).

Power codes influence the choices we make when interacting with others in our social systems. They shape what the RSI model calls **future choosing** (Brown, 1986). Suppose you intern with a local public relations firm. Your supervisor gives you assignments. You face the contending choices of completing all of the assignments, some of the assignments, or none of the assignments. Because of the unspoken power code that governs the *supervisor/intern* relationship, you tend to accept the first choice—completing all of the assignments—because you recognize that the supervisor can shape your future. She can give you challenging or boring tasks; she can write positive or negative recommendations for you; she can hire you when you graduate. By cooperating, you provide her with a valuable worker; in exchange, you gain support for your goals. You could also select to violate power code expectancies and reject the first choice. In so doing, you and the supervisor might negotiate a future in which you no longer intern for the firm. Offering a competing power code challenges social hierarchy and can result in a shift to a relationship organized by threat.

Power codes reduce the complexity of experience by providing an efficient way to make choices (Luhmann, 1979). They simplify reality.

They enable us to make "action or policy decisions without deliberating in the classical sense" (Brown, 1986, p. 181). Interns do not spend time debating whether they should do the assignments, and supervisors do not spend time lecturing interns on reasons to do the assignments. Interns *choose a future* in which they complete the assignments based on a power code that presumes that interns must complete tasks that supervisors require to pass the internship. Much of our future choosing is related to fulfilling "others' wishes, unstated preferences, or direct orders" as opposed to reasoned, logical choice making without regard for relationship (Brown, p. 181).

Two key attributes form power codes, according to Luhmann (1979). First, the preferences of the *power holder* will be selected over the preferences of the *power subject* (Luhmann). In the *professor/student* interdependency, we interpret professors to be power holders and students to be power subjects. Students usually select to follow the preferences of the professor.

Second, challenging the power code or ignoring the preferences of the power holder can lead to **sanctions**—power-holder actions that attempt to force compliance with the code (Luhmann, 1979). An employee who refuses to work might experience the sanction of no pay or being fired to force him to work. Brown (1986) notes that sanctions can range from "(1) suffering the displeasure of the power holder, to (2) disappointment of salient desires, to (3) undergoing violence" (p. 183). When power holders enact sanctions, the system in which the power holders and subjects participate may no longer meet their needs. The employee's need for financial security and the employer's need for a reliable worker go unfulfilled. The relationships that constitute the social system may fail.

Shifting Interdependencies

The power holder and power subject roles are not static entities (Brown, 1986). Which person we name as *power holder* or *power subject* depends on which system interdependencies we foreground and background. Suppose you interpret a professor's actions to be *unfair grading*, an act that violates the *professor/student* power code expectancy that professors will grade students fairly. The professor offers a competing power code. How are professors interdependent with students? Professors need students to fill classes to maintain their teaching position and earn money. They need students with whom they can share knowledge, and they need ideas to generate research. Professors need positive student evaluations to advance in the institutional hierarchy.

In this view of system interdependency, professors are power subjects to the power-holding students.

As power holder, you might enact sanctions such as complaining to the department chair about the professor's actions, dropping the professor's class, or writing negative end-of-course evaluations to *remind* the professor of system interdependency. In so doing, you enact a competitive relationship. By enforcing sanctions, you hope to encourage the professor to cooperate once again with power code. Professors and students, then, share power in negotiating each other's future. Students are interdependent with professors for their future as college graduates and career professionals. Professors are interdependent with students for their futures as candidates for higher levels of rank and positions at other institutions. Without cooperation, their needs will go unmet.

Our interdependencies change as our interpretation of needs changes. Your need for education, as reified in the attainment of a college degree, increases your interdependency with persons such as professors, college administrators, textbook suppliers, and financial aid givers. These power shareholders play a role in mediating your goal of obtaining a college degree. Your choices regarding classes and the amount of free time you have each day will be selected in negotiation with them. But once you have graduated, then what? Your interdependency with the higher education system declines, but your interdependency with other power-sharing systems increases as you seek to meet previously backgrounded or newly attributed needs, such as the need to repay student loans. Shifts in interpretations of interdependency for future choosing and challenges to the power code regulating those interdependencies create social interventions.

Summarizing the Power Subsystem

We symbolically create interdependencies that form social system hierarchy and power codes that transmit choices in future choosing. The power subsystem foregrounds the communication patterns related to interpersonal categorizing. In our symbolizing activity,

- we cooperate and compete to enact relational names and expectancies of symbolically constructed social hierarchy,
- we confirm and disconfirm power code in negotiating and selecting futures, and
- we attribute increased and decreased interdependency with specific power-sharing systems in mediating our needs and choosing futures.

The power subsystem interacts with the attention subsystem: we act together to create interpretations of experience to make comprehensive sense of our experiences (Brown, 1978).

❖ ATTENTION SUBSYSTEM:
    INTERPRETATIVE CATEGORIZING

As we symbolically constitute ideology, we negotiate interpretations of experience in the form of complex naming patterns (Brown, 1978, 1982). As we name needs and power, we also symbolically create templates or worldviews that explain and account for daily experience. The RSI model refers to this subsystem of the ideology-constituting process as **attention** (Brown). We construct interpretations of experience by directing our *attention* to some aspects of experience and away from others.

Perhaps you have encountered a visual perception exercise consisting of an ambiguous black and white picture similar to the one shown in Figure 3.1. You make sense of the picture as *face* or *vase* by foregrounding either the white or the black aspect of the picture and

Figure 3.1   Face or Vase? What Do You Foreground and Background?

backgrounding the other aspect. In like manner, we symbolically create complex naming patterns such as *hard work leads to material success* by foregrounding examples of people who worked long hours and now live in $8 million houses. At the same time, the naming pattern backgrounds examples of people who worked long hours but live in low-income housing projects.

Suppose someone hands you the visual perception exercise in Figure 3.1 and asks, "What do you see?" The expectancy is constituted that you will see *something* rather than ambiguous black and white splotches. Similarly, our ideological system creates the expectancy that we will "see" meaning in experience. For example, the American dream ideology promotes the expectancy that we can create a more perfect life. Participants in this ideology are primed to interpret actions and behaviors in ambiguous experience as contributing to or hindering achievement of the dream. Thus, we interpret the action of *hard work* as an experience that contributes to realizing the American dream by rhetorically linking it with *material success*, an attribute of the dream.

Experiencing Anomalies

At times, however, the expectancies constituted by our complex naming patterns are violated, as in the case of people who work hard but are unable to demonstrate material success in the form of improved housing. Lived experience fails to match the expectancies generated by our naming patterns. The RSI model refers to the difference between our symbolically constituted expectancies about experience and our lived experience as an **anomaly** (Brown, 1982). Rhetorical scholar Russ Corley (1983) explains that an anomaly "arises when someone asserts that an accepted categorization of reality is 'inadequate,' i.e., that the expectancies created by a name are violated by experience" (p. 45). When we encounter *difference* between our symbolically constituted expectancies and day-to-day experience, we become aware of *incompleteness* in our interpretations of experience.

Anomalies are inherent in the naming process because the abstracting process that enables us to categorize symbolically also creates gaps in our naming patterns (Brown, 1978). Because we foreground some aspects of experience and background others to categorize symbolically, our names for experience are always *incomplete*. Our symbolic constructions always direct our attention *away* from parts of experience. To interpret the visual perception exercise as *face*, you avoid attending to experience that could be categorized as *vase*.

To symbolically categorize SUVs as *destroyers of the American dream*, an environmental group might *direct attention to* how SUVs use resources and contribute to global warming, thus violating the expectancy of progress in fulfilling the American dream. The RSI model calls this pattern **anomaly-featuring communication** because we are highlighting anomalies in our interpretations. At the same time, the group *backgrounds* the SUV's role as a symbol that represents *status* and *success*, and by extension, the American dream. The RSI model calls this pattern **anomaly-masking communication** because we mask attention to anomalies in our interpretations. The group's complex name for SUVs is incomplete. By anomaly masking, it ignores aspects of experience that could be symbolically categorized as *success*.

We tend to take for granted that our complex names reflect the whole experience rather than only parts of experience. We code switch by treating *incomplete* names as if they were *complete* names that capture all of experience (Leach, 1976). This is much like our sensory experience. For example, some researchers estimate that less than half of what we see visually is based on experience stimulating the receptor cones on our retinas. Rather, what we expect to see shapes what we actually see (Talbot, 1992). In addition, we "forget" that our visual experience is incomplete, because our eyes have blind spots where the optic nerve attaches. We act as if we see all of experience. Similarly, we "forget" the blind spots in our naming of experience and act as if our names encompass all of experience. We often are unaware of the incompleteness of our naming patterns until we experience expectancy violations or encounter others promoting alternative names.

The RSI model suggests that the more widely we apply our interpretations for experience, the more likely we will encounter anomalies—experiences that cannot be explained or that appear nonfitting with ideology expectancies (Brown, 1982). Because we have an inherent need for order and to make sense of experience, anomalies create discomfort or dis-ease (Brown, 1978). Our interpretations of experience no longer explain and predict events. Thus, the attention subsystem highlights how we rhetorically attempt to compensate for anomalies to satisfy our need to construe an ordered world.

Compensating for Anomalies

The symbolic abstracting process that enables us to categorize symbolically also allows us to compensate for or make sense of anomalies. The abstracting process that creates the anomalies, paradoxically, makes them go away. The RSI model calls this anomaly-compensating behavior an **attention switch** or **attention shift**. Brown (1978) defines an attention switch as a "periodic refocusing of attention . . . compensatory to symbolic gaps and vicious circles" (p. 135). By shifting attention, we symbolically recategorize experience and reconstitute expectancies so that our world once again becomes predictable. We temporarily rid ourselves of anomalies by shifting what we rhetorically background and foreground in experience.

Brown (1982) describes three criterial attributes of attention switches:

- two or more complex naming patterns for interpreting experience,
- each pattern makes sense of experience, and
- systemic shifts from one pattern to another pattern.

First, a minimum of two complex naming patterns must be available for interpreting experience. Suppose you hold to the naming pattern *hard work leads to advancement* to interpret how people become successful and achieve the American dream. However, you become aware of an anomaly. Despite working fifty hours a week, you still maintain the same hierarchical position you had three years ago. You mention your thoughts to a coworker. The coworker responds by offering an alternative naming pattern: *Hard work doesn't matter. Family connections lead to advancement.* Both you and your coworker have constituted naming patterns that make sense of how a person advances in the organization. A third pattern could also be proposed: *Luck leads to advancement.*

Second, each pattern must make sense to the persons negotiating the name for experience. Suppose your coworker had suggested the interpretation *eating algae leads to advancement.* This name might not fit what you take for granted about experience. You see no relationship between *algae* and *advancement* in your work place. But, if you worked for a company that invests in new food sources, then the interpretation might make sense!

Third, an attention switch requires *movement*—from adherence to one interpretation of experience to adoption of an alternative interpretation of experience because the two templates are incompatible. After your coworker foregrounds the experience that only family members appear to attain higher positions in the organization, you might adopt the complex name *family connections lead to advancement* as a better fit to experience. This attention switch compensates for the anomaly you are not advancing despite your *hard work.*

You could also compensate for the anomaly by altering the attributes that constitute the symbolic category *hard work*. You could account for your lack of advancement by deciding that you must not be meeting the organization's expectancy of hard work. Perhaps you define *hard work* as *working fifty hours a week*, and you think that maybe the company defines it as *sixty hours a week*. You alter the attributes of *hard work* from *fifty* to *sixty hours a week* and begin working more hours. In so doing, you forestall an attention shift to a new naming pattern and maintain the old one of *hard work leads to advancement*.

Finally, you could create a third template that combines attributes of your coworker's template and your recategorization of attributes. Perhaps you decide that advancement hinges on both family connections and hard work. Regardless of whether you shift attention to an alternative template or alternative attributes, an attention switch enables you to compensate for the anomalies inherent in your symbolic constructions.

Constituting Continuity and Change

A key assumption of attention switching is that experience itself is assumed to remain the same—only our way of symbolically categorizing experience changes (Brown, 1982). The piece of paper with the visual perception exercise remains unchanged whether you name it *face* or *vase*. Although experience remains constant after an attention switch, it appears different (Brown, 1986). The difference arises from concurrent shifts in how we name need and power. As our attention shifts, our interpretations of need and power also shift. Brown (1978) likens the change brought about by attention switches to the change that occurs in still water when a stone hits it. Attention switches create ripple effects in our rhetorically constituted ideological system.

For example, if you shift attention from the complex name *hard work leads to advancement* to the complex name *family connections lead to advancement*, you might attribute the need to seek employment in an organization where you have family members. Power shifts as you recategorize the organizational hierarchy from *hard workers/slackers* to *family/nonfamily*. The colleagues whom you name as *nonfamily* seem less important now to the choosing of your future. Your interdependency with *family members* as possible mediators of your future advancement increases. Thus, attention switches have ripple effects in intrapersonal and interpersonal categorizing.

Summarizing the Attention Subsystem

Overall, as we symbolically categorize, we—together with others in our social systems—create interpretations of experience. The attention subsystem highlights the communication patterns we enact to cope with the incompleteness of our interpretative categories. In our symbolizing activity, to compensate for anomalies in currently held interpretations of experience,

- we shift attention to alternative naming patterns for experience that seem more *complete*, or
- we rename the expectancies associated with our currently held naming pattern to maintain that interpretation of experience, or
- we both shift attention and rename expectancies.

The rhetorical process of attention switching generates social continuity and change. The symbolic process that enables us to constitute names and expectancies so that we might act as if we live in an orderly, comprehensible world also empowers us to change that symbolically created world. The next chapter lays out the interventional strategies, tactics, and maneuvers we use to promote social change and continuity.

❖ SUBSYSTEMS AS HOLOGRAPHIC SYSTEMS

In our discussion of subsystems, we have treated each as if it were an independent stand-alone system. However, each subsystem embodies and contains information about the other. Each subsystem is a way of describing an aspect of the naming process, which itself is interconnected with the process of creating ideology. This subsystem characteristic has led Brown (1987) to call the interplay among them *holographic*, by which he means that the relationship among the subsystems demonstrates properties similar to a hologram.

A hologram is a three-dimensional record on two-dimensional photographic film of interference patterns created when two laser beams meet (Talbot, 1992). A single laser beam is split into two. One beam is bounced off the side of an object, such as an apple, on to the film. The second beam bypasses the object and shines on the film. Although the recorded image appears as a bunch of swirls on the film, when light illuminates the film, a three-dimensional image of the apple appears. You can look at the left side of the image and see the apple's left side or look at the top to see the apple's top.

An interesting holographic property is that not only does the whole contain the parts, but the parts contain the whole. If you tear an ordinary piece of photographic film in two, each part contains half of the complete picture. But if you cut a holographic film into pieces and shine light through a piece, it still displays the whole, three-dimensional image of the apple, although with less resolution (Talbot, 1992).

In similar fashion, each subsystem holographically contains information about the whole ideological system. In naming our needs, we simultaneously name our relationships with others and our understanding of the world. Our symbolically constructed social hierarchies reflect our interpretations of needs and experiences. The templates we use to make sense of experience tell us who we are and what we need at the same time. The simultaneous existence and interactions of the intrapersonal, interpersonal, and interpretive subsystems holographically constitute and are constituted by an overall ideological system.

In addition, a holographic perspective assumes that everything is interconnected. This assumption will be explored in more detail in the next chapter when we examine how change in one subsystem results in simultaneous changes in all subsystems. We highlight the patterns of communication that generate system process.

❖ CHAPTER SUMMARY

This chapter examined the structure of the RSI model and explained the names and criterial attributes associated with it. The RSI model assumes we have a need to construe an ordered and meaningful world. We meet that need by symbolically constructing ideology to comprehensively explain and interpret experience. Ideology emerges from and regulates three subsystems of naming—need, power, and attention—which form the RSI model structure.

Need involves the awareness and attribution of biosocial and symbolically created needs, the advocacy of those needs, and the seeking out of potential needs-meeting relationships. Ideology creates expectancies about what we need and how to fulfill needs. In our search for needs-meeters, we constitute power in the form of symbolically constructed social system hierarchy and roles that share in choosing futures. We select futures by enacting power codes that arise out of ideological expectancies about how to act with and toward each other. Finally, we symbolically create interpretations of experience in the form of complex names that lead us to foreground certain aspects of experience and background others. Ideology creates expectancies about experience just as our complex names reify ideology.

Anomalies occur when our expectancies of experience appear not to fit our lived experience and our need for order and connection is unmet. We compensate for anomalies by shifting to an alternative interpretation of experience or reconstituting expectancies associated with a naming pattern, or both. Change seems to be a side effect of the symbolic abstraction process. The process of ideological system change—attention switching—is constant; only the content of the attention switch changes. We closed by considering the holographic nature of the ideological subsystems.

Thus far, we have focused on the parts of the RSI model, which foregrounds what we assume to be continuous in human nature—the drive to constitute and enact ideology via the need, power, and attention subsystems. Chapter 4 puts the components of the RSI model together to form a lens through which we can view the rhetorical process of social intervention into ideological and social systems. It provides the background needed for critiquing and for enacting social interventions.

❖ REVIEW QUESTIONS

1. What are the similarities and differences between a specific name for experience and ideology?

2. What criterial attributes form Brown's definition of *ideology*?

3. What three subsystems constitute and are shaped by ideology? What attributes are unique to each subsystem?

4. Distinguish between *biosocial needs* and *symbolically created* needs. Are there any needs that fit both the biosocial and symbolically created categories?

5. How is *power* defined in the RSI model? On what does it depend to work?

6. What is the difference between *reciprocal relationships* and *complementary relationships*?

7. Distinguish among *threat*, *exchange*, and *integry*. Is one of these to be preferred over another? Why or why not?

8. Describe the attributes and process of an *attention shift* or *attention switch*.

9. What rhetorical strategies do we use to compensate for anomalies?

10. What is a *holographic* perspective? How might it be applied to your interpretation of your daily experiences?

❖ CHAPTER EXERCISES

1. Research political candidates' campaigns by examining their Web sites. How do they symbolically attribute and advocate need? Whom do they identify as possible needs-meeters? How do the Web sites name experience? In what ways do they reify the American dream?

2. Discuss an example of a time when you ignored or challenged a power code in school, at work, or with your family. What was the power code? How did you challenge the power code? What competing relational name did you offer? How did other power shareholders respond to the challenge?

3. As a class, observe two classmates role-play the following power-sharing systems: *doctor/patient, political candidate/voter, plumber/home owner, cashier/customer.* How do your classmates constitute the roles? What do they say or do to reify the relationships?

4. Describe a recent event in which your expectancies of experience did not match your lived experience. What were your expectancies? What actually happened? How did you compensate for the anomalies to make sense of the experience? In what way was your original name for experience *incomplete*?

5. As a class, discuss reasons to support and reject this proposition: "No *rights* exist in nature. Rights were constructed when we named—and thus created—the right to vote, own property, speak and worship freely. *Rights* have become a need that most adherents to the American dream ideology take for granted."

6. Research another interpretation of ideology (e.g., Marxist, Hegelian, Gramscian). Write a brief paper that compares that interpretation to Brown's conceptualization of ideology.

❖ SERVICE LEARNING EXERCISE

Interview leaders of the not-for-profit for which you are volunteering. In the interviews, gather information on how the organization names its needs. You can also consult organizational materials, such as an annual report, to identify needs.

Create a chart that describes the roles that the organizational members enact within the organizational system. Then construct a chart that maps out the systems of interdependency in the local community in which the organization shares power. Identify the social organizers (exchange, threat, integry) that form the basis for these interdependencies. Describe the power code expectancies of the interdependencies.

Finally, review the organization's mission statement and goals. Discuss how the statement and goals reflect the organization's interpretation of experience.

Write a brief report that summarizes how the organization interprets its needs, interdependencies, and purpose. Save this information to use with upcoming service learning exercises.

Under the Lens: Abstracting From Experience

Rhetorical scholar Lee Snyder shares this story to illustrate how our talk about everyday experience always omits parts of experience.

Michael travels with his wife Amanda to meet some of her distant relatives for the first time. He finds Amanda's great-uncle, Bob, especially interesting. Bob is an elderly man who had enjoyed immensely driving his large, old, tail-finned Cadillac down country roads, while puffing on a cigar and listening to the radio. Now, no longer able to drive, Bob keeps the Cadillac under a carport. Every day after supper, he goes out, starts the car, cranks up the radio, and smokes his cigar.

A few months after meeting the old man, Michael learns that Bob had died. Now consider that this old man's life, as far as Michael is concerned, and you too, primarily is encapsulated in the cigar-and-Cadillac story. Does this naming pattern for the old man leave out much? Perhaps Bob served his country and was proud of his time in the military. Maybe he was in love many times and was particularly fond of redheads. Perhaps he collected butterflies and wished he lived in Arizona. But that information will be left out when Michael tells of his experience with Bob and will never be recovered.

In the same way, someday your whole life might be summed up by a short phrase on a tombstone. This phrase will abstract from all of your experience. What would you like that phrase to say? Is there something you want to make sure is not left out? When people in the future tell their stories about you, to what aspects of your experience will they attend? In what ways will their naming of you be *incomplete*?

CHAPTER 4

Widening Circles of Intervention

The next time you get into a car, notice the vehicle's safety features such as seat belts, shoulder straps, air bags, and a collapsible steering column. In the 1960s, few automobiles had the safety devices that we take for granted today. At the time, the U.S. social system symbolically categorized cars as already *built as safe as possible* (Martin, 2002). We explained the anomaly of accidents by naming them *driver negligence* or *unsafe roads*. This interpretation of experience generated the expectancy that if we improved driver's training and the roadways, fewer people would be killed or injured. Driving would become a more nearly perfect experience, thus enacting the American dream.

Yet, the more we invoked this naming pattern to explain accidents, the more we became aware of experiences that deviated from expectancies. Despite improved roadway design, driver's education, and traffic law enforcement, automobile fatalities and injuries grew rather than declined (Martin, 2002). These events violated the ideological expectancy of creating a more nearly perfect world. Perhaps you, like lawyer Ralph Nader, might have been attentive to these anomalies. Like him, you might have proposed an alternative interpretation of accidents by rhetorically foregrounding what had been backgrounded in experience.

The problem, Nader (1965) said, was not only drivers and roadways, but also the automobiles. Car occupants were being killed or injured in a "second collision" with the car's unprotected interior after the initial collision with a vehicle or object (Nader). In addition, Nader claimed that automakers produced cars with faulty braking and steering systems, which caused accidents. Thus, he proposed an alternative naming pattern—*automakers design unsafe vehicles*—to explain accident anomalies. Simultaneously with Nader promoting this attention shift, other people and groups were intervening to *maintain* the prevailing interpretation or to *create* alternative naming patterns to make sense of accidents. The vehicle you ride in today is an outcome of those rhetorical social interventions.

Chapter 3 detailed the symbol-based subsystems that form the RSI model structure. This chapter backgrounds the structure and foregrounds the rhetorical process of social intervention. We review assumptions and vocabulary related to the process, and then we focus on the RSI model's three subsystems as starting points for exploring the communication patterns of intervention. We examine the specific rhetorical strategies and tactics associated with each subsystem for promoting and impeding naming shifts. We conclude the chapter with reflections on the overall process of ideologizing and its connection to social intervention.

Throughout, we use Nader's intervention to exemplify the rhetorical process of social intervention. Everyone in the U.S. social system has been affected by the outcome of his intervention—as drivers and as passengers in cars. In addition, the example allows us to consider the long-term ripple effects of Nader's intervention. As you read about the intervention, think about the way in which you interpret automobiles and account for accidents today.

❖   SYSTEM INTERVENTION

As Chapter 3 noted, the RSI model assumes that human beings have an innate need to construe comprehensively an ordered and connected world. We meet this need by creating an ideological system comprising the need, power, and attention subsystems (Brown, 1978). However, because we symbolically abstract from experience to construct ideology, ideology—like all names for experience—is always *incomplete*.

We constitute ideology by featuring attention to certain patterns and orderings of experience. At the same time, we background other patterns and ways of organizing experience. As a result, we can become aware of experience that deviates from ideological expectancies and threatens our ideological assumptions about order and connectedness. The possibility always exists that someone will emphasize elements of experience that we have backgrounded or that we will experience an event that cannot be explained by our ideological system or both. Such anomalies create disorder or disconnection and prompt social intervention.

System Dynamics

When we become attentive to anomalies in our ideological system, we become aware of deviance. **Deviance** is the difference between what our ideology leads us to expect will happen in experience and what actually seems to happen (Brown, 1978). Our name-generated expectancies fail to match lived experience. They *deviate* from experience outcomes. For example, in the 1960s, Nader (1965) and communicators like him called attention to the anomaly that deaths and injuries were increasing rather than decreasing, despite improved driver's training, law enforcement, and highways. He named lived experience as *deviating* from expectancies generated by the naming patterns *driver responsibility* and *poor roadways* used to explain accidents.

Deviance amplification. Because we need our ideological system to make sense of and predict experience, anomalies create discomfort and imbalance. The more we attend to experience that deviates from expectancies, the more disorderly and imbalanced our ideological system seems to become. Our attention to deviance and feelings of discomfort intensify unless we compensate for the anomalies. Our ideological system may become **deviance amplifying** (Brown, 1978).

In a deviance-amplifying system, the components interact continually to increase or amplify the difference between name-generated expectancies and lived experience. Our ideological system seems less and less able to predict experience outcomes. A deviance-amplifying system is like driving down an icy road during winter. Suppose the car hits an icy spot and begins to skid. You steer into the skid, but you turn a little too hard, and the car starts skidding the other way. Again you overcorrect, and each time you do, the fishtailing gets more out of control, and the car quickly lands in a ditch.

Unless a deviance-amplifying trend is halted or reversed, a system's components may begin relating to each other as a **vicious circle**. In a vicious circle, the components interact with each other in maladaptive ways that intensify deviance trends (Brown, 1978). In essence, the system becomes closed—it is unresponsive to change and alteration. A vicious circle can result in the system running down or collapsing. The system can become like the car in the ditch!

Deviance compensation. To reverse this trend toward a vicious circle, we must find a way to compensate for the anomalies. We must reduce deviance. We must enact what the RSI model calls a **trend reversal** (Brown, 1978). A trend reversal reverses or slows the tendency toward deviance amplifying and enables us to regain a sense of comfort and predictability. The system acts as an open system that adapts to change in ways that maintain the system. We enact ideological system trend reversals through attention shifts, power shifts, and need shifts (Brown).

For example, Nader, the automakers, and the U.S. public were components of a power-sharing social system. In this system, the more the automotive industry promoted the interpretation *cars are built as safe as possible*, the more Nader worked to increase the public's attention to experience that deviated from naming-pattern expectancies. He gave speeches, held press conferences, and lobbied Congress. The automotive industry increasingly worked to maintain its interpretation. It explained deviance by blaming workers who built the cars. It also lobbied Congress and worked to discredit Nader.

Without a reversal of the deviance-amplifying trend, the automotive industry, Nader, and the public would be stuck in a vicious circle that could lead to non-needs-meeting outcomes or system failure. The automotive industry and Nader would continue spending time and resources to promote their interpretations while the public would continue to be killed and injured in accidents. In addition, the system could have marginalized Nader and ignored his interpretation, thus prolonging the manufacture of unsafe cars.

We reverse a deviance-amplifying trend by making sense of the anomalies through attention, power, and need shifts (Brown, 1978). We symbolically recategorize experience to *compensate* for or reduce the deviance so it seems not to exist. The ideological system becomes **deviance compensating** (Brown). It regains balance. We recapture a sense of order and feel as if the world makes sense again.

For example, the attention switch from the interpretation *cars-are-built-as-safe-as-possible* to the interpretation *automakers-build-unsafe-cars* reversed the deviance-amplifying trend. The *new* naming pattern compensated for the anomalies of increased automotive fatalities and injuries, auto part failures, and automaker recalls. This alternative interpretation seemed more able to explain events and predict experience. The system for interpreting accident events was again in balance, but it was *different*. Needs and power also altered. The social system differences after trend reversal point to another key assumption of the RSI model—the interconnectedness of attention, power, and need.

System Interconnection

As Chapter 3 noted, the RSI model assumes that the attention, power, and need subsystems holographically form ideology (Brown, 1978). In the intervention process, a change in the attention subsystem brings about simultaneous changes in the need and power subsystems. In like manner, a shift in the need subsystem results in corresponding shifts in the power and attention subsystems, and alterations in the power subsystem connect to alterations in the need and attention subsystems.

The attention switch from *cars-are-built-as-safe-as-possible* to *automakers-design-unsafe-cars* resulted in changed interpretations of need. The public became more attentive to safety features. It now needed new car designs, safety design engineers, and safety feature suppliers. Power shifted with interpretations of increased interdependency among automakers, the U.S. government, and safety feature suppliers. The public now attributed to vehicle manufacturers shared responsibility for accidents. Consumers redefined power codes by challenging automakers' design authority. As part of the revised power code, the manufacturers no longer had final say over car design (McCarry, 1972).

Subsystem emphasis. Although the RSI model assumes that the three subsystems are holographically related and shifts in them occur simultaneously, we must use linear language to discuss social interventions. Thus, when we talk about an intervention, we emphasize one ideological subsystem at a time, as we did in Chapter 3 to describe each subsystem. When analyzing social change, we act as if one subsystem—attention, power, or need—is primary over the other two. Suppose you are analyzing a movie as a social intervention that attempts to shift how its viewers interpret U.S. health care. You must choose a starting point—attention, power, or need—to begin the analysis. If you select *need*, then your analysis emphasizes communication patterns related to the need subsystem. You background the power and attention subsystems as you analyze need. Then you background need to study the side effects of a need shift on the other subsystems. Chapter 5 discusses starting points in more detail.

Intervener emphasis. In addition, the RSI model assumes that all interventions involve multiple interconnected interveners. As one person or group is attempting to influence the naming of experience, another person or group within that system can also be attempting to intervene

(Brown, 1978). However, again, linear language results in our often emphasizing one intervener more than the others when describing an intervention. In this chapter, we treat Nader as if he were the primary intervener who acted as a representative of the U.S. public component of the social system. However, he worked with other people and groups to promote his intervention, just as other people and groups organized to forestall his intervention.

Intervention outcomes. The **holistic** nature of an ideological system and the interconnectedness of multiple interveners mean that we cannot imagine all of the results of a subsystem shift. The entire outcome of any intervention is unpredictable. Although Nader accomplished his interventional goal of promoting a social reinterpretation of car safety, the final outcome of his intervention in terms of laws passed and car redesign was not exactly as he had envisioned (McCarry, 1972). Not every safety proposal he advocated was enacted. Numerous interveners *negotiated* the resulting future of automotive design.

System Intervention Enactment

Because the RSI model emphasizes *intervention into*, rather than control of, how we symbolically constitute ideological systems, it directs our attention to the rhetorical patterns that generate social intervention attempts. Sociologist Barbara Hanson (1995) notes that **holistic** approaches emphasize detecting and exploring the overall patterns of system change and nonchange. The RSI model, as a holistic rhetorical approach, highlights patterns of communication that appear to recur when we intervene into a social system.

Interveners seem to employ particular patterns of communication, which the RSI model calls *maneuvers*, *tactics*, and *strategies*, to enact social interventions (Brown, 1978). The RSI model views these rhetorical actions as a hierarchy, with each more abstract than the other:

- **Maneuvers** accomplish tactics,
- **tactics** bring about strategic results, and
- **strategy** constitutes the ultimate framework for organizing the intervention (Brown).

Maneuvers are the specific texts or actions that we observe or notice when we study an intervention. Nader's (1965) book *Unsafe at Any Speed* is an example of a maneuver to promote his alternative naming pattern.

The examples, statistics, and testimony within the pages of the book are also maneuvers. Rhetorical maneuvers range from using ethos, pathos, logos, metaphor, and arguing by example in discourse, to creating events, writing books, shooting filming documentaries, and organizing protests.

Maneuvers carry out **tactics**, or the plans that an intervener undertakes to promote the intervention. Tactics involve increasing attention to anomalies and disorder in a system's interpretation of experience. *Unsafe at Any Speed* enacted Nader's (1965) tactic of increasing the U.S. public's attention to the need for improved car design by providing it with information that highlighted anomalies in the *built-as-safe-as-possible* interpretation.

From the maneuvers and tactics, we extrapolate or infer the interventional **strategy** or general framework guiding the maneuvers and tactics. The maneuvers and tactics of *Unsafe at Any Speed* (Nader, 1965) strategically shifted our attention *away* from individual-centered needs (driver responsibility) and *to* group-centered needs (automaker responsibility).

In the next sections of this chapter, we use Nader's intervention to exemplify each subsystem's strategies, tactics, and maneuvers. We pick up where we left off in Chapter 3 by first examining attention interventions, then power interventions, and finally need interventions, remembering that the three subsystems form one interconnected ideological system. Overall, the RSI model leads us to search for the communication patterns and cycles that drive long-term social system change.

❖ ATTENTION INTERVENTION

The U.S. ideological system creates the expectancy that certain events and actions will lead to achieving the American dream (Brown, 1970). When we become aware of experience that violates this expectancy, we become more attentive to anomalies in our ideological system. **Attention interventions** occur when we attempt to compensate for the deviance created by anomalies (Brown, 1982). According to the RSI model, attention intervention dynamics involve the encouraging and discouraging of alternative interpretations of experience.

Attention Intervention Dynamics

Strategically, attention interventions involve a shift *away from* naming experience outcomes as being the *same as* the expectancies generated by a complex naming pattern and a shift *to* interpreting the outcomes as *different from* the expectancies and vice versa. The RSI model identifies two rhetorical strategies used to promote and forestall attention shifts—**anomaly-featuring communication** and **anomaly-masking communication** (Brown, 1978, 1982). Anomaly-featuring communication *emphasizes* or *features* attention to the deviance between outcomes and expectancies. It foregrounds the differences and backgrounds the similarities between experience and expectancies. Anomaly-masking communication *de-emphasizes* or *masks* attention to the deviance between outcomes and expectancies. It foregrounds the similarities and backgrounds the differences between experience and expectancies. All attention interventions involve both types of strategies simultaneously.

For example, Nader (1965) attempted to shift attention *away from* the complex name *cars are built as safe as possible* and *to* the interpretation that *automakers design unsafe cars*. Strategically, he promoted the shift by *featuring* anomalies in the *built-as-safe-as-possible* naming pattern. He also *masked* attention to anomalies in the proposed *unsafe-car-design* naming pattern, such as the accident-related experiences of alcohol and driving age.

Deviance amplification. Attention interventions involve cycles of increased and decreased communication related to anomalies in our interpretations of experience. We become more attentive to the *incompleteness* of our naming patterns:

1. The more our attention to deviance between expectancies and lived experience *increases*,

2. the more our advocacy of alternative ways of being, knowing, and valuing *increases*, and

3. the more our openness to a revised interpretation of experience to regain a sense of order and predictability *increases* (Brown).

Thus, as we increase attentiveness to anomalies, we amplify deviance. Our current interpretation of experience seems to make less sense. Figure 4.1 illustrates the deviance-amplifying cycle.

Deviance compensation. To reverse the deviance-amplifying trend, we must explain the anomalies. We do so by symbolically recategorizing experience and by renaming the expectancies associated with a naming

Figure 4.1   Deviance-Amplifying System

This diagram shows a system that has become deviance amplifying. Deviance amplifying occurs when the system's communication patterns emphasize MORE, MORE, and MORE without a rhetorical trend reversal. In addition, although not illustrated, a system could become deviance amplifying when its communication patterns emphasize LESS, LESS, and LESS without a reversal.

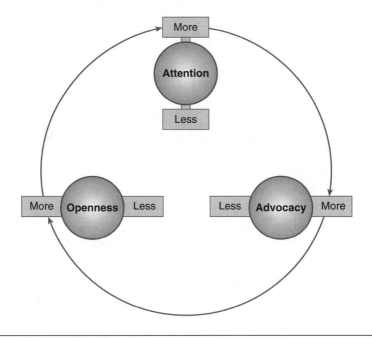

Source: The diagram is based on Brown (1978, Figure 1), © Taylor & Francis, LTD. http://www.infoworld.com.

pattern. In both instances, the attention subsystem becomes more deviance compensating:

1. As our attention to deviance between expectancies and lived experience *decreases*,

2. our advocacy of alternative ways of being, knowing, and valuing *decreases*, and

3. our openness to alternative interpretations of experience *decreases* (Brown, 1982).

Deviance compensation results in the world again making sense. Figure 4.2 illustrates a deviance-compensating system.

Figure 4.2   Deviance-Compensating System

This diagram exemplifies a system that was initially deviance amplifying (MORE, MORE, MORE) but experienced an attention, power, or need shift. Deviance compensating occurs when the system's communication patterns begin emphasizing LESS attention to anomalies, LESS advocacy of anomalies, and LESS openness to alternative naming patterns. However, the RSI model suggests that eventually we will become aware of new anomalies and thus begin the cycle again by shifting back to MORE.

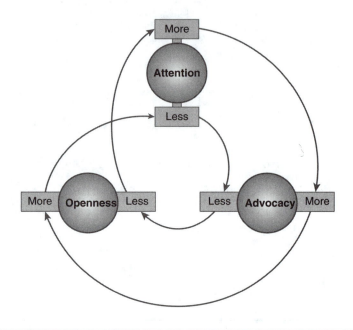

Source: Diagram is based on Brown (1978, Figures 2 & 4), © Taylor & Francis, LTD. http://www.infoworld.com.

Attention intervention strategy is actualized by tactical shifts in axiology, ontology, and epistemology, or in our ways of **valuing, being, and knowing** (Brown, 1978, 1982). Nader's (1965) book *Unsafe at Any Speed* increased the public's attention to anomalies in the interpretation *cars are built as safe as possible* and to alternative ways of valuing, being, and knowing. His attention intervention emphasized an *axiological* shift from valuing automotive *style* to valuing automotive *safety*. The intervention also asked the public to change its sense of *being* from passive consumers to automotive design standard setters. Finally, the intervention shifted the public's way of *knowing* by offering it access to information that previously was the sole domain of automakers or the government. *Safety* became a significant category of information.

With the attention shift to the template *automakers design unsafe cars*, anomalies such as automotive fatality and injury statistics and automotive recalls were explained. Such events fit the expectancies of the naming pattern *unsafe cars*. Adoption of this template led to predictions that, unless car design changed, more deaths and recalls would occur. The interpretative shift from *safe* to *unsafe* eventually encouraged actions such as the passage of the National Traffic and Motor Vehicle Safety and Highway Safety acts in 1966, and the addition of vehicle safety features.

Alternative outcomes. How might automakers have intervened to *maintain* the template *cars are built as safe as possible*, despite the anomalies featured by Nader? To attempt to forestall an attention switch, those interveners would *mask* attention to the anomalies. They might explain the increasing automotive fatality and injury rate by pointing out that more people were driving. Thus, increasing death rates and injuries would be expected outcomes of *an increased number of drivers*. In addition, interveners could rename the attributes of *safe* to include a certain percentage of deaths and injuries. As long as they could make sense of the anomalies, they could forestall an attention switch.

The more we attempt to apply, articulate, and extend a particular interpretation of experience, such as *cars are built as safe as possible*, the more likely we will become aware of backgrounded events and actions that deviate from the expectancies associated with the interpretation (Brown, 1978, 1982). As our attention to anomalies increases, our ability to explain them by renaming expectancies decreases, and deviance amplifies. Without a deviance-compensating attention shift or a renaming of expectancies, the attention subsystem will spiral into a vicious circle. In the end, we might interpret all experience as lacking sense and meaning (Brown).

Attention Intervention Enactment

To *promote* an attention shift, we *emphasize* anomalies in the *currently held* interpretation of events and actions (Brown, 1982). We propose an alternative naming pattern that foregrounds aspects of experience that have been backgrounded in the prevailing interpretation. We also *de-emphasize* anomalies in the interpretation we are promoting. As the automotive safety example illustrates, Nader featured anomalies to create disorder in the template *cars-are-built-as-safe-as-possible* and masked anomalies in his proposed template.

To *forestall* an attention shift, we *emphasize* anomalies in the *proposed* naming pattern (Brown, 1982). At the same time, we *de-emphasize* anomalies in the *currently held* naming pattern (Brown). The automakers invoked anomaly-masking and anomaly-featuring communication to attempt to prevent an attention shift and to maintain the prevailing interpretation of accident events.

Regardless of whether we are promoting or impeding an attention switch, the overall goal is to minimize or mask anomalies and contradictions in symbolically created ideology (Brown, 1982). From Nader's perspective, anomalies would be reduced with an attention shift to the proposed naming pattern. From the automakers' perspective, anomalies would be reduced by featuring attention to contradictions in the proposed naming pattern. By minimizing anomalies, our symbolically constituted expectancies about experience appear to match lived experience, fulfilling our need for order and predictability.

Attention Intervention Cycles

Because we abstract to create interpretations of experience, we always encounter anomalies (Brown, 1982). After we shift from one template for making sense of experience to another, the newly adopted interpretation itself eventually will appear incomplete. Again, we will seek an alternative interpretation that seems more able to make sense of and to predict experience. The American dream ideology entails the expectancy that we can construct the perfect world. We constantly must explain the anomaly that the anticipated world has yet to come into being. Otherwise, we face an attention shift to an alternative ideology or ideological system breakdown.

In the 1960s, the attention shift to *unsafe car design* created the expectancy that if we built safer cars, then we could create a more nearly perfect life. We have developed a variety of automotive safety devices—daytime running lights, child seats, backup cameras—and laws to enforce their use. At the same time, though, we have had to account for the anomaly that the perfect world has yet to come about. Thus, our naming patterns continue to change as we shift attention to experience that was backgrounded in the car *safety* template, such as *cars contribute to oil dependency* or *cars increase global warming*, to mask the anomaly and maintain our ideological expectancies. Perhaps the creation of alternative fuels in addition to safer cars will enable us to build a more nearly perfect world.

Because of the interconnectedness of the attention, power, and need subsystems, any discussion of attention shifts also implies power and need shifts (Brown, 1978). Attention shifts involve changes in interpretations of social hierarchy and needs. Attention interventions become key to reversing deviance-amplifying trends in the power subsystem (Brown, 1986).

❖ POWER INTERVENTION

In the U.S. social system, ideology creates the expectancy of perfection in social order. When we become aware that our power-sharing interdependencies are not meeting needs or that power code violations are creating disorder, we become more attentive to anomalies in our interpretations of power. **Power interventions** occur when we attempt to compensate for deviance created by power anomalies (Brown, 1986). According to the RSI model, power intervention dynamics involve the encouraging or discouraging of alternative interpretations of power-sharing interdependency.

Power Intervention Dynamics

Strategically, power interventions involve a shift *away from* cooperating to enact social hierarchy and power code expectancies and a shift *to* challenging social order by proposing competing interdependencies and codes, and vice versa (Brown, 1986). Power interventions involve strategic shifts of attention to and from interpretations of *cooperation* and *competition*.

Power intervention strategy is actualized by tactical shifts in *exchange, threat,* and *integry* (Brown, 1986). With the publication of *Unsafe at Any Speed,* Nader (1965) attempted to shift the interpretation of interdependency between automakers and consumers *away from* cooperation motivated by exchange and *to* competition motivated by threat. With knowledge gained from the book, consumers could now name automakers as *threatening* their safety and could *threaten* not to purchase cars. They could *compete* with the automakers' standard-setting role by seeking governmental *cooperation* to regulate car design.

Deviance amplification. Power interventions involve cycles of increased and decreased communication related to anomalies in interpretations of social order. We become more attentive to deviance between the expectancies and experience of social hierarchy:

1. The more our attention to non-needs-meeting interdependencies and power code violations *increases,*

2. the more our advocacy of alternative ways of social organizing *increases,* and

3. the more our openness to a revised interpretation of power-sharing interdependency and power code to regain a sense of social order *increases* (Brown, 1986).

Thus, as we increase attentiveness to anomalies, we amplify deviance between our interpretations of social hierarchy and power code and lived experience. Our current interpretation seems to make less sense. Figure 4.1 illustrates the deviance-amplifying cycle.

Deviance compensation. To reverse the deviance-amplifying trend and restore social order, we must minimize the anomalies. We do so by adopting alternative interpretations of interdependency and by recategorizing power code expectancies. In both instances, the power subsystem becomes more deviance compensating:

1. As our attention to non-needs-meeting interdependencies and power code violations *decreases,*

2. our advocacy of alternative ways of social organizing *decreases,* and

3. our openness to alternative interpretations of interdependency and power code expectancies *decreases* (Brown, 1986).

Deviance compensation occurs, and we regain social order. Figure 4.2 illustrates the deviance-compensating cycle.

Roles and expectancies. Prior to interventions such as *Unsafe at Any Speed,* the power-sharing system of automakers, consumers, media, and U.S. government gave the automakers the authority to set vehicle design standards (Nader, 1965). In exchange, the public and government expected automakers to produce quality vehicles to meet society's transportation needs. Consumers performed the power-sharing role of ratifying automakers' choices by purchasing vehicles. Consumers relied on automaker-supplied information and media reviews to enact the role of informed ratifiers. The media fulfilled consumers' information needs with articles on automotive styles and features. In exchange for the reports, automakers purchased advertising and gave the media test vehicles and mechanical specifications (Nader). The government enacted the role of regulating driver behavior and developing road designs. The power-sharing system appeared to mediate the power share-holders' needs and goals. System participants cooperated to maintain social stability by affirming the automakers' authority to set standards in choosing the future of automotive design.

With the publication of *Unsafe at Any Speed*, Nader (1965), as a representative of the U.S. public, increased attention to anomalies. He challenged social order by offering an alternative interpretation of interdependency. His book offered numerous examples to reason that automakers violated power code by designing unsafe automobiles and by withholding information that limited consumers' ability to act as informed ratifiers. It reported that automakers impeded the media's ability to provide automotive safety information by threatening to withdraw advertising and test cars. These actions resulted in the media affirming the automakers' designs by offering driving tips and car handling advice rather than spotlighting design flaws. The book illustrated how the current power-sharing system failed to meet ideological expectancies. Rather than helping consumers mediate their transportation needs and make the world a more nearly perfect place, automakers were killing consumers with unsafe car designs.

To compensate for the anomaly, Nader (1965) proposed a revised social hierarchy, one in which the public, through the government, would set car design standards. Consumers would *sanction* the automakers for violating power code—the public's trust—by legislatively forcing them to provide safety features and safety information. Using legal channels, the power-subject consumers would *remind* the power-holding automakers of their interdependency and power code obligations. At the same time, the public would attribute to the government an increased power share to intervene and regulate U.S. businesses.

To continue satisfying their profit need, automakers would have to cooperate with government requirements and include safety as a design consideration, or they would face threats such as decreased sales, increased lawsuits, and new competitors offering safer cars. Armed with information provided by interveners such as Nader, consumers could now enact their role of informed ratifiers by attending to both safety and style in purchase decisions. Congress later reified the alternative power-sharing system by passing the National Traffic and Motor Vehicle Safety and Highway Safety acts.

Alternative futures. Suppose the power-sharing social system had back-grounded Nader's intervention and maintained the interdependencies. If automakers had continued violating power expectancies by producing unsafe vehicles, then social order challenges, such as lawsuits and new competitors, might have increased. Automakers would have to spend more money to respond to these challenges, reducing their ability to fulfill profit needs. Uninformed consumers would continue purchasing automobiles that increased their risk of accidents and increased social costs such as deaths and hospital bills. Without a deviance-compensating reinterpretation of social hierarchy, the power-sharing system would spiral into a vicious circle, with the power share-holders' needs and goals remaining unsatisfied.

As an alternative, the public and government could have maintained social hierarchy by revising power expectancies to compensate for the anomaly. System participants could have renegotiated the attributes of the automakers' role. They would no longer expect automakers to produce safe vehicles in exchange for design control. Consumers could also have shifted the basis of their relationship with automakers—from exchange to threat—without a legislative mandate for automakers to build safe cars. They could have simply quit buying cars named *unsafe*. In the end, though, automakers, consumers, media, and government adopted the trend-reversing interpretation of interdependencies promoted by interveners such as Nader.

Power Intervention Enactment

To *promote* a power shift, we *foreground* anomalies in the current interpretation of social hierarchy (Brown, 1986). We symbolically categorize the apparent behavior and actions of power shareholders as *deviating* from power-related expectancies. We propose an alternative interpretation of interdependency that seems to better fit the behaviors and actions we observe. We also *background* anomalies in the alternative hierarchy we are promoting.

Unsafe at Any Speed was a rhetorical maneuver to encourage a power shift. The book detailed how the automakers' actions violated the consumers' expectancies for quality products to reason that the power-sharing social system was non-needs-meeting. It described how automakers limited the public's and media's ability to enact their roles in the future choosing of automotive design. It symbolically categorized the existing power-sharing system as *different* from a system that fulfilled needs and power code expectancies.

To *forestall* a power shift, we *emphasize* anomalies in the *proposed* social hierarchy (Brown, 1986). At the same time, we *de-emphasize* anomalies in the *existing* interpretation of interdependency by reinterpreting roles and expectancies. Automakers attempted to maintain the social hierarchy by renaming Nader's role. General Motors (GM) hired a private investigator to research Nader's personal life and find whether Nader was acting in socially unacceptable ways. If so, then GM could threaten to publish this information if Nader continued to challenge its authority (McCarry, 1972). GM believed that Nader would shift from challenging social hierarchy to cooperating with it to protect his reputation.

Also, if the investigator discovered that Nader would profit from lawsuits encouraged by *Unsafe at Any Speed*, then GM could reason that Nader was violating the power expectancies of a citizen acting for the good of the public (McCarry, 1972). GM could feature anomalies in Nader's motives for acting as the public's representative and shift the public's attention away from the revised interdependency proposed by Nader. Thus, power interventions can both promote and forestall the reinterpretation of interdependencies and power code.

Power Intervention Cycles

We constitute social hierarchy and power code by symbolic abstraction. Thus, we always encounter anomalies. After we shift from one social hierarchy to another, the newly adopted social order eventually will appear non-needs-meeting. Again, we will seek an alternative interpretation of social order that seems to minimize anomalies. The American dream ideology creates the expectancy that we can build a social order to enact the perfect world (Brown, 1970). We attempt constantly to compensate for the lack of creating that world by symbolically constituting *alternative* interdependencies and power codes as necessary to achieve perfection.

Shifts in our interpretation of interdependencies involve attention switches. In addition, power-sharing systems undergo revision to meet alternative interpretations of need (Brown, 1986). Thus, power interventions become key to reversing deviance-amplifying trends in the need subsystem (Brown).

❖ NEED INTERVENTION

In the U.S. social system, the American dream ideology creates the expectancy that if we fulfill certain needs, we can achieve a more nearly perfect life (Brown, 1970). When we become aware of experience that violates this expectancy, we become more attentive to anomalies in our interpretations of needs. **Need interventions** occur when we attempt to compensate for deviance created by such anomalies (Brown, 1987). Need intervention dynamics involve the encouraging and discouraging of alternative interpretations of need.

Need Intervention Dynamics

Strategically, need interventions involve a shift *from* emphasizing individuality-stressing needs and *to* foregrounding collectivity-stressing needs, and vice versa (Brown, 1987). Need interventions involve strategic shifts of attention to and from these interpretations of needs.

Deviance amplification. Need intervention tactics involve cycles of increased and decreased communication related to needs. We become more attentive to anomalies in our interpretation of needs:

1. The more our attention to unmet or attributed or denied needs *increases*,

2. the more our advocacy behavior toward those we name as possible needs-meeters *increases*, and

3. the more our openness to those who can respond to attributed or denied needs *increases* (Brown, 1987).

Thus, as we increase our awareness and advocacy of needs and our search for needs-meeting responses, we amplify deviance, and our current interpretation of needs seems to make less sense. Figure 4.1 illustrates the deviance-amplifying cycle.

Deviance compensation. To reverse the deviance-amplifying trend, we must make sense of the anomalies. Potential needs-meeters can reduce deviance by responding to needs advocacy. We also compensate for needs anomalies by symbolically recategorizing needs expectancies. In both instances, the need subsystem becomes more deviance compensating:

1. As our attention to unmet or attributed/denied needs *decreases*,

2. our advocacy behavior *decreases*, and

3. our openness to others *decreases* (Brown, 1987).

Deviance compensation occurs, and our needs seem satisfied. Figure 4.2 illustrates the deviance-compensating cycle.

Nader's (1965) intervention promoted a strategic shift *away from* the individuality-stressing need for drivers to improve their driving skills and *to* the collectivity-stressing need for governmental regulation of car design. Tactically, his book *Unsafe at Any Speed* increased the public's attention to the anomaly of unmet safety needs, important for growth and survival. It attributed to consumers the need to take action against automakers that were denying their safety needs. Nader advocated this need to consumers who could mediate the need by pressuring legislators to regulate automotive design. The legislators exhibited open-channel behaviors by enacting legislation. With the passage of the National Traffic and Motor Vehicle Safety and Highway Safety acts and the inclusion of safety features on automobiles, *less* attention was given to the need for design regulation. Advocacy behavior related to auto safety diminished. Nader no longer sought a response from legislators. *Unsafe at Any Speed* went out of print.

Alternative futures. Suppose, though, that Nader had continued to experience non-needs-meeting responses such as he encountered in his early days as an advocate. Nader had been promoting the need for car design regulation several years before the publication of *Unsafe at Any Speed* (Nadel, 1971). Rather than promote an alternative interpretation of needs, Nader could have recategorized needs expectancies to explain anomalies. He could have renamed the attributes of *driver responsibility* or foregrounded the role of alcohol and age in accidents. Nader's continued advocacy of the need for safer automotive design, despite the initial needs-meeter closed-channel behavior, indicates that for him only the adoption of an alternative interpretation of needs would compensate for the deviance to which he attended.

Typically, interveners advocate needs in socially agreed-on ways (e.g., appealing to courts, grievance boards, and customer complaint desks) (Brown, 1987). When language tutors teach us the names for needs, they also teach us the social system's expectancies for *appropriate* actions to communicate needs. Nader wrote magazine articles, testified before state and federal legislatures, gave speeches, and eventually published a book to promote a need intervention. His actions followed the social code for appropriate needs advocacy.

If needs advocates continually encounter what they interpret to be closed-channel behavior, however, they sometimes begin enacting socially *inappropriate* rhetorical maneuvers in the search for open-channel responses (Brown, 1987). These increased advocacy behaviors may incur social damage and costs such as social disruption, violence, and even terrorism. If the U.S. Congress had enacted closed-channel behavior by refusing to listen to or acknowledge Nader, Nader could have organized protests against automakers or physically damaged automobiles he named *unsafe*. Automakers might have been harmed by reduced vehicle sales, and commuters might have been hurt by interference in traffic patterns. Government officials would have to spend money to respond to social disruption.

When we advocate needs, we *remind* others that they are *interdependent* with us for meeting all needs (Brown, 1987). Automakers can meet their need to sell cars only because we agree not to blockade or vandalize their car lots. Commuters can meet their need to drive safely only because we agree not to throw bricks at their cars or to park trucks in the middle of the freeway. Governments function peaceably only because we agree not to disrupt social order. Thus, the lack of needs-meeting responses may spawn advocacy behavior that violates the social system's expectancies for appropriate behavior and amplifies deviance in the system.

Need Intervention Enactment

To *promote* a need shift, we *emphasize* anomalies in the *current* interpretation of needs to show the deviance between lived experience and ideological expectancies (Brown, 1987). We offer an alternative interpretation of needs that seems to more closely fit experience by directing attention to aspects of experience that had been backgrounded. We mask attention to anomalies in the proposed interpretation of needs.

Nader (1965) advocated the need for safer automotive design through the rhetorical maneuver of writing *Unsafe at Any Speed*. In it, he used the Corvair as a case study. He described how GM gave much thought to the Corvair's design, marketability, and cost, but little thought to its safety. Consequently, it marketed a car that oversteered, flipped over, and handled in uncontrollable ways. Nader reasoned that the consumers' safety needs would go unmet unless they attended to the need for government and public involvement in car design.

To *forestall* a needs shift, we emphasize anomalies in the *proposed* interpretation of need (Brown, 1987). We also *mask* attention to anomalies in the *existing* interpretation of needs by reinterpreting the attributes of needs. Interveners opposing Nader's proposed naming of needs pointed out that the number of automobile accidents caused by alcohol and persons under age twenty-five exceeded the deaths and injuries attributable to poor car design (de Toledano, 1975). Also, production flaws instigated by unmotivated workers rather than design problems could explain second-collision deaths (de Toledano). These interveners, then, attempted to *prevent* the attribution and advocacy of the need to regulate car design. Thus, need interventions can both promote and forestall the reinterpretation of needs.

Need Intervention Cycles

Once we have minimized or compensated for anomalies related to a specific need, our attentiveness to that need diminishes. At the same time, our attention to backgrounded needs increases (Brown, 1987). For example, after the need for automotive design regulation appeared satisfied, Nader began increasing public awareness and advocacy of the need for revised meat inspection standards to fulfill the need for safe food (Martin, 2002). The awareness, advocacy, and meeting of needs seem to be a constant cycle. Only the specific needs to which we attend at any given moment change.

Because the American dream creates the expectancy that we can build a perfect and ideal life, we attempt constantly to compensate for the anomaly that we have yet to accomplish the ideal. One way we account for the anomaly is by symbolically constituting *new* needs that must be satisfied to achieve perfection. For example, regulating automotive design has not led to perfection in driving. But rather than question the ideological expectancy, we maintain ideology by constituting other needs that must be fulfilled to create the perfect world.

As our interpretation of needs shift, power and attention also shift. Attention shifts as we move to and from individuality-stressing and collectivity-stressing interpretations of need (Brown, 1987). Our interpretations of cooperative and competitive power interdependencies shift as we seek out new needs-meeters (Brown).

Thus far, we have examined continuity and change in the ideological subsystems of attention, power, and need. Figure 4.3 summarizes the interconnected communication patterns of the ideological subsystems.

To highlight the subsystems, we backgrounded the overall ideological system that arises out of and constitutes the subsystems. To close, we examine the dynamics of ideologizing.

❖ IDEOLOGY INTERVENTION

In the U.S. social system, communication patterns tend to promote the American dream ideology as a superordinate name for organizing

Figure 4.3   Subsystem Communication Patterns

This diagram summarizes the communication patterns related to interventions in the (A)ttention subsystem, the (P)ower subsystem, and the (N)eed subsystem. Subsystem interventions shape and are shaped by the (I)deological system.

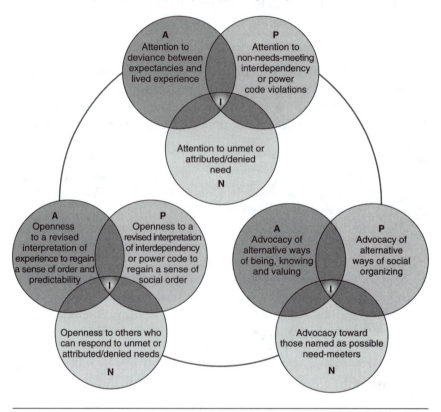

Source: Gregory Opt and authors.

experience. We participate collectively through conversations, movies, blogs, and so forth in an ongoing quest to create a more nearly perfect life. According to this ideology, perfection can be achieved by reifying symbolic categories such as *freedom, individualism, success, equality,* and *progress* (Brown, 1970; Kochan, 2006; Robertson, 1980).

Ideology Anomalies

Throughout the automotive safety narrative, the attention, power, and need anomalies also created anomalies in the overall ideological system. Unexpected experience outcomes, power code violations, and unmet needs promote attention to the lack of fit between lived experience and the American dream expectancies. We compensate for these anomalies by maintaining or changing the ideological system to meet our innate need for comprehensive order and predictability (Brown, 1978).

As noted with the attention, power, and need subsystems, we reverse deviance-amplifying trends by symbolically recategorizing experience or revising outcome expectancies, or both. In the case of ideology, we account for ideological anomalies in two ways:

1. We shift attention to an alternative superordinate name that seems more comprehensive and fitting with lived experience.

2. We mask attention to anomalies in the current ideology by reinterpreting the attributes that constitute the superordinate name.

Unlike attention, power, and need subsystem shifts, an ideological shift entails "*a* difference that relates to *many* differences" (Brown, 1982, p. 22; emphasis in original). It involves a comprehensive shift in our "theory" of life.

Ideology Shifts

Adherents to the American dream ideology tend to name their experience, relationships, and needs in terms of the overall ideological expectancy of creating a perfect world and life. Imagine, though, that you participate in an alternative ideological system in which the end goal is *other than* working toward a more nearly perfect world.

Can you conceive of alternative purposes, or an ideology that has no end goal? Can you imagine a world in which symbolic categories such as *freedom, progress,* and *equality* have no meaning, or a world without social hierarchy? How about a world without symbolically created need? Although you might find envisioning an alternative ideology challenging, the RSI model predicts that the more we apply our current superordinate name, the more likely we will encounter anomalies that one day might lead to an ideological shift to meet our innate need of construing an ordered and connected world.

Ideology Maintenance

Alternatively, we can rhetorically mask attention to anomalies to maintain our current ideological system. For example, although Nader (1965) promoted alternative interpretations of experience, power, and needs, his interventions, like those of the automakers, maintained the American dream ideology. Rather than feature anomalies in the overall ideological expectancy of creating a perfect world, Nader featured anomalies in expectancies about *how* that perfect world would be achieved. It would be enacted by regulating car design. The attention, power, and need shifts related to automotive safety masked attention to the ideological anomaly that the perfect life has yet to be reached.

Attention, power, and need shifts rename the attributes that constitute the American dream ideology. For example, after Nader's intervention, *success* would now be measured by how safe vehicles were rather than only by the sophistication of their style. *Progress* would be redefined from features that only added to a car's styling to technological innovations that increased a car's safety. Thus, we explain ideological anomalies by reinterpreting how the ideological expectancies will be made real and by redefining the attributes of symbolic categories that constitute the ideology.

Ideology Cycles

The RSI model offers neither a timeline for determining when ideological shifts might occur nor judgment about the content of specific ideologies. The model simply provides a framework that enables us to act as observers of our social system's rhetorical dialogue to create, maintain, and change ideology. The model leads us to pay attention to the rhetorical strategies, tactics, and maneuvers that underlie our efforts to promote and forestall ideological shifts.

Brown (1978) remarks that the rise and fall of particular ideologies "are objects neither for blame nor praise, mourning nor rejoicing" (p. 139). Ideologies come and go as we feature and mask attention to anomalies in our incomplete symbolic systems. Brown explains, "Their rising and falling, given the function of human symbol-use, simply *are*" (p. 139). Nevertheless, the overall process of ideologizing, as outlined in the RSI model, continues (Brown).

What interests RSI scholars, therefore, are the long-term rhetorical patterns of social continuity and change. Much like systems theorists, RSI critics concern themselves not with the progress or advancement of a particular ideology, but rather with understanding communication patterns of change and nonchange in social systems (Hanson, 1995). As we will see in Chapter 5, RSI critics examine communication patterns of specific interventions to theorize about long-term patterns of social change.

❖ CHAPTER SUMMARY

This chapter introduced the RSI model as a lens through which we can explore the process of social continuity and change. We examined the characteristics of a holistic approach for understanding rhetorical intervention and the dynamics of deviance amplification and deviance compensation. We discussed the need for rhetorical trend reversals to hinder the growth of vicious circles that arise from anomalies and could lead to system breakdown.

The RSI model also emphasizes the holographic interconnectedness of attention, power, and need subsystem change during trend reversals—a shift in one subsystem brings about simultaneous shifts in the other subsystems. Because we use linear language, we foreground one subsystem as a starting point for interpreting interventions and consider interventional side effects in the other subsystems. In addition, multiple interveners are involved in any intervention, although linear language leads us to emphasize one component as primary intervener in discussions of intervention. The RSI model assumes that we intervene into, rather than control, our symbolic interactions to negotiate interpretations of experience, interdependencies, and needs. Thus, the specific outcomes of an intervention are unpredictable. However, the RSI model leads us to be aware of likely side effects of an intervention.

The RSI model's three subsystems provide starting points for observing the communication patterns involved in social interventions to compensate for anomalies. Attention interventions occur when we promote and impede attention shifts to alternative interpretations of daily events and actions. We encourage and discourage attention switches via the strategies of anomaly-masking and anomaly-featuring communication. Tactically, attention switches involve awareness of deviance; advocacy of alternative ways of being, knowing, and valuing; and openness to alternative interpretations of experience.

Power interventions occur when we rhetorically promote and impede alternative interpretations of social hierarchy and power code. Power interventions involve strategic shifts from cooperative to competitive interdependencies and back. Tactically power interventions involve shifts in the exchange, threat, and integry social organizers, which depend on calling attention to non-needs-meeting interdependencies and power code violations.

Need interventions occur when we rhetorically promote and impede alternative interpretations of need, strategically shifting from individuality-stressing to collectivity-stressing needs and back.

Tactically, need interventions involve the awareness and attribution of need, advocacy of need, and the seeking of open-channel needs-mediating behaviors.

Attention, power, and need shifts are reified in rhetorical maneuvers that range from argumentative forms, to media pseudoevents, to actions and behaviors that disrupt social order. The overall process of intervention to prompt and forestall attention, power, and need shifts serves to create, maintain, and change symbolically constituted ideology.

In all, the RSI model points to the continuity of change. If ideology as symbolic abstraction is always incomplete, then we will forever be enacting attention, power, and need shifts to compensate for ideological anomalies. Only the rhetorical process by which we constitute, maintain, and change ideology remains constant.

How have we, the authors, acted as rhetorical interveners in this chapter? Also, think about the relationship between the American dream ideology and the RSI model. Are we, the authors, like Ralph Nader, masking attention to ideological anomalies in how we conceive and promote attention to the RSI model? Does our discussion feature attention to anomalies in our American dream expectancies? What rhetorical actions do you find yourself enacting in response to our social intervention?

❖ REVIEW QUESTIONS

1. What are the *strategies, tactics,* and *maneuvers* for the attention subsystem?

2. What are the *strategies, tactics,* and *maneuvers* for the power subsystem?

3. What are the *strategies, tactics,* and *maneuvers* for the need subsystem?

4. How are interventions within a subsystem *holographic*?

5. How are the three subsystems interdependent with the naming process? How does naming create subsystem expectancies?

6. What did Ralph Nader background in order to foreground the problem of unsafe automobile design? What strategies, tactics, and maneuvers did he employ to do this?

7. How did the automotive industry attempt to impede Nader's social intervention? What strategies, tactics, and maneuvers did it employ?

8. Suppose that in the revised interpretation of power, consumers and the government now always distrust automakers. How might this scenario evolve into a deviance-amplifying system? What other deviance-amplifying systems can you envision based on the chapter's narrative about car safety?

9. The chapter discussed *deviance amplifying* as increasing attentiveness to anomalies. What if attention never shifts to awareness of anomalies? In what way might that system become deviance amplifying?

10. Suppose your ideology lacks the expectancy that the world should make sense and be predictable. What implications might it have for the RSI model's explanation for the motivation underlying social change?

❖ CHAPTER EXERCISES

1. Describe the power-sharing system involved in purchasing a house, car, or computer. What are the roles and the nature of the interdependencies that connect the power shareholders? Give examples of power-related anomalies that might occur. How might the system respond to deviance?

2. Suppose you are a nonsmoker (or smoker). Your favorite restaurant does not distinguish between smoking and nonsmoking sections. Discuss how you might attempt a need intervention to encourage the restaurant to create a smoke-free section (or to encourage it to maintain its smoking section to counter the intervention of those advocating a smoke-free environment).

3. Identify a public figure who is currently attempting to intervene to bring about social change. What type of intervention does the person seem to be enacting? Describe the strategies, tactics, and maneuvers of this person's intervention. What interveners appear to be attempting to counter the intervention? Describe their strategies, tactics, and maneuvers.

4. In a small group, discuss the idea that the RSI model offers neither a timeline for determining when ideological shifts might occur nor judgment about the content of specific ideologies. How might these RSI model expectancies support or violate expectancies associated with the American dream or both? What are the ethical implications? Share highlights from the group's discussion with the class.

5. Look for current books and articles that discuss the American dream. In what ways do the writers maintain or offer revisions of the attributes associated with the American dream or both? What alternative ideologies to the American dream, if any, are proposed?

❖   SERVICE LEARNING EXERCISE

Select a recent example of a attention, power, or need intervention that the not-for-profit organization for which you are working this semester has attempted. Perhaps the organization has conducted fundraising, held membership drives, recreated its image, or lobbied the government.

Analyze the rhetorical strategies, tactics, and maneuvers of the intervention. As a class, compare the analyses and identify common rhetorical patterns that the organization seems to use to promote its interventions. Share the results of the analyses with the not-for-profit organization.

Under the Lens: Compensating for Social Order Challenges

In this chapter, we have acted as if Ralph Nader were the primary intervener and that his book *Unsafe at Any Speed* brought about social system change related to naming accident events. However, he was but one of numerous interveners who attempted to challenge the social order. In the following two examples, notice General Motors' (GM's) actions to compensate for the deviance that the interveners attempted to foreground.

During the first four years that GM produced the Corvair, independent automotive specialists designed and sold add-on devices and offered modifications to improve the car's stability and handling (Nader, 1965). These specialists *threatened* the existing social hierarchy by *competing* with GM's role as standard setter. Their actions also potentially increased the public's attention to safety concerns. The need for devices and modifications suggested anomalies in the expectancy that *cars are built as safe as possible*. These actions could have resulted in a reinterpretation of interdependency between automakers and consumers.

GM responded to the specialists' competitive behaviors by revamping the 1964 Corvair. The redesigned Corvair incorporated the specialists' safety features, making their add-ons and modifications unnecessary (Nader, 1965). GM's actions backgrounded public attention to the anomaly. GM forestalled a power shift and maintained its *standard-setter/ratifier* relationship with the public.

Another challenge to social order appeared in the form of lawsuits. By 1965, more than 100 Corvair owners had filed suits against GM because of accidents that violated the *built-as-safe-as-possible* expectancy (Nader, 1965). In three cases brought to court that year, GM denied the charges of instability problems with the Corvair and invoked the prevailing naming pattern of *driver negligence* to explain accident events (Nader). Only one court case decided against GM in a default judgment when the company refused to comply with court orders to make Corvair test and engineering data available (Nader).

Overall, the legal system cooperated with GM to maintain social order by affirming its authority to create design standards. The legal system agreed to attribute accident events to *driver responsibility*. Thus, the role of automakers in contributing to automotive accidents through poor safety design remained backgrounded. GM maintained its power-holding role to set design standards and the interpretation that it *built cars as safe as possible*.

In both instances, GM was able to deflect the social order challenges. Consider, though, the time and resources GM spent to maintain a social order that appeared to be increasingly non-needs-meeting.

CHAPTER 5

Process and Practice of RSI Criticism

In daily life, we are constantly involved in the rhetoric of social intervention. Consider the interventions related to furthering one's education. Recruiters intervene by rhetorically reasoning that the college they represent will best meet prospective students' needs. College course work results from curriculum committee interventions to categorize certain courses as fulfilling the expectancies of a particular symbolically created major.

How students symbolically categorize themselves—*interested, disinterested, hardworking, creative*—is influenced by professor and peer interventions that name their actions and behaviors. Community interpretations of campus events such as the resignation of a popular professor involve social interventions related to naming the events. In all, daily life is a continual process of social intervention to make sense of experience, with everyone serving as both change agent and audience of interventions.

The Rhetoric of Social Intervention (RSI) model concepts you have learned empower you to assume a new role in the intervention process—that of an RSI critic. As a critic, you search for and reflect on the communication patterns that interveners use to promote and impede social change. You speculate on the outcomes and side effects of those interventions. You undertake your own RSI investigations and construct your own narratives of social change and continuity.

An RSI analysis relates to a variety of situations. You might need to write an academic paper that demonstrates your understanding of the RSI model. You might use the RSI model as a methodology for a thesis. You might employ the RSI model to interpret workplace alterations or to critique a public relations campaign that promotes change.

This chapter guides you through the steps of an RSI model critique. First, we discuss the preanalysis process—how to select a social intervention and data to analyze. Next, we focus on the analysis process. We provide questions to assist your exploration of need, power, and attention interventions. Finally, we examine the postanalysis process and outline a narrative form for reporting the findings from an RSI analysis.

The result of this process is a critical essay that contributes to our knowledge and understanding of human symbolizing activity. Your RSI analysis can also enhance your role as a participant in the process of social continuity and change. It can improve your ability to reflect on and respond to your social system's future choosing.

❖   PREANALYSIS: NAMING THE SOCIAL INTERVENTION

To begin enacting the role of an RSI critic, choose a social intervention to analyze. It can be a past, present, or possible future intervention. It can be one that seems to have succeeded as well as one that appears to have failed. The preanalysis process involves selecting symbolizing activity, collecting data, defining social system boundaries, and reviewing scholarly literature. As an outcome of this process, you name the intervention you plan to critique.

Selecting Symbolizing Activity

To identify a social intervention, start with this question: **What interests me?** Reflect on events, actions, and experiences that capture your interest. Pay attention to what you attend to.

Perhaps you watch news coverage about a particular event that relates to social change. Maybe you engage in heated discussions about certain social issues. Perhaps you have read a book or seen a movie that has influenced your interpretation of experience. Maybe you are impressed by the actions and behaviors of a particular celebrity or politician who rallies around a social cause. Perhaps you have been complaining about a local policy change that seems wasteful. Think about the events, texts, and people that catch your attention.

You can also consider topics or questions that you have addressed in other fields, such as history, political science, or business. However, recategorize the topic or question as a rhetorical one. For example, how did the Romans handle the anomaly they must have observed when so-called barbarians destroyed the West's greatest empire? How did Frederick Douglass invite his listeners to see an anomaly in their interpretation of events as he gave his 1852 speech "What, to the Slave, Is the Fourth of July?" How did economist Thomas L. Friedman intervene through his book *The World is Flat* to make globalism seem inevitable and outsourcing a good move for U.S. business? Thus, pay attention to symbolizing activity in which you notice different viewpoints being expressed or communication that makes you wonder why social change happened and how it was received.

As you narrow your interests, ask this question: **How does my interest relate to social change?** Consider how the symbolizing activity that captures your attention appears to encourage or discourage particular interpretations of needs, relationships, or experience, or all of these. Identify the *change* being prompted or impeded. What *differences* have occurred as a side effect of the symbolizing activity? What *differences* were promoted by the intervention but *failed* to result in change?

Suppose that symbolizing activity about space exploration interests you. You frequently read articles and watch television programs that discuss returning to the moon and creating missions to Mars. You connect your interest to social change by considering how the articles and programs promote or impede the public's interpretation of the need for space exploration.

Finally, in developing a topic to analyze, address this question: **What specific intervention associated with social change will I emphasize?** In other words, link the *change* you identify in the symbolizing activity to a specific event, text, or person or group that you can analyze. If you are researching the space exploration topic, you might observe numerous attempts to shape social interpretations of space exploration, such as NASA press conferences, books and documentaries, and speeches by government officials. If you were writing a book, you could examine all these various attempts. For the purposes of writing a critical essay, however, choose a specific attempt to investigate as an intervention.

For example, you could analyze media coverage of the International Space Station to examine how interpretations of it have shifted since its launch. You could critique a book or documentary that commemorates the fortieth anniversary of the moon landing to search for the interpretation of the event being promoted or impeded. You could analyze George W. Bush's 2004 speech as an attempt to affect public interpretations of moon and Mars explorations. You could study feature films that involve space exploration for how they name experience. Overall, narrow your area of interest to a specific intervention you find interesting and worthy of critique.

Collecting Data

How you focus your investigation depends on your answer to this question: **What data about the intervention are available to me?** To conduct an RSI critique, you need access to symbolizing activity—such as written, spoken, and visual communication. Symbolizing activity is also known as **rhetorical artifacts**. You must locate rhetorical artifacts that communicate the intervention's strategies, tactics, and maneuvers.

Intervention data include rhetorical artifacts such as articles, books, newsletters, correspondence, speeches, transcripts, memos, video, audio, and Internet communication. The artifacts can be produced by the interveners or reported by observers of the intervention, or both. To analyze interventions related to an international conference on space exploration, you could collect newspaper articles, Internet reports, and television news transcripts about the event. To analyze a text such as a book or documentary about space exploration, you need access to that book or documentary. To analyze a person or group, you could search for articles, speeches, and books that report the actions and thoughts of that person or group and conduct interviews.

In determining data availability, you must discover if the desired rhetorical artifacts exist and whether you can access them. Perhaps you heard a speech about space exploration, but if you have no recording or written record of the speech, you cannot study it. For example, Patrick Henry's "Give Me Liberty or Give Me Death" speech was reconstructed by his biographer decades after it was given. The original text does not exist. Sometimes rhetorical artifacts exist but are not accessible in the time you have to complete your analysis. Thus, allow adequate preparation time in case you encounter challenges in accessing intervention discourse.

In addition, collect background information on the intervention you plan to analyze. Background material can create a context for the intervention and clarify the social change being encouraged or discouraged by the intervention. To study Ralph Nader's intervention, we reviewed books and articles written by observers of the intervention. Their reports indicated how power shareholders responded to Nader's attempted intervention. The writings also provided background on the social system's interpretations of experience prior to Nader's intervention. Thus, search for background data that give insight into the social system before, during, and after the intervention you plan to investigate.

To find data for your study, consult electronic databases such as Academic Search Premier, FirstSearch, Lexis Nexis, MasterFILE Premier, Newspaper Source, and ProQuest Newspapers. In addition, Business Source Premier, *Los Angeles Times, New York Times,* NetLibrary, *Wall Street Journal,* and *Washington Post* may be useful databases. Internet search engines can also help you locate written, audio, and visual material related to the intervention. Finally, librarians can provide a wealth of information about resources and search strategies for finding and identifying appropriate data.

Defining Social System Boundaries

As you review the data you are collecting, consider this question: **What social system will I emphasize in my research?** Recall from Chapter 1 that a social system is a network of individuals and groups that affect each other. In RSI terms, it is a collection of power shareholders that mediate each other's needs and influence future choosing. However, because *social system* is a symbolic construction, we must define the experience that we view as constituting a social system. You must name the power shareholders you consider as the system you plan to investigate and describe their connections. In essence, you abstract from experience to create social system boundaries by stating what components you will include and those you will exclude.

For example, in Chapter 4 we defined the social system as consisting of these power shareholders: Ralph Nader, the U.S. public, U.S. automakers, and the U.S. government. We excluded potential system components such as insurance companies, automotive workers, lawyers, and foreign automakers. Although these elements influenced and were influenced by the interpretive shifts, the intervention we selected to study—*Unsafe at Any Speed*—was primarily geared toward the power shareholders we included. In addition, they appeared to be the key responders to the intervention in the background material about the intervention. Throughout Chapter 4, we indicated how the components we selected related to and influenced each other.

To define the social system components, think about the intervention you plan to analyze and review the data that you have collected about the intervention. What people and groups are generating the symbolizing activity related to the intervention? What people and groups seem to be the most affected by the intervention? What people and groups appear to be communicating about and responding to the intervention? Around what goal or need related to the intervention do the people and groups seem organized? How do they potentially influence each other? Look for recurring mention of people and groups in the symbolizing activity about the intervention.

Finally, because of the limitation of linear writing, you must name one component of the social system as the primary *intervener*—as the person or group that you will treat as initiating or starting the intervention. This does not mean that the person or group is the only intervener—all interventions include multiple interveners. However, when analyzing an intervention, you act as if one person or group *begins* the intervention, even though that person or group may have been intervening in response to interventions on the part of others.

The symbolizing activity you have elected to study as intervention usually dictates the *starting* intervener. Because we selected the book *Unsafe at Any Speed* as an intervention, we treated its author, Ralph Nader, as the intervener. The public, automakers, and government became the *audience* of the intervention. If we had focused instead on General Motors' (GM's) hiring of a private detective as the intervention, then we would have named GM as the intervener, and we would have named Nader, the public, and the media as the intervention's audience. Furthermore, we can view Nader's intervention as initiated or influenced by earlier GM or other system component interventions.

Overall, define the social system that you will analyze by addressing these questions:

- What symbolizing activity will I consider as the intervention (e.g., events, books, films, speeches)?
- What will I name as the social system components influenced by the intervention?
- What system component will I consider as the intervener (i.e., intervention initiator)?
- What system components will I consider as the audience of the intervention? (i.e., power shareholders influenced by the intervention)?

A wide variety of social systems are available to study. Thus, you must make choices about naming the system's boundaries, the intervener, and the audience. Your selections must make sense to the readers of your analysis. You must be able to reason for the components and connections that you choose. Clearly state your choices in the paper that you write.

Reviewing Scholarly Literature

After choosing an intervention to analyze, consider this final pre-analysis question: **How have other scholars studied my topic?** Review scholarly literature databases to locate articles that might relate to the intervention you plan to study. In addition, look for scholarly articles that use the RSI model to see if their findings suggest insights useful to your research. This scholarly background provides a context for your own original research and helps to place your critical voice into the ongoing conversation about the particular intervention and the use of the RSI model as a method of critical analysis.

If scholars have not studied the intervention you plan to investigate, then your analysis might add new knowledge to scholarly literature. If scholars have studied it, but from approaches other than the RSI model, then your RSI analysis might contribute a new understanding of the intervention. Nevertheless, the other scholars' findings might lend insights to your investigation. If the intervention has been critiqued using the RSI model, then study an alternative social system related to the intervention or examine some discourse previously unconsidered, so that your analysis increases our understanding of the intervention or the RSI model, or both.

Electronic databases such as Academic Search Premier, Communication and Mass Media Complete, Expanded Academic Index, ERIC (Education Resources Information Center), JSTOR, ProQuest Research Library, and Project Muse archive articles from communication journals and related areas. These databases might contain communication studies on your topic area and RSI studies in general. In addition, review *Dissertation Abstracts International* if you plan to write a master's thesis or doctoral dissertation using the RSI model.

If we run the search term "Ralph Nader" in the Communication and Mass Media Complete database, we find two scholarly articles on the topic. Stein (1990) compares and contrasts Nader's muckraking style with other social activists. Bishop and Kilburn (1971) look at Nader's use of public relations techniques in advocating automotive safety. These articles might provide useful insights into Nader's intervention maneuvers and suggest a social system to be analyzed. We search several more databases using terms such as "Ralph Nader," "automotive safety," and "Corvair." We find no additional articles on the intervention or that analyze it through the lens of the RSI model. This finding helps to justify the need for our study.

In addition, we run search terms such as "social intervention," "rhetorical intervention," and "RSI model" to locate scholarly articles that use the RSI model. These articles might provide additional understanding of the model or suggest ways to analyze the intervention. The Additional Readings section at the end of this book lists some RSI studies that might be useful for your research.

Finally, review the three scholarly articles by RSI theorist William R. Brown (1978, 1982, 1986), cited in this book's references. Brown developed the RSI model concepts in these articles, so they provide direct access to his ideas. This book reflects only a summary and interpretation of the RSI concepts. You should quote from the original source for the RSI model, especially when you discuss your approach and methodology for doing the analysis. Using the original writings lends more authority and credibility to your analysis. In addition, you might discover that you differ from the book's authors on your interpretation of Brown's concepts.

So far, we have described the initial process of enacting the RSI critic role. Although we have acted as if each step or question comes one after another, you might follow a different order. As you select symbolizing activity, collect data, define the social system boundaries, and review scholarly literature, you might discover that the ideas and information overlap and interconnect. The preanalysis goal is to identify an intervention that has interest to you, has accessible discourse, and has not been analyzed using the approach you plan to take or, at least, has not found the insights that you will write about.

Once you have completed the preanalysis, you are ready to begin analyzing the intervention through the lens of the RSI model. The RSI model is designed to be a search model—one that guides you to seek communication patterns as you read, watch, observe, and listen to the symbolizing activity that you have named as the *intervention*. Initially, you might interpret uncovering patterns as *challenging*. As you become a more practiced critic, though, pattern discovery will become easier. As you write your essay, you will likely experience an epiphany in which the model and its application suddenly become clear. To assist in your explorations, the next section provides lists of questions and pointers to guide your analysis.

❖   ANALYSIS: ASKING CRITICAL QUESTIONS

To conduct the analysis, examine both the naming and subsystem processes that generate the social intervention. Use concepts discussed in Chapter 2 to identify specific naming patterns that support the strategies and tactics of the social intervention. For the subsystem analysis, draw on concepts discussed in Chapters 3 and 4 to search for rhetorical patterns of change and continuity.

We first present questions to consider as part of the naming analysis. Then we list questions geared to the subsystem analysis. Although we discuss the naming analysis first, you can begin with the subsystem analysis and refer back to the naming analysis as you work through the data. You can also start with the naming process and extrapolate the subsystem patterns.

Naming Analysis

The RSI model's naming foundation provides a method for analyzing the details of the intervention discourse. This analysis can help you identify the specific naming activity that underlies attention, power, and need interventions. It can reveal the rhetorical maneuvers that promote the strategies and tactics of an intervention.

As you review the data you have collected, pay attention to the specific names being given to experience related to the intervention. Think about how interveners create, maintain, and change symbolic categorizations of experience. Look for the patterns of rhetorical reasoning used to generate names. For example, as you analyze discourse about a possible return-to-moon space flight, you notice that interveners name the moon as both a *scientific frontier* and a *tourist destination*. You attend to how interveners reason for these names for experience.

Consider these questions, based on Chapter 2, as you search the data for naming activity:

1. What name(s) is the intervener proposing in the symbolizing activity?

2. Is the intervener attempting to offer an alternative name for an already named experience? Maintain a current name for an experience? Create a name for an unnamed experience?

3. How does the intervener rhetorically reason for the appropriateness of the name?
   a. What criterial attributes does the intervener identify as constituting the proposed name? What is *the difference that makes a difference*?
   b. How does the intervener demonstrate that experience fulfills the expectancies associated with the proposed name? How does the intervener reason *this-is-the-same-as-that* or *this-is-different-from-that*, or both?

4. How does the proposed name function rhetorically?
   a. How does the name clarify ambiguous experience?
   b. How does the name suggest approach and avoidance behavior?
   c. How does the name create expectancies about what is transcendent (same) and blindering (different) about experience?

5. How does the naming activity link to attention, power, or need interventions?

A naming analysis highlights our actions as interveners to influence how others symbolically categorize specific events, people, and objects associated with a social intervention. It offers insight into the rhetorical maneuvers that interveners use to generate social interventions.

At the subsystem level, we shift to analyzing the communication patterns underlying social change. To begin a subsystem analysis, ask this question: **What subsystem—attention, power, or need—will I emphasize as a starting point?** All subsystems offer equally valid ways of interpreting an intervention. Select the subsystem that seems to make the most sense to you given your review of the symbolizing activity; then look at the list of questions in the following sections that corresponds to your starting-point subsystem.

Each list begins by asking you to name the intervention and social system that you intend to analyze. Next, it guides you through the process of reflecting on the before- and after-intervention situations and identifying the strategies, tactics, and maneuvers of the intervention. Each list ends with questions that relate to interventional side effects. As you conduct your analysis, keep in mind that interventions both encourage and discourage social change.

Attention Subsystem Analysis

As you review the data you have collected, you might notice that the symbolizing activity emphasizes interpretation. Perhaps the communicators appear to describe *differently* the same experience. Maybe they debate *different* understandings of what an action or event *means*. Perhaps the data contain explanations of *why* an event or action has or has not occurred. The data might be organized around *comparing* and *contrasting* various opinions about an experience.

If these types of symbol exchanges stand out in your perusal of the data, then the *attention subsystem* might be an appropriate starting point for conducting your analysis. As you search your data for

communication patterns related to an attention intervention, consider
these questions, based on Chapters 3 and 4:

1. What components will you define as the social system? Whom
    will you treat as the intervener? What will you treat as the
    intervention? Whom will you consider as the audience of the
    intervention?

2. How will you describe the naming pattern (interpretation
    of experience) of the social system *before* the attempted
    intervention?
    a. What expectancies about experience does the naming pattern
        create?
    b. What ways of knowing, being, and valuing does the naming
        pattern convey?
    c. What, if any, other influences encourage or inhibit interpre-
        tations within the social system that the naming-pattern
        expectancies are or are not being met?

3. How will you characterize the attempted attention intervention?
    a. What rhetorical maneuvers does the intervener employ to pro-
        mote or impede the intervention? What does the intervener
        say or do, or what events does the intervener enact, to consti-
        tute the intervention?
    b. What tactics do the rhetorical maneuvers serve? Increasing
        or decreasing attention to naming-pattern anomalies? Encou-
        raging or discouraging shifts in ways of knowing, being, and
        valuing? Facilitating or impeding openness to alternative
        naming patterns?
    c. What overall strategy underlies the tactics? Anomaly-featuring
        communication? Anomaly-masking communication?

4. How will you characterize the social system's potential or
    actual naming pattern *after* the attempted intervention?
    a. What expectancies about experience does the naming pattern
        create?
    b. What ways of knowing, being, and valuing does the naming
        pattern convey?
    c. What, if any, other influences encourage or inhibit interpre-
        tations within the social system that the naming-pattern
        expectancies are or are not being met?

5. Given this attempted attention intervention, what appear to be the systemic side effects for need and power?
   a. What, if any, need shift has been involved?
   b. What, if any, power shift has been involved?

6. How does the attempted attention intervention maintain or challenge the ideology of the social system?

In all, an analysis of an attention intervention can provide insight into how we constitute, maintain, and change our symbolic interpretations of reality. This understanding can also enhance knowledge of our ideology, which, in turn, constitutes our interpretations of experience.

Because attention switches involve shifts in how we interpret our interdependencies, attention interventions result in power interventions (Brown, 1987). Thus, the power subsystem provides another starting point for analyzing social intervention.

Power Subsystem Analysis

As you review the data you have gathered, you might notice that *power* seems to stand out. Perhaps words such as *player, voice, marginalize, class, power, role, clash, struggle, social movement,* or *influence* frequently appear in the data. Maybe you find yourself thinking about how this person or group is *connected* to that person or group as you dissect the discourse. Perhaps the data contain reports of behaviors such as strikes or protests that seem to *challenge* social hierarchy or actions that are being named *threats*. Maybe you notice violations of power code or enactments of sanctions.

In such instances, beginning your analysis with the *power subsystem* might be appropriate. Consider these questions, based on Chapters 3 and 4, to detect the strategy, tactics, and maneuvers of a power intervention:

1. What components will you define as the social system? Whom will you treat as the intervener? What will you treat as the intervention? Whom will you consider as the audience of the intervention?

2. How will you describe the power-sharing interdependency in this social system *before* the attempted intervention?
   a. How does each power shareholder appear to mediate the needs and goals of the other shareholders?
   b. What motives organize the interpretations of interdependency (exchange, integry, threat)?

     c. What, if any, other influences encourage or inhibit interpretations within the social system that the interdependencies are or are not needs-meeting, or that power code is or is not being enacted?

3. How will you characterize the attempted power intervention?
    a. What rhetorical maneuvers does the intervener employ to promote or impede the intervention? What does the intervener say or do, or what events does the intervener enact, to constitute the intervention?
    b. What tactics do the rhetorical maneuvers serve? Increasing or decreasing awareness of non-needs-meeting interdependencies and power code violations? Encouraging or discouraging shifts in exchange, integry, and threat? Facilitating or impeding openness to revised interpretations of interdependencies and power code?
    c. What overall strategy underlies the tactics? Emphasizing or de-emphasizing cooperation to maintain the current interpretation of social hierarchy? Emphasizing or de-emphasizing competition to offer an alternative version of social hierarchy?

4. How will you describe the potential or actual power-sharing system *after* the attempted intervention?
    a. How does each power shareholder appear to mediate the needs and goals of the other shareholders?
    b. What motives organize the interpretations of interdependency (exchange, integry, threat)?
    c. What, if any, other influences encourage or inhibit interpretations within the social system that the interdependencies are or are not needs-meeting or that power code is or is not being enacted?

5. Given this attempted power intervention, what appear to be the systemic side effects for attention and need?
    a. What, if any, attention shift has been involved?
    b. What, if any, need shift has been involved?

6. How does the attempted power intervention maintain or challenge the ideology of the social system?

In general, a power intervention analysis can enlighten our understanding of the rhetorical process by which we constitute, maintain, and change social hierarchy. In addition, it can increase our knowledge of how we create, maintain, and change ideology, which constitutes and is constituted by power.

Because we and others are interdependent for the meeting of needs, power interventions result in need interventions (Brown, 1987). Thus, the need subsystem offers a starting point for analyzing social intervention.

Need Subsystem Analysis

As you review the data you have collected, you might find yourself thinking about *need*. Perhaps the communicators talk about *need, satisfaction, desire, requirements,* or *wants.* Maybe the intervention discourse seems organized around the *lack* of something, something that is *missing,* or something that needs *to be done* or *fulfilled.* The data might include descriptions of events and actions that appear to be advocating for or denying a need. The discourse might also address questions related to what it means to be human and what human beings need or do not need.

If you notice these types of patterns, then beginning your analysis with the need subsystem might be appropriate. Consider these questions, based on Chapters 3 and 4, as you search the data for the communication patterns related to need intervention:

1. What components will you define as the social system? Whom will you treat as the intervener? What will you treat as the intervention? Whom will you consider as the audience of the intervention?

2. How will you characterize the social system's interpretation of needs *before* the attempted intervention?
   a. How are the needs advocated?
   b. Toward what others (power shareholders) does the social system express openness as potential sources of needs-meeting responses?
   c. What, if any, other influences encourage or inhibit interpretations within the social system that such responses are or are not needs-meeting?

3. How will you characterize the attempted need intervention?
   a. What rhetorical maneuvers does the intervener employ to promote or impede the intervention? What does the intervener say or do, or what events does the intervener enact, to constitute the intervention?

b. What tactics do the rhetorical maneuvers serve? Affirming or denying needs? Encouraging or discouraging advocacy of need? Facilitating or impeding openness of the social system to potential needs-meeters?

c. What overall strategy underlies the tactics? Increasing or decreasing awareness of individual need? Increasing or decreasing awareness of collective (group) need?

4. How will you characterize the social system's potential or actual interpretation of needs *after* the attempted intervention?

a. How are such needs advocated?

b. Toward what others (power shareholders) does the social system express openness as potential sources of needs-meeting responses?

c. What, if any, other influences encourage or inhibit interpretations within the social system that such responses are or are not needs-meeting?

5. Given this attempted need intervention, what seem to be the systemic side effects for power and attention?

a. What, if any, power shift has been involved?

b. What, if any, attention shift has been involved?

6. How does the attempted need intervention maintain or challenge the ideology of the social system?

In all, a need intervention analysis can increase our knowledge of how we create, maintain, and change social interpretations of needs. In addition, it can provide insight into how we support or shift ideology that both constitutes and is constituted by needs. Underlying need shifts are shifts in attention and power (Brown, 1982). Thus, all three subsystems provide ways to begin an RSI analysis.

When using the lists of questions, you need not follow the question order. You can begin the analysis with any of the questions. You might also develop additional questions to assist in the analysis. Whether you start with a naming or subsystem analysis or begin with Question 1 or Question 6, the analysis goals are the same— to increase our understanding of human beings as symbolizing creatures and to increase our knowledge of the RSI model and its usefulness for interpreting experience. Your goal also might include the pleasure of pondering the intervention and what made it *work*. The last step you enact in the role of RSI critic is to share your analysis with others.

❖ POSTANALYSIS: WRITING THE CRITICAL ESSAY

The RSI model is an interpretative approach to studying human symbolizing activity. You *interpret* experience that you have called an *intervention* through the lens of the RSI model. Then you communicate that interpretation to other people. You become both critic and intervener because, in writing the analysis, you attempt to intervene in how others interpret the intervention.

Meeting Format and Audience Expectancies

As part of enacting the role of RSI critic, address this question: **How will I share my interpretation with others?** You can communicate your interpretation in a variety of forms. You could write a first-person account as a participant in an intervention. You could write your analysis in dramatic form with characters and plot. You could present your findings following a format similar to a scientific report. You could communicate your analysis as a video, documentary, audio commentary, or Web site.

In selecting a form to present the analysis, your primary consideration should be this question: **Who is the audience for my analysis?** To whom am I communicating my analysis findings? Traditionally, rhetorical critics write scholarly papers to share their research findings with other rhetorical scholars. Thus, this chapter's questions and discussion focus on writing a critical essay. We assume that the audience for your analysis is an academic one—professors and students.

Also, you might share your analysis with audiences outside the classroom by submitting your paper to a communication convention or journal. These audiences have expectancies about what constitutes the symbolic category *quality scholarly paper*. The essay that you produce must embody the criterial attributes that the audiences associate with that symbolic category for them to recognize your work as being scholarly and of high quality. Thus, the writing guidelines we provide are geared toward meeting those expectancies.

Enacting Style Expectancies

As you write your essay, address this question: **What academic style should I use?** Academic style refers to writing guidelines such as the *Publication Manual of the American Psychological Association* (APA), the *Modern Language Association Handbook* (MLA), and the *Chicago Manual of Style*. Academic styles provide rules for how to format the paper (e.g., margins, headings, cover page) and how to cite sources used in the paper (e.g., quotations, paraphrases, references, works cited). Academic style choice is determined by professors' preferences, school requirements, or the journal to which you submit your paper.

Following an academic style is important to creating the *look* that an academic audience expects. It ensures that the essay includes the reference material that scholars attend to when reading critical essays. It enables the audience to focus on the content of the analysis rather than be distracted by the format of the analysis and permits the audience to easily find information in the paper. By enacting proper academic style, you build your own credibility and demonstrate that you fit the criterial attributes of *scholar*.

Regardless of the academic style used, the RSI paper organization remains the same. Traditionally, academic papers are organized into three main sections—introduction, body, and conclusion. The writing pattern we describe is a symbolic construction, one that can be negotiated with others to create alternative frameworks and expectations for the analysis presentation. Thus, you can adapt this pattern to meet professor and journal preferences.

Writing Section I: Introduction

The first section of your paper introduces the topic and purpose of your research. It also describes the importance of the topic you are presenting and gives your audience a reason to want to read your paper. The introduction also provides a blueprint for the narrative that follows in your paper. In general, the introduction should address these questions:

- What is the topic of the analysis?
- What is the purpose of the analysis?
- Why is examining this intervention interesting or important to my audience?
- How does the paper present the analysis?

Typically, an RSI paper opens by offering a brief overview of the intervention situation that is the *topic* of the analysis. It should refer to an aspect of the intervention that will capture the audience's interest and attention. Think about how the change encouraged or discouraged by the intervention could connect to your audience's experiences. Highlight this connection in the introduction. Avoid revealing too much of your analysis in the introduction: save the main narrative you plan to write for the body section.

The introduction also indicates the *purpose* of the analysis. It lets your audience know why you studied the topic. Usually that goal includes increasing your audience's knowledge and understanding of human symbolizing activity. Summarize your purpose in one or two sentences. For example, a purpose statement for a paper analyzing Ralph Nader's intervention might read this way:

> This paper uses the RSI model to analyze the intervention *Unsafe at Any Speed* to understand and explain how Ralph Nader promoted a shift in social interpretations of accident events.

The introduction also relates the topic of your study to your *audience's interests*. You conducted your analysis because the intervention was interesting and important to you. However, the introduction needs to explain why the audience should find your topic worthy of research. The importance of doing the study may be implied in your opening description of the intervention and purpose of the analysis.

You can also directly state reasons for the topic's importance. Those reasons might involve the importance of the resulting social change or lack of change related to the intervention, the social change insights that an RSI analysis offers, the need to test or expand the RSI model concepts, and the contributions the analysis can make to the practice of intervention. In all, the audience expects you to answer the question, "Why?"

Finally, the introduction should *preview* what will follow in the paper. A preview is two or three sentences that describe the thesis and the main sections of the paper. It tells the audience the paper's main idea and organization. It also helps you stay organized by reminding you of the paper's purpose and main points. Write a succinct thesis statement that summarizes the argument you will present in this analysis. Follow it by a preview of the paper's organization. The remainder of the paper fleshes out the reasons for your interpretation.

Overall, the introduction creates audience expectancies about your topic, its importance, your approach, and your presentation.

Writing Section II: Body

The body of the paper fulfills the expectancies you have created in the introduction. It describes in detail the intervention you have previewed. It presents the findings of your analysis. When your audience finishes reading the body of your paper, it should have increased its understanding of and insight into the intervention that you have analyzed. The body addresses these questions:

- How have other scholars researched the intervention topic?
- How did I research the topic?
- What are the results of my research?

The question of *other scholars' research* reflects the audience's expectation that you are knowledgeable about previous scholarship on the topic and that your research differs from or contributes to that scholarship, or both. Reviewing the literature is a way of building your own credibility, of showing that you have *paid your dues* by reading and understanding what others have said. In addition, it shows that you will have something fresh to contribute to the ongoing conversation about the particular topic or the use of the RSI model as a criticism method.

The length and depth of your discussion about other research will depend on the intervention you are analyzing. It may be as short as a sentence that reads something like this:

Although scholars have examined Ralph Nader's muckraking activities (Stein, 1990) and contributions to public relation strategy (Bishop & Kilburn, 1971), none has studied his interventional strategy, tactics, and maneuvers through the lens of the RSI model.

This sentence could also be incorporated in the introduction of the paper as a justification for researching the topic.

Alternatively, if you review the scholarly databases and discover that a number of scholars have written interpretations of the intervention (e.g., Lincoln's Gettysburg Address), then your answer to the question may run longer. However, you might also choose to interweave some of this information into the narrative you write about the intervention, thus indirectly acknowledging other research about the intervention.

Finally, if the intervention you analyzed has been critiqued previously using the RSI model, then you must indicate how your analysis adds to or challenges the earlier work, or both. Again, this information might appear in the introduction as a justification for doing the study.

The academic audience also expects you to answer the question of *how you researched the topic*—how you selected and interpreted the intervention discourse. It needs this information to understand your approach and to critique the quality of your results. The extent of your explanation depends on the specific audience of your paper.

If you are writing the essay for professors and students who are familiar with the RSI model, then you need only briefly discuss it. You may be able to describe how you selected the intervention discourse you analyzed in one or two sentences. You also need to mention the subsystem starting point you used. For example, we could make this statement in a paper about Nader's intervention:

> To understand how Ralph Nader acted as a social intervener to shift society's interpretations of accident events, this paper examines his book *Unsafe at Any Speed* using the Rhetoric of Social Intervention (RSI) model. This book was selected because it provides a summary of Nader's rhetorical maneuvers that he had been using in articles and in speeches before social groups and congressional committees in the years before the book's publication. In addition, the book was widely read and critiqued during that period. The essay will discuss the strategies, tactics, and maneuvers of Nader's intervention from the starting point of *power*.

If you plan to submit the essay to a conference or journal, then assume that your audience is unfamiliar with the RSI model. Briefly summarize the model's major concepts so that the audience understands the assumptions you are making to do the analysis. Define vocabulary associated with the model that you use, such as *attention switch* and *anomaly masking*, so that the audience understands your terms. Reference Brown's (1978, 1982, 1986) articles about the RSI model in the summary. In addition, indicate why you have selected this approach to examine the symbolizing activity. What does the RSI model enable you to "see" that other approaches might not?

The majority of the paper's body is devoted to *reporting the results of your analysis*. Construct a narrative about the communication patterns of the social intervention that you have observed through the lens of the RSI model. The narrative should discuss three aspects of the intervention experience—*preintervention, intervention*, and *postintervention*. Your answers to the search questions in the analysis section of this chapter can form the basis of your analysis.

For the *preintervention* part of the narrative, describe the social system prior to the intervention. Provide a brief background or context to help the audience understand the system's communication patterns prior to the intervention. If you are analyzing symbolizing activity such as a book, movie, or speech, then provide details about the context in which that activity was produced.

Next, discuss the *intervention* in terms of the person or groups whom you have named as initiating the intervention and the rhetorical strategies, tactics, and maneuvers used to enact the intervention. Use the concepts of one of the RSI model subsystems to interpret the intervention discourse. Show how the intervener(s) attempted rhetorically to promote or impede a shift in attention, power, or need. Support your observations of the patterns with examples from the symbolizing activity that you are examining.

Finally, describe the social system *postintervention*, in terms of need, power, or attention. Discuss the outcomes of the intervention—what did or did not change. In addition, consider the side effects of the intervention. Reflect on the shifts in the two subsystems that were backgrounded in the subsystem you emphasized.

Writing Section III: Conclusion

As the introduction opens the intervention narrative, the conclusion closes it. The conclusion shows your audience that the purpose and goals of your research have been accomplished. In addition, it meets the scholarly audience expectation that your research contributes to the ongoing conversation that is considered *knowledge*. In general, the conclusion responds to these questions:

- What was learned about the specific intervention as a result of the analysis?
- What was learned about human symbolizing activity in general as a result of the analysis?
- Where do we go from here?

Conclusions often begin with *a brief review of the major findings* or *conclusions of the analysis*. This section of the paper gives meaning to the results of your research. You reflect on the knowledge that you have gained from examining the intervention through the lens of the RSI model. Also, you consider how you have intervened in the audience's interpretation of the intervention. If you have analyzed an intervention that has been critiqued by others, discuss how your analysis supported, challenged, or added to the previous research, or all of these.

In addition, discuss how the analysis contributes to the broader understanding and interpreting of human symbolizing activity. Comment on the insights gained about the process of social continuity and change. Think about the long-term implications of the communication patterns occurring in the intervention you have analyzed. Reflect on your use of the RSI model, indicating strengths and weaknesses of this approach as well as offering extensions or modifications to it. If appropriate, connect your comments to other works that have used the RSI model.

Finally, conclusions often end with thoughts about further explorations and comments on ideas introduced in the introduction. Suggest additional directions that research might take as inspired by your analysis. Point out interesting details you noticed in your research but did not have time to investigate. You can also write an ending to the narrative that you started in the introduction by concluding with some aspect of the intervention that seems to summarize the story as a whole.

Fulfilling Other Critical Essay Expectancies

Overall, academic audiences expect to read a well-researched, well-reasoned, and well-written essay that provides insight into the human symbolizing process. The audience critiques the quality of your analysis based on how effectively your work fulfills these expectancies. It determines the quality of your work based on the sources and depth of your preanalysis research, the evidence used to support the claims and findings of your analysis, and the writing style and organization of your paper.

As you review and revise your paper, ask these questions:

- Have I clearly indicated and reasoned for the choices I have made while conducting this analysis?
- Are the main points of my analysis clearly supported by evidence from relevant symbolizing activity?
- Are the promises I announced in the essay's introduction fulfilled in the body and conclusion of the essay?
- Have I accurately cited and recorded all sources used in the essay, following the pertinent academic style?

Print a hard copy of your paper to review before submitting it. Computer spell and grammar checkers miss some errors. You might discover items to correct or rethink that were unnoticed on the computer screen. Also, ask a friend to proofread your work, or take it to a writing center for review to improve quality. Finally, back up computer files after every writing session. Power outages and computer crashes wipe out weeks of hard work in a blink.

The critical essay format that we have outlined addresses the types of questions that academic audiences expect a rhetorical critique to answer. However, the format we suggest is just that—a suggestion. You can modify the pattern or develop an alternative pattern as long as it communicates your analysis in a way that demonstrates the criterial attributes of *quality researching, reasoning,* and *writing.*

As you are working on your essay, look at examples of RSI critiques. At the end of this book is a bibliography of suggested additional readings that lists numerous published articles using the RSI model. In addition, the second section of this book includes four RSI essays. As you review the journal articles and this book's essays, consider how the authors address the critical essay questions and expectancies detailed in this chapter. Notice how their essays demonstrate alternative ways of analyzing and organizing. Think about which ones most clearly fulfill the RSI research purpose of contributing to our knowledge and understanding of ourselves as the naming beings.

Like these writers, you might choose to share your analysis outside the classroom. Presenting or publishing your analysis gives other scholars the opportunity to learn from and expand on your work. In turn, you receive feedback about your research that might improve the quality of and inspire new directions for your research. Together the power-sharing system of communication scholars negotiates understandings and interpretations of human symbolizing activity. For more information about contributing to conventions and journals, consult the National Communication Association (http://www.natcom.org), the International Communication Association (http://www.icahdq.org), or the Rhetoric Society of America (http://rhetoricsociety.org) Web sites, and talk to your professors.

❖ CHAPTER SUMMARY

This chapter introduced the role of an RSI critic and the expectancies associated with writing an RSI essay. We described the preanalysis, analysis, and postanalysis processes that RSI critics enact to analyze and critique social interventions. For each stage, we provided questions that RSI critics typically address to meet audience expectancies of scholarly research.

Key questions to address as you research and write your own RSI analysis include the following:

Preanalysis

- What interests me?
- How does my interest relate to social change?
- What specific intervention associated with social change will I emphasize?
- What data about the intervention are available to me?
- What social system will I emphasize in my research (intervener, intervention, audience)?
- How have other scholars studied my topic area?

Analysis

- What subsystem—attention, power, or need—will I emphasize as a starting point?
- What naming patterns do the questions related to my subsystem highlight in the intervention data?
  - o Preintervention system?
  - o System intervention?
  - o Postintervention system?

Postanalysis

- How will I share my interpretation with others?
- Who is the audience for my analysis?
- What academic style should I use to write the essay?
- What organizational expectancies should my essay fulfill?
  - o Introduction expectancies?
  - o Body expectancies?
  - o Conclusion expectancies?
- What other critical essay expectancies should my essay fulfill?

This chapter emphasized developing your role as an RSI critic and ability to apply the RSI model concepts to analyze and interpret social interventions. What you learn as a critic of social intervention will enhance your ability to act as a participant in and initiator of interventions. The final chapter of this book examines how the RSI model might guide you in creating social interventions.

❖ REVIEW QUESTIONS

1. What are the *preanalysis steps* to starting an RSI critique?

2. What are the *analysis steps* for interpreting an intervention?

3. What are the *postanalysis steps* for sharing the results of an RSI analysis?

4. Why is *context* significant when analyzing an intervention? How do you balance describing the context versus emphasizing the analysis in an RSI critical essay?

5. What are the similarities and differences between a *naming* analysis and a *subsystem* RSI analysis?

6. Why should you consider your critique of an intervention as part of an *ongoing conversation about* rather than the *definitive analysis of* the intervention?

7. How is reviewing the published analyses of others who have examined the same intervention or used the same method important to your development as a researcher?

8. What are the common questions that you will find in any subsystem analysis—whether you start the analysis based on need, power, or attention?

9. How can the analysis of a specific short-term intervention, such as *Unsafe at Any Speed*, be connected to patterns related to long-term social change?

❖ CHAPTER EXERCISES

1. List some challenges that you might experience when trying to identify and locate intervention data to analyze. Share your list with class members. As a class, make suggestions and recommend techniques for managing these challenges.

2. Identify a recent social intervention reported in the media. Define the social system boundaries encompassing this intervention based on your review of media reports. What symbolizing activity related to this intervention could you study for an analysis?

3. The company for which you work plans to revamp its product line so that its products are interpreted as more environmentally

friendly. Discuss how this action might involve social intervention to both promote and prevent change. Identify social systems you could study as part of this intervention. Describe the types of rhetorical artifacts you could use to analyze the intervention.

4. Search an online database to locate a scholarly article that uses the RSI model; then critique the article on how well it meets the scholarly expectancies outlined in this chapter.

5. As a class, pick a recent documentary to examine as a social intervention. Divide yourselves into three groups—need, power, and attention. Meet as a group and review the chapter's analysis questions related to the group's assigned subsystem. Then watch the documentary, taking notes on rhetorical maneuvers you observe. Afterward, meet again as a group and draft responses to the subsystem questions. Reconvene as a class and share each group's findings.

6. Outline an alternative format to a scholarly essay that could be used to present an RSI analysis (e.g., as a play, video, Web site). Share your ideas with the class.

❖ SERVICE LEARNING EXERCISE

Using the intervention that you analyzed for the service learning exercise in Chapter 4, expand your analysis to address the subsystem questions listed in this chapter. In addition, determine criteria by which you could name the interventional attempt of the organization with which you are volunteering as *successful* or *unsuccessful* or both. Reflect on the ethical side effects of its interventional attempt. Share the results of your analysis with the class and with the not-for-profit organization.

Under the Lens: Finding Inspiration

Students often say they have difficulty identifying an intervention to analyze. Inspiration can come from everyday experience. Here are examples of events that gave the book authors ideas for interventions to critique:

Opt was living in Germany in 1992 when more than 170 world leaders gathered to discuss sustainable development issues at the first Earth Summit. She occasionally read newspaper articles about the event but did not pay much attention to them until she made a brief visit to the United States. She was surprised to see a *difference* in the way that U.S. media reported on the Earth Summit compared to how German media reported on the same event. As a result, she used the RSI model to investigate the two countries' media coverage to understand how they symbolically constituted alternative narratives and to reflect on side effects of those naming patterns (Opt, 1997).

In another instance, Opt overheard several students discussing a suggestion box that the university had installed. The submitted suggestions and the administrators' responses were posted monthly near the box. The students reading a recent posting complained to each other that the administrators never listened to them. These comments captured the author's attention because they violated the expectancy that a suggestion box would be named as *an attempt by administrators to listen*. She used the RSI model to understand the *difference* in the students' interpretation (Opt, 1998). In both the media coverage and suggestion box cases, *differences* in the symbolizing activity sparked the author's curiosity and led her to ask, "Why?" Opt eventually presented her findings at conferences and submitted her analyses for publication (Opt, 1997, 1998).

Gring's life experience provided inspiration for research. He spent several formative years on the Texas-Mexican border and in Guatemala and El Salvador. Years later when significant political changes affected that region of the world and the United States, he used the RSI model as a lens to gain insight into the dynamics of the sociopolitical events. His analysis formed the basis of his dissertation (Gring, 1993).

Gring's initial research led to work that examined how individuals combined religious convictions with Marxist revolutionary discourse to bring about the 1979 revolution in Nicaragua. He became interested in this revolution because it combined two ideas that had previously been named *diametrically opposed* to each other, namely Marxism and religion (Gring, 1998). Gring, like Opt, also presented his findings at a conference and eventually published his work (Gring, 1993, 1998).

Thus, keep your eyes, ears, and mind open to experience around you to discover interventions to analyze.

CHAPTER 6

Process and Practice of Intervention

Recently you notice that your school or workplace cafeteria is offering new foods—foods that you symbolically categorize as *unhealthy*. The change violates your ideological expectancies about how a more nearly perfect life might be achieved. You rename yourself, from *consumer* to *change agent*. How might knowledge of the Rhetoric of Social Intervention (RSI) model guide your actions as an intervener to encourage the food service and institutional administrators to attend to and satisfy your need for more healthful menu choices?

Perhaps you took a course that uses this book on the rhetoric of social intervention because the class was offered at a convenient time or fulfilled a degree plan requirement. Although you find rhetorical criticism interesting, you are majoring in another subspecialty of communication. Still, how might the RSI concepts you have learned be relevant in other communication areas besides rhetorical criticism? Or how might they be relevant to other disciplines in general?

This final chapter examines the proactive and practical use of the RSI model to guide the creation of interventions. We reflect on the process we enact when intervening and responding to others' interventions. We also consider the model's relevance to other communication areas—such as organizational, public relations, and public speaking—and to fields outside communication. Finally, we invite you to join us in considering this book as an attempted intervention.

❖ THE MODEL AS PRACTICAL INTERVENTION

Throughout your life, you will often act as a social intervener or change agent—sometimes to promote social change, sometimes to maintain social continuity. At times people might name you as initiating the intervention; at other times, you might interpret your actions as responding to their interventions. Regardless, your voice is one among many that interact to influence social system dynamics (Brown, 1978). No techniques exist to ensure that your intervention will result in your hoped-for outcomes. However, knowledge of the RSI model can reveal the possibilities for an intervention in a situation, guide the development of the intervention, and enable you to consider the possible side effects of your interventional attempts. In addition, it allows you to reflect on your responses to others' interventional attempts in social systems in which you participate.

. We tend to become change agents when experience appears to deviate unpleasantly from the expectancies created by our ideologically generated names for experience (Brown, 1978). For example, what if product sales decline after a company introduces a reengineered soft drink that has been named *the means to ensure the company's growth*? Suppose a cat or dog dies after eating pet food that has been symbolically categorized as *nutritious and life extending*. Such nonfitting experiences prompt interventions to rename experience to compensate for the anomalies that threaten the continuity of ideology.

The RSI model suggests choices that change agents make when enacting interventions. We describe these choices as questions to consider when developing the strategies, tactics, and maneuvers of an intervention. These same questions can also help you recognize others' interventional attempts as you attempt to intervene. We exemplify these questions in a narrative about a college-based intervention.

Increasing Anomaly Awareness

Suppose you complete a doctorate in communication. You enter the field because you name *communication* as a key to achieving the American dream. An understanding of communication leads to more effective relationships, more tolerance for others, and more career opportunities, and, by extension, a more nearly perfect world. Hence, you *profess* communication as the basis for understanding human identity.

You teach at a small commuter college that you categorize as *a good place to work*. The students are interesting and interactive. Your colleagues are friendly and supportive. The administration provides adequate pay and benefits. These experiences form criterial attributes of the symbolic category *a good place to work*. The college power-sharing system meets your needs.

During the past year, however, you become aware of events that bother you. Program enrollment has been declining, with 30 percent of students transferring after their sophomore year. Also, although you receive good teaching evaluations, students frequently comment "interesting course, but the theory stuff isn't very useful," or "need more hands-on work." Finally, local employer surveys frequently rate your graduates as "excellent" in researching and critical-thinking skills but "needs improvement" in the flexibility and adaptability categories. These events violate the expectancies you associate with the communication program, which you have categorized as providing *excellent preparation for the future*.

You discuss these anomalies with your colleagues. They seem unconcerned. They attribute the enrollment decline to the implementation of higher program standards. They account for the teaching evaluation comments by saying that students will recognize later the value of what they have learned. Finally, they remark that employers always complain because they feel important when they can complain.

Despite your colleagues' explanations, you fear that the trends of enrollment drops and student dissatisfaction with program knowledge might continue. In addition, employers might refuse to hire your students if they name them *inadequately prepared*. If the trend continues, the program could be downsized or discontinued. You would lose your job and ability to achieve the dream. The college would no longer be *a good place to work*.

Identifying Naming Patterns

You become more open to an alternative way of symbolizing experience to explain the anomalies you are encountering. By embracing openness, you begin the process of social intervention. The starting point for enacting a social intervention is an analysis of the social system's current naming patterns. In this instance, you have been observing these system components that influence each other—the communication faculty, the current students, and potential employers. The RSI model suggests asking these types of questions about the system:

- How am I naming experience? How are the system components naming experience?
- What anomaly-featuring communication or anomaly-masking communication, or both, are the components emphasizing?

- What aspects of experience do their current naming patterns background or foreground, or both?
- What ideological expectancies do their naming patterns reflect?

You identify your colleagues' naming pattern as one that categorizes the college's communication program as providing *excellent preparation for the future*. You detect this pattern in their conversations as well as in the program's mission statement and recruitment materials. Thanks to your knowledge of the RSI model, you recognize the unease you have been feeling as related to anomaly-featuring communication—the inability of the current naming pattern to make sense of the declining enrollment, student comments, and employer complaints. These events violate the expectancies generated by the naming pattern *the program provides excellent preparation for the future*.

Other power shareholders—students and employers—seem to be advocating a competing template—*the program provides inadequate preparation for the future*. They constitute this name by featuring anomalies in your colleagues' template. They communicate these anomalies in actions and symbolizing activity, such as changing schools, completing course evaluation forms, and completing employer surveys. They appear to be acting as interveners to promote an attention shift.

As you reflect on how your colleagues account for the enrollment drops, student remarks, and employer responses, you recognize their explanations as examples of anomaly-masking communication. They have responded to the anomaly-featuring communication by finding ways to mask attention to the anomalies. Thus, they have been able to maintain the naming pattern *the program provides excellent preparation for the future* and reject the alternative interpretation being proposed. They have been intervening to prevent an attention shift.

You examine the symbolizing activity to understand how the faculty constructs its naming pattern. Your colleagues emphasize behaviors and activities defined as *scholarly* as the criterial attribute of *excellent preparation*. They foreground completing theory and research courses, participating in the undergraduate research symposium, and writing senior theses as aspects of experience that reify the symbolic category *excellent preparation*. In this interpretation of experience, the American dream is achieved by scholarly preparation. But what does this naming pattern background?

To reveal backgrounded experience, you examine the students' and employers' naming patterns. How do they appear symbolically to construct *excellent preparation*? To what aspects of experience do they refer to reify *excellent preparation*? How does that influence their interpretation of the communication program? How do they make sense of the American dream? In answering these questions, you observe that, for them, *practical* knowledge is a criterial attribute of *excellent preparation*.

You are prompted to intervene because you project that if the students and employers continue their anomaly-featuring communication to promote the name *inadequate preparation* and the faculty continues its anomaly-masking communication to promote the name *excellent preparation*, deviance will amplify. These naming patterns can result in neither group fulfilling the others' needs and goals. Without a rhetorical trend reversal, the system components might become less needs-meeting and might disband. Thus, you begin enacting the role of change agent.

Making Choices

The RSI model suggests questions for interveners to consider when planning an intervention:

- What is the nature of my intervention? Am I promoting change? Impeding change? Both?
- In what way am I trying to reverse or compensate for a rhetorical trend that I interpret to be deviance amplifying?

These questions require you to think about choices. Perhaps the faculty interpretation of experience makes sense to you. You agree that *excellent preparation* means emphasizing scholarly knowledge. You choose to intervene to *maintain* this interpretation. To reverse the deviance-amplifying trend of lower enrollment, you create an intervention that attempts to *change* how students and employers symbolically categorize *excellent preparation*. You intervene to shift the students' and employers' attention *away from* emphasizing practical knowledge and *to* emphasizing scholarly knowledge. What could you do or say to these power shareholders to promote a shift in their interpretations of needs, interdependencies, and experience? What might be the side effects of such an intervention?

Alternatively, you might choose to adopt the alternative naming pattern. Practical skills attainment as a criterial attribute of *excellent preparation* makes sense to you. You attempt to intervene to *change* how your colleagues symbolically categorize *excellent preparation*. You intervene to shift attention *away* from scholarly knowledge and *to* practical knowledge. What could you say or do to promote a shift in your colleagues' interpretation of needs, interdependencies, and experience? What might be the side effects of such an intervention?

In either case, you intend the renaming to reverse the deviance-amplifying trend. However, these two choices are *either-or* options. One foregrounds scholarly activity and backgrounds practical experience; the other highlights practical skills and downplays scholarly knowledge. What about a third option—one that symbolically categorizes *excellent preparation* as attaining *both* scholarly *and* practical knowledge?

What your colleagues need to do, you decide, is to rename the criterial attributes associated with *excellent preparation*. Rather than focusing on *either* scholarly *or* practical knowledge, you will encourage them to extend the attributes of the symbolic category *excellent preparation* to include practical activity. In this alternative version of experience, the American dream will be achieved through a program that provides excellent preparation by emphasizing *both* scholarly *and* practical achievements. How will you promote this shift?

Again, you make choices about how to enact the combination of scholarly and practical activity. Will you do it through new skills-oriented courses? Internships? Service learning? You decide that one way to reify scholarly and practical activity is to add a student newspaper to the communication program. You select this choice because you worked on a student newspaper as an undergraduate and you name that experience as contributing to your own success. However, you support that choice by finding research and professional sources that emphasize the need and value of student newspaper experience. How might producing a student newspaper incorporate both your colleagues' expectancies of scholarly activity and the students' and employers' expectancies of practical activity associated with *excellent preparation*?

Deciding on Audiences

As you consider the nature of your intervention, you must also identify the social system components with which you are interdependent for the enactment of your intervention. The RSI model leads you to ask this question:

- Who is the primary audience of my intervention?

Although your long-term interventional goal is to shift how current students and future employers name the communication program, your method of achieving that goal (developing a student newspaper) requires attention to a different system of power shareholders. To identify your primary audience, you must identify the social system components with whom you are interdependent to achieve your goal. Because you want to introduce a student newspaper in a college setting, you examine components within the college, such as students, faculty, staff, administrators, alumni, board of trustees, and donors. Which of these components, or audiences, seem most able to mediate your future—in this case, the creation of a student newspaper?

Suppose you name your colleagues as your primary audience. You interpret their support as being most critical to achieving your goal of extending the criterial attributes of *excellent preparation* to include practical activity in the form of a student newspaper. That is not to say that you consider the other system components unimportant. You could increase your interdependency with alumni and donors by advocating the need for funds to operate a student newspaper. In addition, other components, such as faculty outside the communication program, administration, and students will become important as the intervention progresses. However, time and resources often temper our selection of audiences. You decide that unless your colleagues interpret a need for a student newspaper to enact practical experience, they will be unlikely to provide the logistical support necessary to ensure the newspaper's future.

Selecting a Starting Point

As you determine your audience, you consider the starting point for your intervention. The RSI model suggests that you pose this question:

- With which subsystem will I begin my intervention?

Will you gear your intervention toward increasing your audience's attention to unmet needs, non-needs-meeting interdependencies, or anomalies in its interpretation of experience? Often we appeal to the same need, power, or attention anomaly that is already apparent to us.

You choose *need* as your starting point because the anomalies you have noticed suggest that the communication program is not satisfying students' or employers' needs. You select to focus your intervention on making your colleagues aware of the need to extend the program's preparation to include practical knowledge. You do this by advocating the creation of a student newspaper. You reason that this action will meet the growth-and-survival need of the communication program. Related to the subsystem question is this consideration:

- What strategies and tactics will I use to promote my intervention?

Strategically, you select to feature anomalies in your audience's accepted way of interpreting need. You seek to shift the faculty's emphasis *away from* the collectivity-stressing need for scholarly activity that contributes to the knowledge base of the communication field as a whole. You attempt to shift the faculty's emphasis *to* the individuality-stressing need for both scholarly and practical experience that contribute to the holistic development of the student. Common to both emphases is the symbolically constituted need for *excellent preparation* as a means to reify the American dream. Only the interpretation of *how* that need is met changes as the emphasis shifts.

Tactically, you plan to create awareness of and attribute to your colleagues the need to revise the communication program to offer both scholarly and practical activities. You advocate the creation of a student newspaper as a way to satisfy the need to include practical knowledge. You encourage your colleagues to open channels of communication with potential power shareholders, such as students, administrators, and others who will be important to establishing a student newspaper.

Because the RSI model emphasizes the dynamics of system intervention, you assume that, at the same time you are intervening, others will also be intervening. For example, some of your colleagues might intervene to attempt to prevent change. They deny the need for practical experience or for a student newspaper. Thus, you must consider how you will respond to others' interventional attempts as you create the rhetorical maneuvers of your intervention.

Creating Rhetorical Maneuvers

As you determine the strategies and tactics of the intervention, your knowledge of the RSI model leads you to pose these questions:

- What rhetorical maneuvers will I employ to enact the intervention?
- How will I reason to promote my naming of experience?

Enacting an intervention requires developing rhetorical maneuvers that communicate the strategies and tactics of the intervention. Think about what you will say or do to reach your intended audience.

In developing messages, keep in mind your overall strategy—in this case, to shift the audience's interpretation of needs. You employ rhetorical maneuvers that feature anomalies in your colleagues' interpretation that the program must emphasize only scholarly activity to ensure its growth and survival. At the same time, you use rhetorical maneuvers that mask attention to anomalies in the interpretation of needs that you are promoting.

To create rhetorical maneuvers, you gather materials such as statistics, examples, and testimony. These materials highlight experiences that violate expectancies associated with your colleagues' interpretation of needs. You might identify several universities that symbolically categorize *excellent preparation* as including both scholarly and practical knowledge. You show how their enrollment numbers are increasing. You might find examples of programs similar to yours that define *excellent preparation* as scholarly knowledge only. You show how their enrollment numbers are decreasing. What other aspects of experience might you foreground to feature attention to anomalies in your colleagues' interpretation of needs?

In anticipation of other interveners' messages, you reflect on how to mask anomalies in the interpretation of needs that you are advocating. Suppose your colleagues say that practical activities will *dilute* the program and make it *the same as* a technical school. What if they note that students can volunteer on the college's yearbook to get practical experience? They might point out that creating a student newspaper will draw resources away from other activities and courses, thereby reducing the program's ability to provide *excellent preparation*. How will you respond? How will you show that practical activity is not opposed to scholarly activity and that scholarship can emerge from practical involvement?

Choosing Channels

You also make choices about the channels of communication for conveying your messages to your intended audience. You could write a book on the need for both scholarly and practical activities to enhance *excellent preparation*—but think about the time and cost of that maneuver. You could post flyers around the campus that summarize your anomaly-featuring messages—but your colleagues might ignore the flyers because they interpret flyers to be communication intended only for students. You could create a PowerPoint show and invite the faculty to a formal presentation—but you notice that only administrators seem to give formal presentations on issues. You could march around campus carrying a sign that advocates the need for change—but your colleagues might symbolically categorize you as *weird* and ignore your messages.

In the end, you select to communicate your intervention in two ways: informal discussions with departmental colleagues and a presentation at the department's monthly meeting. You choose these communication channels to convey your message based on your observation of the college system. You notice that the system has an institutionalized or *socially accepted* method for professors to advocate change in program curriculum. Thus, you hope that by following a similar process with the student newspaper proposal, your colleagues will name the proposal as *the same as* changing curriculum and focus on its contributions to students' academic experience.

To change curriculum, a professor first discusses the proposed change with colleagues. If the colleagues seem receptive, then, following institutional policy (power code), the professor presents the proposed change to the department. If the department approves, then the professor's interdependency with three additional power shareholders increases—the division dean, the curriculum committee, and the full faculty. All three must approve the proposal and may require the professor to enact additional interventions.

Considering Subsystem Side Effects

In this narrative, we have acted as if the interventional goal is to promote a need intervention—*away* from the need to emphasize scholarly activity *to* the need to emphasize both scholarly and practical knowledge to enact *excellent preparation*. However, the RSI model points to asking additional questions:

- What are the potential subsystem side effects of my intervention?
- How will a shift in one subsystem (need, power, or attention) simultaneously lead to shifts in the other subsystems?

In this instance, you consider the side effects for power and attention. If the departmental faculty accepts the interpretation of needs you are advocating and the remaining components of the college system approve the student newspaper, how might power shift within the department? How might interdependencies be revised? Who becomes *more* important in future choosing? Who becomes *less* important in future choosing? In what ways does the need shift challenge the current departmental hierarchy? How might this influence the overall development of the department system?

No doubt, the communication program will become more interdependent with a person who can advise and students who can write and edit newspapers. The program will also become more interdependent with people willing to talk to the student reporters and with advertisers willing to buy ads to support the newspaper. Increased interdependency will be formed with printers or web masters. Faculty with technical skills to facilitate the newspaper's production might need to be hired.

At the same time that you urge your colleagues to rename needs, you also encourage them to reinterpret their experiences. How will the shift *away from* emphasizing only scholarly activity and *to* emphasizing both scholarly and practical activity influence how your colleagues interpret the program as a whole? How will their sense of being shift? How will their ways of knowing change? How will the need intervention alter what they value?

Furthermore, what additional interventions might be needed to attempt to shift the students' and employers' interpretation of *excellent preparation*? How will you encourage those system components to rename the attributes of *excellent preparation* to include both practical and scholarly work, or interpret the student newspaper as practical experience, or both? What if the trend of enrollment drops and employer dissatisfaction continues after reorganizing the department to include a student newspaper?

Alternatively, suppose the audience agrees to maintain its current interpretation of needs and rejects the proposed interpretation. Your colleagues deny the need for preparation that includes both scholarly and practical activity. How might the power shareholders interpret your attempted intervention? How might that influence your interdependencies with them? How will you account for your inability to bring about change? What price might you pay for your attempted intervention? How might you next intervene if you continue to interpret a need for both scholarly and practical activity to ensure the program's growth and survival?

Finally, suppose your colleagues agree that the communication program needs to include practical experience to provide *excellent preparation*, but suppose they intervene to propose alternative ways to satisfy that need, such as creating a literary magazine or a student public relations firm. What if other power shareholders in the college system respond to your attempted intervention by choosing to ensure the institution's growth and survival by eliminating the communication program? These possible side effects remind us that we *intervene*, rather than *control*, when we attempt to bring about social change.

Overall, the RSI model provides a framework to guide the actions of change agents. The model's use does not ensure that the intervention will result in the intended outcome. As you promote your interpretation of experience, others will advocate theirs. Together, you and the other interveners negotiate the choosing of futures.

Thus far, we have examined the questions that the RSI model leads you to ask when acting as an intervener. Now we consider how the RSI model applies in other areas of communication besides rhetoric.

❖ THE MODEL AS RHETORICAL INTERVENTION

The RSI model directs our attention to the rhetorical nature of social interventions. This does not mean, however, that the RSI model is relevant only to rhetorical criticism. The model offers insights into a wide range of communication areas. To demonstrate its applicability across the field of communication, we briefly discuss three areas that might relate to your experience in communication. We examine the RSI model's connections to organizational communication, public relations, and public speaking.

Connecting to Organizational Communication

Organizational communication scholars often emphasize the importance of understanding the change that organizations must undergo to grow and survive (Bergquist, 1993). Organizations must be able to initiate and adapt to apparent changes in their external and internal environments to maintain their goals of providing services or producing products. For example, when airplanes began replacing ships as the main means of overseas travel, the ocean cruise line industry changed and adapted by emphasizing *entertainment* instead of *transportation* to stay in business (Eisenberg & Goodall, 1997).

Through the lens of the RSI model, organizational change occurs because events violate the expectancies generated by the organizational members' naming patterns. Organizational members attempt to compensate for the anomalies by renaming experience or the criterial attributes of experience. Thus, organizations transform as their members promote need, power, and attention shifts (Opt, 2003).

When organizational members conceive of new ways to make old products, develop new products, find new uses for old products, and shift management styles, they engage in attention switching (Opt, 2003). Organizations grow and survive because their members symbolically recategorize experience. From the perspective of the RSI model, Apple Computer, Inc., came into being when its founders renamed the computer from *industrial product* to *hobbyist toy* and eventually to *home appliance* (Opt).

The RSI model interprets the decline or dissolution of an organization in terms of vicious circles. If an organizational system is unable to compensate for deviance-amplifying naming patterns, then the organization might no longer meet other system components' needs and might go out of business (Opt, 2003). What if the ocean liner industry had continued to name its business as *providing transportation*, despite the anomaly of an increasing number of its customers electing to fly?

Finally, the RSI model suggests that to understand and intervene in organizational change, we should pay attention to the organization's naming patterns (Opt, 2003). We might attempt to anticipate the direction of organizational change by attending to anomaly-masking and anomaly-featuring communication in superiors' and subordinates' conversations. We might identify organizational interveners by watching for needs-advocacy behaviors and challenges to the organization's power code. We could analyze the organization's adaptation to its internal and external audiences by comparing its interpretations of need, interdependencies, and experience to the naming patterns that external publics constitute about the organization.

Linking to Public Relations

Like organizational communication researchers, public relations scholars emphasize the importance of understanding organizational change processes so that organizations can proactively, rather than reactively, respond to their environments (Opt, 2008). As public relations theorist Derina Holtzhausen (2000) comments, "Practitioners' ability to deal with changes in society will enable those who work in institutions to contribute to their organizations' survival and effectiveness" (p. 110). The RSI model provides practitioners with a framework for comprehending and interpreting the organizational change needed for growth and survival.

Public relations professionals often monitor the environment in search of events that might influence the public's interpretation of the organization. The RSI model directs practitioners to pay attention to how the organization names itself and its publics, and how the publics, in turn, name themselves and the organization (Opt, 2008). These professionals would compare the organization's and the public's communication patterns in terms of what they foreground and background in experience. They would reflect on how similarities and differences in the patterns might shape the relationship between the organization and its publics.

For example, a pet food public relations professional monitoring the media might notice an increase in articles that foreground attention to the deaths of cats and dogs after the animals had consumed certain pet foods. To account for the anomaly, some consumers rename the pet foods *unsafe*. This shift in interpretation, from *safe* to *unsafe*, constituted in the symbolizing activity, suggests to the professional that consumers' interdependency with the organization is about to change—from one based on *exchange* to one organized by *threat*.

Thus, public relations practitioners can look through the lens of the RSI model to anticipate changes in the interdependency between an organization and its publics. In addition, the RSI model suggests a way for practitioners to envision side effects that might occur as a result of rhetorical renaming (Opt, 2008). For example, what potential systemic side effects might result from an interpretive shift from *safe pet food* to *unsafe pet food*?

In their role as change agents, public relations practitioners often attempt interventions to create, maintain, and change the relationship between an organization and its publics. The RSI model indicates that professionals should develop interventions by analyzing the public's current ways of naming needs, interdependencies, and experience. The RSI model provides practitioners with a framework for constructing interventional strategies, tactics, and maneuvers and considering the side effects of the attempted change (Opt, 2008).

Relating to Speech Communication

Like organizational and public relations scholars, speech communication scholars also emphasize understanding change, but often from the point of view of the speaker as change agent. For example, speech textbook authors Steven Beebe and Susan Beebe (2006) note that speaking with competence and confidence is empowering. "To be empowered is to have the resources, information, and attitudes that allow you to take action to achieve a desired goal" (p. 2). In achieving a desired goal, the speaker seeks change, which suggests a connection to the RSI model.

In the RSI model's interpretation of experience, public speakers are *interveners* (Gring, 2006). They attempt to influence interdependencies with audiences so that the speakers' needs might be met and desired goals achieved. Speakers attempt to shift or maintain how their audiences symbolically categorize experience. Think about speeches you have given, perhaps in a class or an organizational setting. Can you identify the shifts in need, power, or attention that you tried to promote or impede in those speech-making events?

Through the lens of the RSI model, all public speaking events are *interventions*. Giving a speech is not a static experience—rather, it is an intervention into an ongoing dialogue negotiating the symbolic categorization of experience. More specifically, a speech enacts the rhetorical maneuvers that promote the strategies and tactics of an intervention. For example, an HIV/AIDS speech given to college administrators tactically attributes and advocates the need for an HIV testing center on campus and promotes the strategy of stressing group need.

In addition, the RSI model allows a speaker to develop the speech around the intervention-constructing questions posed earlier in this chapter. As part of an audience analysis, the speaker examines the system components' naming patterns and compares them to his or her own. How does the audience talk about the topic? How does it symbolically categorize its needs, interdependencies, and experience? What anomaly-masking and anomaly-featuring communication is occurring? How have the audience's naming patterns changed over time? By addressing such questions, the speaker gains clues as to how to intervene and which type of intervention to emphasize—need, power, or attention.

Finally, the RSI model enables the speaker as intervener to consider the side effects of the attempted intervention. Traditionally, speech communication scholars discuss ethics—the need to be truthful, fair, and accurate, and to consider sources and values—based on the assumption that speeches can influence audiences (Beebe & Beebe, 2006). The RSI model also directs speakers to attend to the potential subsystem side effects of their rhetorical interventions. For example, if you as a speaker attempt a needs intervention, how might that influence the system's interpretation of its interdependencies and experience?

As we discussed the RSI model's connection to organizational communication, public relations, and speech communication, perhaps you also thought of RSI model links to other subspecialties of communication. Maybe you see relationships between the RSI model and communication areas such as family, health, intercultural, interpersonal, mass media, political, risk, crisis, and small group. In addition, perhaps you considered how the RSI model could be used to organize and make sense of the historical development of communication theory. These connections offer opportunities for you to explore as you grow in your role of RSI scholar.

Connecting to Other Fields

As you learn about the RSI model, maybe you notice ties between the RSI model and disciplines in addition to communication—such as psychology, marketing, economics, sociology, and history. As your thinking about the model develops, you might act as an innovator in these other fields by introducing the RSI model as an alternative framework for interpreting experience examined in these disciplines.

You might also find that the RSI model has applicability in fields that are attempting to make sense of human experience using a **holographic** metaphor. Although we have referred to the RSI subsystems as holographic, the model itself is a holographic approach to understanding human symbolizing activity. It assumes that all experiences, like the swirls on holographic film, are dynamically interconnected. We create the appearance of separateness in and give order to experience when we symbolically categorize. The RSI model, though, directs our attention to the holistic nature of experience by emphasizing the interconnectedness and interdependence of our communication patterns. Like the light that shines through the holographic film patterns reveals the apple, the RSI model enables us to reveal our symbolic patterns that divide and unite experience.

Over the past few decades, scientists, scholars, and philosophers in fields such as physics, chemistry, neuroscience, biology, psychology, anthropology, medicine, and organizational design have been negotiating the merits of a holographic metaphor for making sense of human experience (Banner, 1994; Bekenstein, 2003; Bohm, 2002; Johnston, 2006; Pribram, 1971; Susskind & Lindesay, 2005; Talbot, 1992; Wagner, 2001; Wilbur, 1982). Physicist David Bohm, an advocate of the holographic template, believes that "our almost universal tendency to fragment the world and ignore the dynamics interconnectedness of all things is responsible for many of our problems, not only in science but in our lives and society" (quoted in Talbot, p. 49). Such thinking enables us to start wars and bury toxic wastes without reflecting on the long-term impacts of our individual actions on the whole system (Talbot). Thus, as you develop in your role as an RSI scholar, you might act as an intervener to contribute to our understanding of a holographic template. You might also contemplate the side effects for a social system that symbolically recategorizes the universe as a hologram.

We, the authors, hope that one side effect of our intervention is that you increase your reflectivity about the communication processes that underlie every aspect of our lives. By way of closing, we mention a few other ways we hope this book intervenes in your naming patterns.

❖ THE BOOK AS INTERVENTION

If we, the authors, restricted ourselves to philosopher Thomas Kuhn's (1996) model of scientific change, we would name ourselves as *cumulators*. Kuhn views *cumulators* as power shareholders whose task in the academic social system is to choose the concepts and models to be passed down to the next generation of scholars. Cumulators compile these ideas into forms such as books and articles. In this book, we have summarized and compiled RSI model concepts from the original articles to pass on to you. However, in the process of being cumulators, we, the authors, are also interveners. Let's contemplate how we have attempted to intervene in your symbolic reality through writing this book.

Promoting an Attention Intervention

Consider how we, the authors, attempted to promote or impede a shift in your interpretation of experience. How did you name the communication process prior to reading this book? How do you name it now?

Perhaps you foregrounded marketplace forces, technological advancements, or psychological attitudes as the drivers of social change. You rhetorically backgrounded the role of communication in prompting and forestalling social change, treating it as something added, a tool of occasional use in shaping the world. Maybe now you name *communication*—more specifically, the human ability to transform experience into symbols—as the *catalyst of social change*. When individuals, organizations, societies, and cultures experience change, we ascribe the generator of that change to shifts in how they symbolically construct interpretations of needs, interdependencies, and experience. To promote this attention shift to the interpretation that communication drives social change, we attempted to shift your ways of knowing, valuing, and being.

The book highlighted the rhetorical nature of our knowledge of the world—that much of what we call *reality* has been symbolically constructed. It emphasized valuing the understanding of alternative interpretations of experience and the process by which we rhetorically construct those interpretations. Finally, it directed attention to the symbolic nature of our being—we are the naming beings.

Rhetorical theorist Kenneth Burke (1966) ties together knowing, valuing, and being when he poses these questions related to defining human beings as symbol-using creatures:

> [C]an we bring ourselves to realize . . . just how overwhelmingly much of what we mean by "reality" has been built up for us

through nothing but our symbol systems? Take away our books, and what little do we know about history, biography, even something so "down to earth" as the relative position of seas and continents? What is our "reality" for today (beyond the paper-thin line of our particular lives) but all this clutter of symbols about the past combined with whatever things we know mainly through maps, magazines, newspapers, and the like about the present? . . . And however important to us is this tiny sliver of reality each has experience firsthand, the whole overall "picture" is but a construct of our symbol systems. (p. 5)

Finally, what power-related and need-related attention shifts might have occurred? Perhaps prior to reading this book you named yourself as *independent*. Now you name yourself as *interdependent*. Perhaps you interpreted all of your needs as *real*. Now you interpret many of them as *symbolic constructions*.

Encouraging a Power Intervention

In what way has this book attempted to promote a power shift? Perhaps you purchased this book because a professor assigned it for a class. You followed a power code that says that you obtain the books that the professor requires. Maybe you read the chapters because of a power code that says you complete the assignments required by the professor. By agreeing to buy and read this book, you entered a power-sharing system that includes us, the authors.

The book promotes an interpretation of experience that we, the authors, believe compensates for anomalies in currently held naming patterns about social change. We are interdependent with others, such as you, to read, ratify, and advocate this proposed interpretation. By presenting our interpretation of experience, we offer a choice—an alternative way to name experience and for the social system to develop.

Perhaps your professor previously cooperated with other authors by purchasing their books. If your professor names this book as one that offers an interpretation that seems to make more sense of experience, then the professor reduces interdependency with other authors and increases interdependency with us. In this exchange-based relationship, we, the authors, provide a communication-based view of change that might enable your professor to better do his or her job. In turn, your professor agrees to adopt the new book and distribute this view of change.

Although you might have followed a power code in acquiring this book, you have power code expectancies related to book authors. You probably expect academic book authors to offer information that prepares you to participate more fully in society by being a more informed citizen. You might expect the authors to provide knowledge that enhances and expands your life and career opportunities. You might expect them to use a writing style that is understandable, and so forth.

You become a power holder when you give feedback on the professor's choice of books. If you and other students agree that the authors have violated power code expectancies, you can advocate change. The professor might discontinue using this book and become interdependent with other authors or become a competitor by writing his or her own book about social change. What you learn from books is part of your future choosing, just as your evaluation and recommendation of books are part of future choosing for authors.

Finally, how has your role in social hierarchy shifted now that you can enact the roles of *RSI critic* and *social intervener*? With what groups, courses, and theorists might you now seek increased interdependency as a result of your renaming? With what groups, courses, and theorists might you be less interdependent if you adopt the alternative names for yourself?

Prompting a Need Intervention

In what ways have your interpretation of needs shifted? If you are using this book in a course, perhaps you initially focused on your individual need to get through the material to pass the course. You needed to do well on examinations and papers, so you needed to learn about the RSI model to meet that need. Perhaps you advocated that need by asking the professor questions about exam designs and paper requirements. How have we tried to encourage you to rename your needs from the individual need of simply passing this class to the social need of learning more about a communication-driven interpretation of social change?

Think about how we linked an understanding of social change to American dream attributes such as the *need for success*. If you comprehend and can critique social change, you can more effectively participate in the social system as critic and intervener. Such knowledge might enable you to enhance the social good and fulfill the need to accomplish a more nearly perfect life for all. We have advocated the RSI model as a way for you to meet this need to understand and analyze social change.

Finally, consider how some of your other needs might have shifted after reading this book. Maybe now you support a need to make others aware of the symbolic nature of social change. You might interpret a need to pay attention to people's dialogue and discussions to glimpse the rhetorical processes of social intervention. Perhaps you become an advocate of the RSI model by writing papers and theses based on the model. You also might see a need to reinterpret or expand the model. Of course, after reading this book, you might interpret the model to be non-needs-meeting, return the book to the bookstore, and advocate an alternative approach.

Overall, this book has been an attempt to intervene in your interpretations of social change, interdependencies, and needs. It attempts to nudge you in the direction of naming social change as rhetorically driven and of defining naming as the essence of being human. However, we recognize that, as interveners, we do not control the intervention's outcome. We simply present one choice among many for understanding human experience. We are interdependent with you in choosing the future.

❖ CHAPTER SUMMARY

This chapter has considered how the RSI model offers a framework for constructing social interventions. Using the narrative of a college-setting intervention, we highlighted some of the questions that the RSI model suggests that interveners consider when organizing interventions:

- How am I naming experience? How are the system components naming experience?
  - What anomaly-featuring or anomaly-masking communication, or both, are the components emphasizing?
  - What aspects of experience do their current naming patterns background or foreground, or both?
  - What ideological expectancies do their naming patterns reflect?
- What is the nature of my intervention? Am I promoting change? Impeding change? Both?
- In what way am I trying to reverse or compensate for a rhetorical trend that I interpret to be deviance amplifying?
- Who is the primary audience of my intervention?
- With which subsystem will I begin?
- What strategies and tactics will I use to promote my intervention?
- What rhetorical maneuvers will I employ to enact the intervention?

- How will I reason to promote my naming of experience?
  - o What messages or symbolizing activity will I create to communicate the intervention?
  - o What channels of communication will I use to communicate the intervention?
- What are the potential subsystem side effects of my intervention? How will a shift in one subsystem (need, power, or attention) simultaneously lead to shifts in the other subsystems?

Overall, the RSI model can guide intervention development. It can also provide a framework for reflecting on others' attempts to intervene in systems in which you participate.

Next, we examined the RSI model's connections to communication subspecialties and other disciplines. The RSI model offers a rhetorical way to understand and interpret the organizational change that is necessary to an organization's growth and survival. It provides a methodology to enable public relations professionals to anticipate shifts in the *organization/public's* relationship and create interventions to attempt to shape those shifts. The RSI model also suggests a way to reinterpret public speaking events by naming speakers as *interveners*, speeches as *rhetorical maneuvers* that promote interventions, and ethics as *reflection* on the side effects of interventions. In addition, the model potentially links to disciplines advocating the hologram as a metaphor for making sense of experience, both as a holographic approach and as a method to explore that interpretive shift.

Finally, the chapter concluded with thoughts about this book as a social intervention. We reflected on how we, the authors, have attempted to promote need, power, and attention shifts in your interpretations of experience. We have sought to expand how you name your role in the social system—from *participant* to *critic* to *intervener*. We have foregrounded communication as the driver of social change. We have advocated the interpretation that understanding social change from a rhetorical perspective will enable us to build a more nearly perfect world and enact the American dream.

How will we, the authors, evaluate the response to and side effects of our intervention? We will pay attention to the social system around us. We will review symbolizing activity such as letters to the editor, magazine articles, and news broadcasts for shifts in how people talk about social change. We will examine scholarly journal articles for the types of communication models being used to interpret social change. We will listen to daily conversations for evidence of new or redefined words, such as *anomaly-masking* and *anomaly-featuring*, prompted by the RSI model. We will search for social hierarchy changes, such as newly created positions with titles like *intervention specialist*.

In sharing our interpretation of the rhetoric of social intervention, we have contributed to the ongoing human dialogue to construe a world of ordered experience. Now it is your turn.

❖ REVIEW QUESTIONS

1. What are the similarities and differences in using the RSI model as a method of criticism versus a method of intervention?

2. How does your attention shift when renaming yourself from *critic* to *change agent*? What are the implications for needs and power?

3. What types of choices must you make when acting as an intervener?

4. When intervening, are there times when interveners may be pushed or forced to do something that they did not want to do? Are there times when the power code prevails over what seems to be the free will or choice of the intervener?

5. When acting as an intervener, what might be your ethical responsibilities for any unintended side effects of your intervention?

6. Think of a field outside of communication. In what ways might the RSI model be used to provide insight into that field?

7. How does knowledge of the rhetorical patterns of social intervention enable you to participate more fully within a social system?

8. How might the RSI model, a *holographic approach*, be used to understand some disciplines' shifts to interpreting the universe as a hologram?

9. Is this textbook an *ethical intervention*? Which power code conventions does it follow and violate? How would you deem its effectiveness at promoting need, power, and attention interventions?

❖ CHAPTER EXERCISES

1. Using the chapter's example of the college need intervention, redesign the intervention from the starting point of power or attention.

2. Reflect on a speech or presentation that you have given recently. Analyze that event through the lens of the RSI model.

3. Visit the Web site American Rhetoric (http://americanrhetoric .com). Choose two speeches on a related topic (e.g., race relations, global warming, homeland security). Compare and contrast the interventional strategies, tactics, and maneuvers of the two speeches.

4. Suppose you work for a company that wants to boost sales for its new line of all-natural, organic yogurts. How might your knowledge of the RSI model assist you in developing and implementing a marketing campaign to increase sales?

5. Select an organization that has been in the news recently. Find newspaper and magazine articles that have been published about the organization during the past six months. Analyze the articles for anomaly-featuring or anomaly-masking communication, or both. What trends do you notice? If you were a public relations professional for that organization, how would you advise it to respond to the trends in light of your knowledge of the RSI model?

6. Divide the class into need, power, and attention groups. Each group should analyze the strategies, tactics, and maneuvers of this book's attempted intervention into the group's assigned subsystem. Group members should discuss how they individually have responded to the attempted intervention. Share the group's findings with the class.

❖ SERVICE LEARNING EXERCISE

Propose an intervention for the not-for-profit organization for which you have been working. Respond to the questions in this chapter. Explain the purpose and nature of the intervention; its audience; the strategies, tactics, and maneuvers to enact the intervention; and possible side effects from the intervention. Present an oral and a written version of the proposal to the organization.

Under the Lens: Interpreting Scholarship

Review the following narrative that rhetorical scholar Lee Snyder shares with his students. Consider these questions as you read: What is the nature and purpose of his intervention? What are the strategies, tactics, and rhetorical maneuvers of his intervention? What side effects might result from his attempted intervention? What kind of alternative intervention might you construct to accomplish similar goals?

There is a great ship, chartered by philosopher Sir Francis Bacon, and still in operation, traveling continually around the world. The ship contains many spacious rooms, each filled with great men and women of the world who have lived in all times from ancient days to the present.

Some of these people are scientists. Others are philosophers. Some are farmers. Others are business entrepreneurs. Some are professors. And among the men and women are some students.

These people are remarkable—you would recognize some of them—and their faces seem to radiate a light of understanding. Also remarkable is that, although these people often disagree in their discussions, they do not discriminate against others. Wherever in the world the ship docks, new passengers are welcomed based only on their merits. Race and sex are irrelevant, and young students are treated with the same dignity as the old sages.

Often, a new person tries to board the ship. This person presents to the porter a paper, a book, or a speech. After the porter examines the work carefully and approves it, the person is welcomed aboard and given all rights of the ship. The new passenger immediately notices that the air is rich and exhilarating here.

Sometimes a wealthy person tries to buy passage, or a famous person asks for special admission, but he or she is always rejected. The ship has only one door through which passengers can enter, and it is barred to everyone except those who qualify for admission.

Sometimes people on shore laugh at the "unrealistic" people on the ship. "It's a wonder they are able to tie their shoes without a manual," they say. But these critics fail to understand that all of their political ideas, their education, most of their entertainment, their art, their good health, and even much of their food come from those who have learned at the feet of these passengers.

Now, the gangplank is extended, and you enter. A few of you may want to stay all your lives; most will visit and enjoy the company just for a while. All of you will remember the experience throughout your lives.

One student was able to enter the ship because he decoded the meaning expressed by a dollar bill. Another was able to explain the power of Norman Rockwell's paintings of the Four Freedoms. Another student was admitted because she had mastered an E. E. Cummings poem. Still another had unique insight into the meaning communicated by the way a black woman's hair is styled. Perhaps a few of you have dropped in before.

This ship really exists. It is called *Scholarship*. In your work on social intervention, you have been earning the credentials to visit it. But you must demonstrate that you can think like a scholar—that is the only way to get aboard.

First, have the attitude of the learner. Question everything, especially what all people know, even what *you* know. But that is not enough. You must also not be content with questions; you must *want* to know.

Second, pay your dues. Master what those who entered the ship before you have learned. All geniuses onboard built on what came before. Show respect to your predecessors, even if you have discovered they were wrong.

Third, acknowledge your debt. Give credit to those from whom you have learned and borrowed. Failure to do this means expulsion from the ship. A scholar who plagiarizes is instantly cast overboard, and his or her career is finished. No school will hire a thief as a teacher, and no journal will publish anything written by a plagiarist, even if the plagiarism happened only once.

Fourth, learn a method of inquiry, such as the RSI model. The method of inquiry will serve as a lens through which you can understand and interpret the world.

Fifth, by using your method, discover something fresh and take a position on it. Argue for your position.

Sixth, communicate your position clearly. This requires learning the customs of your discipline, such as the appropriate writing style, and working at the writing process.

In this way, you earn the right to take passage with the rest of us. Welcome aboard!

SECTION II

RSI Criticism Essays

RSI Essays Introduction

The second section of this book contains four examples of critical essays that use the Rhetoric of Social Intervention (RSI) model to interpret a social intervention. These essays demonstrate the variety of social interventions that can be analyzed through the lens of the RSI model. In addition, they illustrate the different ways critics apply the model to make sense of symbolizing activity. Finally, they show how critics might choose to organize their essays in a manner similar to the format described in Chapter 5 or might develop alternative organizational patterns to present their findings.

In Essay 1, graduate student Shannon DeBord tracks communication patterns associated with how the U.S. social system has named *Down syndrome*. She explores how two young authors, whom she designates as interveners, attempted to shift the naming patterns of parents, doctors, the U.S. public, and others with Down syndrome. She names their book as the intervention and highlights the rhetorical maneuvers within the book. She organizes her essay in the preintervention, intervention, and postintervention format.

In Essay 2, graduate student Seth Phillips and professor Mark A. Gring name a specific speech as an intervention and its speaker, Margaret Thatcher, as the intervener. They study her attempt to encourage a change in the communication patterns of a social system consisting of her political party, the opposition, and the British public. The essay provides detailed examples of rhetorical maneuvers often used by public speakers to promote attention interventions. In addition, it shows the importance of background and context for understanding interventional patterns.

In Essay 3, undergraduate student Omolara Oyelakin focuses on an intervention that is described within the pages of a book. Rather than viewing the book itself as an intervention, she attends to the process of a power intervention revealed in the book's story. She explores the actions of the Mirabel sisters, whom she names as interveners, as they challenge social hierarchy to shift relationships between the government and its citizens. Her analysis highlights the intrapersonal shifts that persons might experience to prompt them to begin acting as interveners and the social system responses to interveners' efforts. In addition, her analysis contemplates the side effects of interveners' choices.

In Essay 4, professor Lee Snyder examines the symbolizing activity of the Posse Comitatus, a group that he names as acting as intervener in the attempt to shift social hierarchy in the United States. His essay details the rhetorical maneuvers related to a power intervention. It also shows how a critic might draw on a variety of symbolizing activity to understand the communication patterns of an intervention. In addition, the essay provides an example of a social intervention that has yet to result in any overall shift in the larger social system.

Each essay concludes with a Reflections section that provides insight into the author's selection of the intervention and thoughts about the RSI model. The Reflections section includes questions to prompt your critical evaluation of the essays. Critiquing the strengths and weaknesses of the essays' claims, supporting evidence, and organization can enhance your growth as a scholar, critic, and intervener.

From Count Them Out to
Count Us In

Renaming the Expectancies of Down Syndrome

Shannon DeBord

In the early 1970s, two families joyously anticipated their babies' births. But after the boys were born, doctors told them that they should institutionalize them (Kingsley & Levitz, 1994). Both boys had Down syndrome. The doctors' advice reflected the social interpretation that people with Down syndrome had little possibility for a good life and little ability to contribute to society. However, the parents and doctors symbolically categorized the experience differently, and the parents took their sons home. About twenty years later, the two boys, Jason Kingsley and Mitchell Levitz, published the book *Count Us In: Growing Up with Down Syndrome*.

The year their book was published, 1994, I gave birth to a son with Down syndrome. Like Kingsley's and Levitz's mothers, I was asked whether I planned to take my child home. Like them, I refused to believe that my child's disability would limit him, and I began to search for information to help me understand his possibilities. I ran across *Count Us In* and discovered an alternative interpretation of experience—one that, for me, made better sense of experience than the medical community's interpretation of Down syndrome and one that chose an alternative future for my son.

This essay analyzes how the two young authors of *Count Us In* promoted a revised interpretation of experience that encouraged me to see my son in new ways. By examining their effort to bring about social change, I can understand the process of my own change. I can gain insight into the nature of and side effects of my own symbolic reality. I use the Rhetoric of Social Intervention (RSI) model (Brown, 1978) to showcase the communication patterns involved in promoting and impeding interpretive shifts.

The essay first discusses the prevailing social template for making sense of Down syndrome prior to interventions such as Kingsley's and Levitz's (1994). I review the expectancies associated with the Down syndrome naming pattern at the time when they and my son were born. Next, I analyze Kingsley's and Levitz's attempted intervention through the lens of the RSI model, specifically focusing on attention-switching (Brown, 1982). I examine the revised interpretation of *Down syndrome* the young men propose, the audiences to which they appeal, and the strategy, tactics, and rhetorical maneuvers they used to promote an attention shift. Finally, I consider the outcome and side effects of their intervention and my own personal attention switch.

❖ TEMPLATE ONE: NONCONTRIBUTING MEMBERS OF SOCIETY

Because my analysis focuses on attention switching, I begin by examining the template I encountered when my son was born. I consider how the U.S. social system symbolically constituted the name *Down syndrome* and the attributes it traditionally associated with that name. The template creates the expectancy that children with Down syndrome will be *incapable of contributing to society and having potential*.

The Name *Down Syndrome*

The term *Down syndrome* comes from the name of the British physician—J. Langdon H. Down—who, in 1866, created the symbolic category *Down syndrome* by describing its physical characteristics (Leshin, 2003). Down was a superintendent of a mental asylum for children (Leshin). Children with Down syndrome had been placed in the asylum because, at the time, society named them as being *the same as* other mentally challenged children because of their apparent inability to learn or, ultimately, to live independently (Ward, 2002).

Down noticed physical differences that seemed common among some children at the asylum (Leshin, 2003). He eventually categorized children with these types of visually apparent characteristics as being *different from* those with other types of mental challenges (Ward, 2002). In addition, he identified these physical features as being *the same as* characteristics he associated with people from Mongolia (Leshin). Thus, he symbolically categorized the children who exhibited these features *Mongoloids* (Leshin).

Down's initial description of children with Down syndrome as *Mongoloid* promoted attributes that would be associated with the symbolic category *Down syndrome* for the next few generations (Leshin, 2003). Down viewed such children as reflecting a degeneration of ethnic features. As Leshin explains, in the late 1800s, Westerners assumed that the Mongoloid race was intellectually inferior to the Caucasian race. Thus, children who exhibited Mongoloid features were assumed subordinate to Caucasians. In the 1970s, the U.S. medical community would officially rename the chromosome disorder as *Down syndrome*, but the old expectancies of inferiority remained.

Name-Generated Expectancies

In naming his observations, Down created a template for making sense of the children who appeared different. The attributes he used to constitute *Down syndrome* created the expectancy that individuals so categorized would be incapable of thinking abstractly, learning, developing relationships, living independently, initiating actions, and making decisions. Although by the 1970s scientists had found the cause of Down syndrome—a chromosome disorder—and were beginning to revise the attributes they associated with the name to include the capability to learn, the general public tended to maintain the old naming pattern. The doctors who asked in 1994 whether I would take my son home enacted the expectancies of the template that had been promoted since the days of Langdon Down's initial naming of the experience.

In the introduction to *Count Us In*, Mitchell Levitz's mother, Barbara, describes her doctor's prognosis, which reflected this template: "[T]he doctor told us that our son's mental retardation would be a burden to us and recommended that the baby be institutionalized"

(Kingsley & Levitz, 1994, p. 2). In 1974, when Jason Kingsley was born, his mother, Emily, remembered how her doctor named the event:

> Your child will be mentally retarded. He'll never sit or stand, walk or talk. He'll never be able to distinguish you from other adults. He'll never read or write or have a single meaningful thought or idea. The common practice for these children is to place them in an institution immediately. (Kingsley & Levitz, 1994, p. 3)

She adds that the doctor recommended that she tell everyone that her child had died in childbirth (Kingsley & Levitz). Such advice was not uncommon in the 1970s and earlier, given how Down syndrome had been symbolically constructed.

Side Effects of Naming

By naming these children as *different from* so-called *normal* children and by associating them with a race presumed to be subordinate in the social hierarchy, the interpretation that these children should be institutionalized made sense. In this template, both the families and the children would be better off by institutionalizing the children. However, Riccitiello and Adler (1997) point out an anomaly in this interpretation—that "unnumbered thousands of children perished in neglect" (p. 46) in institutions where life expectancy was only about nine years.

Parents typically followed the doctors' advice to institutionalize their children because, in U.S. social hierarchy, doctors are power holders. Parents expected doctors to know what is best for their families and for their children. Parents based their decision to institutionalize their children on the expertise they attributed to the doctors and on information doctors gave them. As a side effect of this naming of experience, society focused more on the need for institutions in which to place the children. It gave less attention to needs such as integrating a baby with Down syndrome into the home environment or educating the child. In addition, neither parents nor doctors interpreted a need to develop a relationship with a child who had Down syndrome.

However, in the 1970s, societal interpretations of Down syndrome began to change (Riccitiello & Adler, 1997). Parents began challenging the power code that said, "Do what the doctor says." They started bringing their children home against their doctors' advice. The Kingsleys and the Levitzes were part of this social attention shift, which would later encourage their sons' attempted intervention. The publication of *Count Us In* promoted an alternative template for making sense of *Down syndrome* and revised expectancies for the future of children with Down syndrome. It would shift how I viewed the experience of my son.

❖   TEMPLATE TWO: CONTRIBUTING
      MEMBERS OF SOCIETY

Since the 1970s, public attention increasingly has been directed to an alternative template for making sense of Down syndrome and other disabilities (Riccitiello & Adler, 1997). This template proposes that, despite disabilities, individuals can *be contributing members of society and have potential*. The Rehabilitation Act of 1973 and the Individuals with Disabilities Education Act in 1975, which granted children with disabilities access to education, are evidence of this emerging shift to the alternative template, at least for the legal community. However, the naming patterns I encountered at my son's birth suggest that the traditional *noncontributing member* template was still prevailing. It is a template that I might have used to organize my experience with my son had I not encountered the book *Count Us In*.

The Book

   Kingsley and Levitz (1994) titled the book *Count Us In: Growing Up with Down Syndrome* as a rhetorical maneuver to encourage an attention shift in the attributes constituting the name *Down syndrome*. Levitz said the name *Count Us In* focuses on what is important: "People consider you an individual with rights. People respect you for who you are. Not just your disability. The person who you are makes it. That's what counts" (p. 14). To him, the book's name reflects its purpose to "make the future better for people with disabilities" (p. 14).
   In the book's introduction, the young men's mothers discuss anomalies in the expectancies associated with *Down syndrome* that had become apparent to them. Examples of anomalies include the young men's abilities to handle social and educational challenges previously believed incapable of people with Down syndrome. Also, the two can conceptualize and reflect on their disability, violating naming-pattern expectancies of diminished mental capacities. Other anomalies the mothers highlight are the young men's desire to advocate for themselves and their ability to handle public speaking engagements. Again, such actions are nonfitting with the expectancies of the traditional

template for *Down syndrome*. Attention to these anomalies prompted the mothers to encourage Kingsley and Levitz to write the book, which consists of transcripts of the young men's conversations and essays they have written.

The Audiences

Kingsley and Levitz direct their attempted attention intervention toward several audiences of the book. They gear their message to parents of children with Down syndrome and doctors who interact with the parents and children. They also intend to reach individuals with Down syndrome and society in general. Insight into these audiences appears in an *Exceptional Parent* magazine interview and in the book (Kingsley & Levitz, 1994; Role models: Jason Kingsley and Mitchell Levitz, 1994).

The authors target parents as a primary audience of the intervention. The authors attempt to shift the expectancies that parents associated with Down syndrome—*away* from dependence and lack of hope and *to* independence and success. In the *Exceptional Parent* interview, Levitz explains, "I would like to tell parents that they should give us a chance to be ourselves and to make decisions on our own. It is understandable that parents can be overprotective" (Role models, 1994, p. 18). Kingsley concurs, saying, "I also would like parents to learn to let go of their children, give us the same opportunities parents had as children" (p. 18). Kingsley adds that he expects to be treated *the same as* his parents were when they were growing up and to be given the same chance to succeed in life. He attempts to rename the social hierarchy expectancies associated with Down syndrome from *inequality* to *equality*.

By expressing their desires, the young men are, at the same time, violating expectancies associated with Down syndrome by what they choose to say to parents. Their words challenge the power code in which parents treat children with Down syndrome as incapable of independence. The young men's words and actions as persons with Down syndrome present anomalies in the current interpretation of the power code.

The book *Count Us In* also indicates that Kingsley and Levitz (1994) view doctors as an audience. Kingsley discusses what he would say if he could speak to the obstetrician who recommended his institutionalization. He would tell the obstetrician how smart he is and that "people with disabilities *can learn!*" (p. 27; emphasis in original). The book demonstrates how the young men's actions create anomalies in the doctors' interpretation of experience. Doctors had assumed that children with Down syndrome should be institutionalized. Kingsley's and Levitz's actions suggest otherwise.

The authors also target individuals with Down syndrome in this intervention. Kingsley emphasizes that this audience should "be proud . . . and be happy. . . . Be motivated. You can realize now: You can do everything yourself from now on" (Kingsley & Levitz, 1994, p. 44). The book and the young men's apparent success feature anomalies in how other individuals with Down syndrome might interpret their experience—that they could not accomplish and contribute to life. The book showcases how two young men with this chromosome disorder have become active participants in and contributors to society.

Finally, the authors target the public as an audience for their intervention. In the book tour interview, Levitz said, "My message is that people with disabilities want to be accepted. They want to have opportunities for life. I just want to erase all the negative attitudes in society" (Role models, 1994, p. 20). Levitz encourages those without Down syndrome to rename people with Down syndrome from *noncontributing* members of society to *contributing* members of society by giving them opportunities. Again, the young men's ability to do interviews and write a book features anomalies in the expectancy that people with Down syndrome are unable to contribute to society.

❖ THE ATTENTION SWITCH

In this intervention, two templates exist for making sense of the experience of people with Down syndrome. One is that people with Down syndrome are *incapable of contributing to society and having potential*. The other is that they are *capable of contributing to society and having potential*. Both templates can make coherent the experience of people with Down syndrome. In their intervention, Kingsley and Levitz attempt to *move* their audiences from interpreting experience with the first template to interpreting it with the second template.

Attention switches are promoted and impeded through the rhetorical strategies of anomaly-featuring and anomaly-masking communication (Brown, 1982). In *Count Us In*, Kingsley and Levitz primarily enact the attention-switching strategy of anomaly-featuring communication to highlight anomalies in the *noncontributing* template. The experience of people with Down syndrome does not change—they still have Down syndrome. But the interveners attempt to shift the meaning that society attributes to Down syndrome and the expectancies it has of people with Down syndrome.

Attention switches entail tactical shifts in social ways of knowing, being, and valuing (Brown, 1982). Kingsley and Levitz primarily promote a shift in *knowing* by giving the public first-hand information about the experience of people with Down syndrome. The book is filled with new information that potentially alters what the public knows about Down syndrome. At the same time, though, the authors also promote a shift in *being*—to naming people with Down syndrome as being *the same as* other contributing members of society. Finally, they promote a shift in *valuing*—to appreciating the contributions that people with Down syndrome can make to society.

Rhetorical Maneuvers and Expectancy Violations

Attention-shift strategy and tactics are actualized with rhetorical maneuvers (Brown, 1982). In this analysis, the primary rhetorical maneuver is the book. Within the pages of the book are numerous examples of events and actions that feature anomalies in the *noncontributing* template. In addition, the book itself is an anomaly.

The book addresses the expectancy that people with Down syndrome are unable to choose, initiate, or participate in everyday activities. It features attention to anomalies in this expectancy by giving numerous examples of how the two young men initiate and participate in activities. A photo in the book shows Kingsley voting, and another shows him painting a landscape; both activities require skill and initiation. Kingsley calls painting his hobby and indicates he has painted on his own initiative on numerous occasions (Kingsley & Levitz, 1994). Levitz talks about playing on a soccer team, and a photo visually reinforces that experience.

The book also deals with the expectancy that people with Down syndrome are unable to live *normal* lives. It highlights anomalies in this expectancy by discussing *normal* activities in which Kingsley and Levitz engage. Kingsley writes about the activities that he has done or plans to do, all of which violate expectancies associated with the *noncontributing* template. He has traveled all over the world with his parents and other people with disabilities, he reads and writes, he intends to get married and live in his own apartment, and he wants to go to college. Kingsley also discusses his appearance on the NBC television program *Dateline*, which showed video of him playing baseball and video games, and participating in many other social activities expected of *normal* children.

In addition, the book uses the rhetorical maneuver of expert testimony to support the credibility of the interpretation of experience it is promoting. Joan Ganz Cooney, originator of *Sesame Street* and cofounder of the Children's Television Workshop, wrote the book's foreword. She praises Kingsley's and Levitz's heroic efforts to change the world by writing the book: "Jason Kingsley and Mitchell Levitz make abundantly clear, to those who still may not know, what people with disabilities want. They want exactly what the rest of us want" (Kingsley & Levitz, 1994, pp. xiii–xiv).

The book also incorporates examples of analogies that the young men use. For example, Kingsley compares himself and Levitz to the story of the tortoise and the hare. He said that he is the tortoise, going slowly, step by step—and that Levitz is the hare, going too fast and wanting to skip college (Kingsley & Levitz, 1994). The use of analogies violates the expectancy that people with Down syndrome are incapable of complex and abstract thinking.

Overall, the book itself is a form of anomaly-featuring communication. Kingsley and Levitz, by writing the book together, demonstrate they can communicate with each other and their audiences. The young men's book-writing capabilities violate the expectancy that people with Down syndrome are incapable of communicating freely, much less publishing a book. The book also reflects Kingsley's and Levitz's awareness of their own disability, something that doctors and teachers thought people with Down syndrome could not do. By publishing a book, the two young men with Down syndrome encourage society to pay attention to their intelligence and accomplishments.

Trend Reversal

Kingsley and Levitz attempt to break out of the vicious circle of naming people with Down syndrome as *noncontributing members of society*. This vicious circle naming pattern contributes to increasing the low self-esteem and lack of expectations experienced by people with Down syndrome. Their actions, then, reinforce the parents', doctors', and public's interpretation that they are incapable of contributing to society, creating a vicious circle.

At the time that Kingsley and Levitz wrote the book, Mitnick (1997) notes that a social interpretative shift was beginning. Interventions to reverse the deviance-amplifying trend began freeing people with Down syndrome, their parents, doctors, and the public to begin expecting more of people with disabilities. The shift in naming patterns helped to create the expectancy that people with Down syndrome *could* make meaningful contributions to society.

Other Interveners

The RSI model assumes that, at the same time a person is intervening to promote change, other interveners will attempt to impede the change (Brown, 1982). In terms of the *Count Us In* intervention, few negative responses to the book appear in the popular media. A consumer reviewer on Amazon.com said she had nothing in common with the young men with Down syndrome and could not relate to their male points of view (Janicen, 2006). The reviewer recommended that women read a more "uplifting" book (Janicen).

A potential intervener attempting to forestall a shift in how society names individuals with Down syndrome could highlight attention to anomalies in Kingsley's and Levitz's proposed interpretation of experience. For example, how many people with Down syndrome share the same abilities that Kingsley and Levitz demonstrate? Perhaps Kingsley and Levitz were atypical because they met legislators, traveled a lot, and most importantly, initiated this intervention. Maybe their accomplishments were due to parental attention and assistance.

Alternatively, an intervener supporting the proposed shift could account for these anomalies by pointing out that, prior to the book's publication, people with Down syndrome might have been unaware of their capabilities. Low self-esteem and lack of social expectation encouraged by society's naming pattern might have led them to focus on their limitations, rather than on their ability to overcome boundaries. In essence, the way in which society named people with disabilities was itself a disability.

❖ INTERVENTION OUTCOMES

The RSI model leads the critic to reflect on the outcomes and side effects of an attention intervention and consider the long-term ripple effects of the intervention. Book reviews and social discourse provide clues about how others responded to the young men's intervention.

Reviewers' Responses

Book reviewers serve the role of *ratifying* alternative interpretations of experience as well as highlighting anomalies in those interpretations to maintain the old naming pattern. For example, *Kirkus Reviews* named *Count Us In* as a "worthwhile inspiration and insight for Down syndrome children, as well as for their families, teachers, friends, and advocates" (Book Review, 1993). The words *inspiration* and *insight* suggest that the reviewer interprets the template offered in the book as having approach value.

Another reviewer, Craig (1994), writes that the book will "open eyes" (p. 162). Again, this naming implies promotion of the interpretation of experience advocated by Kingsley and Levitz. In *Down Syndrome Quarterly*, Mitnick (1997) describes *Count Us In* as contributing to increasing social understanding of people with Down syndrome. The reviewer notes that the book won numerous awards from the Down syndrome and mainstream communities. Winning awards outside the Down syndrome community suggests wider social system acceptance of the book's interpretation of experience. A *Booklist* reviewer writes, "Hearing about Down syndrome directly from these young men has a good deal more impact than reading any guide from a professional or even a parent" (Donavin, 1993, p. 586). The word *impact* implies that Kingsley's and Levitz's intervention was making a difference.

Social Discourse Shifts

Another way to consider interventional outcomes is to examine changes in social discourse. For example, some people in the Down syndrome community have adopted an alternative name for the syndrome, which Kingsley and Levitz proposed in the book. Levitz (Kingsley & Levitz, 1994) says, "We should call each other Up syndrome" (p. 44). Their renaming is an attempt to emphasize the positive rather than the negative qualities of the syndrome.

Several organizations today use the *Up* term instead of *Down* syndrome, following Kingsley's and Levitz's lead of renaming the name for the symbolic category *Down syndrome* (Forts, 2002; Upside!, n.d; What is the UP! Club, 2006). Use of the term *Up syndrome* seems to be limited to the Down syndrome community, however. The medical and general publics appear not to have adopted the term. *Down syndrome* has remained the medically recognized name because the disorder is named after the person who first constituted its attributes—Langdon Down.

Subsystem Side Effects

Brown's (1982) notion of "circles of influence" suggests that critics consider possible side effects of an intervention (p. 21). In this case, attention switches have side effects for social interpretations of need and power (Brown). For example, as the authors of *Count Us In* apply the revised template of people with Down syndrome as *contributing members of society*, they begin opening communication channels with new people and groups in the social system to meet newly attributed needs. The authors start building cooperative interdependencies with needs-meeting individuals and groups.

The book attributes to individuals with Down syndrome the need for more familial attention and education. It advocates the need for parents to see their children with Down syndrome as contributing members of the family and to treat them as capable individuals. It also advocates the need for educational programs adapted to the children's learning abilities. At the same time that the book prompts a need shift, it also encourages a power shift. Children with Down syndrome become more interdependent with their families and with school systems to meet their advocated needs.

Furthermore, the book promotes a power shift by providing parents with information to challenge doctors and school administrators who might still maintain the previous interpretation of Down syndrome. In addition, interdependencies as a whole between people with Down syndrome and U.S. society shift. As the public begins renaming people with Down syndrome *contributing members of society who have potential*, the need to include and develop cooperative relationships between those with and those without Down syndrome increases in importance.

Long-Term Shifts

When the book was reissued in 2007, Kingsley and Levitz added an afterword that described what they had been doing since 1994. Kingsley, nineteen at the time the book was originally published, was thirty-two years old. He had lived on his own in a co-op and later with roommates in a group home. Kingsley had continued to speak publicly about stereotypes of people with disabilities. At the time the book was republished, Kingsley was working at a Disney store and was still hoping to marry one day (Kingsley & Levitz, 2007).

Levitz, then age twenty-two and now thirty-five, had worked as a disability specialist for national organizations and used self-advocacy to promote people with Down syndrome as contributing to society. He also continued to speak and give interviews. He notes, "Our book is recommended reading for schools, colleges, and universities. It encourages students with disabilities to pursue their futures and desires" (Kingsley & Levitz, 2007, p. 193). This suggests that the book's intervention has had lasting effects.

In their daily lives, Kingsley and Levitz accomplished many things, including lobbying for disability legislation, participating in documentaries, acting in television shows, promoting other actors with Down syndrome, and working in jobs to encourage living independently (Mitnick, 1997). Their actions tied into a larger ongoing social intervention—the attention shift from naming people with disabilities *incapable of contributing to society and of having potential* to naming them *capable of contributing to society and of having potential*. The authors' continued promotion of this interpretation of experience in their lives outside the book demonstrates their dedication to the intervention.

These days, the experience for children with Down syndrome is different from when Kingsley and Levitz were born. Today, children with Down syndrome expect to receive a public education. From birth on, they can participate in early intervention programs and begin public school at age three (Smith & Luckasson, 1995). Inclusion into regular education is common, although some programs still offer self-contained special education classrooms.

New Anomalies

Yet people with Down syndrome still face barriers to living fully as people who are capable of contributing to society, especially after their formal education ends. In a recent newspaper article, Mixon (2007) describes life after high school for one young woman with Down syndrome. The young woman faces being on a waiting list up to ten years to receive money and services she needs to integrate into society after high school. This problem could indicate that although society now interprets people with disabilities as needing education to become contributing members of society, it does not fully recognize the needs of people with disabilities after education. Interventions such as *Count Us In* open society's eyes to the need for equal educational opportunities regardless of disability, but do not address life after education.

❖ CONCLUSION

In this essay, I used the RSI model to highlight the communication patterns involved in constituting and promoting templates about the experience of Down syndrome. The model also provided a way to think about the side effects of that symbolizing activity. The model could be used to understand how society continues to make sense of what it means and what is required to be a *contributing member of society*. Through its lens, communication patterns about what is needed to help people with Down syndrome and other disabilities to enact more perfectly their place in the social hierarchy as *contributing members* could be foregrounded and gaps in those patterns identified. This might result in another revision of social interpretation related to Down syndrome.

As for myself, examining this intervention from two perspectives has enriched both my life and my son's life. The first perspective is as a parent of a child with Down syndrome, and the second is as a communication researcher. As a parent, reading the book *Count Us In* enlightened me to the possibilities of children with Down syndrome. I learned that I should not put limits on my expectations of my son. This has proved fruitful, because he exhibits many of Kingsley's and Levitz's characteristics. For example, he chooses his own activities, contributes to his own education and to our family, and continues to learn academic subjects.

Preintervention, as a parent just after his birth and before I read the book, I thought my son Jared might have trouble walking or talking. I was completely unschooled on Down syndrome. After reading the book, I was able to consider all sorts of new possibilities. The book taught me not to impose my own preconceived limitations, but instead to empower and enable my son. Jared contributes to society in ways that others might not perceive as contributing. By participating in public education and on sports teams, he changes social interpretations of people with disabilities, and in effect, becomes a self-advocate.

In addition, he facilitates communication between people who would not necessarily communicate. For instance, he does not observe all the unstated rules of communication and he does indeed talk to strangers when I am there. On many occasions, this bold communication on his part has prompted conversations and advocacy on my part for his abilities. Thus, the intervention has fueled my need for advocating Jared's needs.

As a communication researcher, after experiencing *Count Us In*, I realize the power that interventions can have. The RSI model enables me to explain how change occurs and how people attempt to intervene to bring about change for the better. The RSI model enables understanding of the medical community, the education community, and others' preintervention worldview and the side effects of those choices. It helps showcase alternatives for society as posited in the postintervention worldview. The power of written communication, such as *Count Us In*, appears limitless in terms of choosing futures.

The intervention I examined is but one example of how a community's interpretation of experience can change from *noncontributing* to *contributing members of society*, simply by interveners advocating a renaming of expectancies—from *less* to *more*.

❖ REFERENCES

Book review: *Count us in: Growing up with Down syndrome*. (1993, November 1). *Kirkus Reviews*. Retrieved June 24, 2007, from LexisNexis database.

Brown, W. R. (1978). Ideology as communication process. *Quarterly Journal of Speech, 64*(2), 123–140.

Brown, W. R. (1982). Attention and the rhetoric of social intervention. *Quarterly Journal of Speech, 68*(1), 17–27.

Craig, J. (1994, June). Book review: Adult books for young adults. *School Library Journal*, p. 162. Retrieved June 24, 2007, from Academic Search Premier.

Donavin, D. P. (1993, November 15). Social sciences—*Count us in: Growing up with Down syndrome* by Jason Kingsley and Mitchell Levitz. *Booklist*, p. 586.

Forts, A. (2002). Annie's favorite comments. *The Annie Forts Up Syndrome Fund, Inc.* Retrieved June 26, 2007, from http://www.anniefortsupfund.org/inspiring_comments.html.

Janicen (no last name listed). (2006, July 22). As a mom, I couldn't relate. Amazon.com. Retrieved June 26, 2007, from http://www.amazon.com.

Kingsley, J., & Levitz, M. (1994). *Count us in: Growing up with Down syndrome*. New York: Harcourt & Brace.

Kingsley, J., & Levitz, M. (2007). *Count us in: Growing up with Down syndrome*. New York: Harcourt & Brace.

Leshin, L. (2003). Trisomy 21: The story of Down syndrome. *Down Syndrome: Health Issues*. Retrieved April 16, 2007, from http://www.ds-health.com/trisomy.htm.

Mitnick, B. M. (1997). High expectations of myself. *Down Syndrome Quarterly*. 2(3), 3–5.

Mixon, M. (2007, June 2). Life after high school: Special education students try to transition to what's next. *Austin American–Statesman*. Retrieved July 20, 2007, from http://www.statesman.com/search/content/news/stories/local/06/02/2transition.html.

Riccitiello, R., & Adler, J. (1997, Spring–Summer). Your baby has a problem. *Newsweek*, pp. 46–49. Retrieved July 2, 2007, from Academic Search Premier database.

Role models: Jason Kingsley and Mitchell Levitz. (1994, April). *Exceptional Parent*, pp. 17–20. Retrieved June 26, 2007, from Proquest Research database.

Smith, D. D., & Luckasson, R. (1995). *Introduction to special education: Teaching in an age of challenge*. Boston: Allyn & Bacon.

Upside! (n.d.). *UPSIDE! Down syndrome society*. Retrieved June 26, 2007, from www.telebyte.com/upside/.

Ward, C. (2002). John Langdon Down and Down's syndrome (1828–96). *Learning about intellectual disabilities and health.* Retrieved June 4, 2007, from http://www.intellectualdisability.info/values/history_DS.htm.

What is the UP! club. (2006). *Down Syndrome NSW.* Retrieved June 26, 2007, from http://www.dsansw.org.au/index.php?pg=60.

Reflections

Shannon DeBord is a doctoral candidate at Texas A&M University.

I have a son, Jared, who has Down syndrome. At his birth, doctors asked if I planned to take him home. I thought that was a strange and offensive question. Of course I would take my child home, so I set out to learn all I could about Down syndrome. When I encountered *Count Us In*, the book shifted my expectations about him from *limited* to *unlimited*. Later I analyzed the book as an intervention for a master's seminar on the RSI model.

Kingsley and Levitz's intervention enabled me to consider new possibilities for Jared outside of the boundaries of how society had been naming children with Down syndrome. Today, he reads, does math, has a wonderful sense of humor, and gets along with people of all backgrounds and cultures. He continues to excel in ways unimagined in the template of the doctors who attended his birth.

1. DeBord analyzed *Count Us In* as the primary symbolizing activity. What might be the strengths and limitations of focusing on one book versus a variety of symbolizing activity to make sense of a social intervention?

2. How might DeBord's own experience with Down syndrome influence the choices she makes as an RSI critic, such as materials to analyze and rhetorical patterns to which she attends?

3. DeBord suggests that society was *disabling* those with Down syndrome by its choice of criterial attributes to symbolically constitute *Down syndrome*. How did using the RSI model enable her to reach this conclusion? How might this finding be relevant to other naming situations? What does it teach us about human symbolizing?

4. In what ways does or does not DeBord's essay fulfill critical essay expectancies?

ESSAY 2

"The Lady's Not for Turning"

Margaret Thatcher's Attention Intervention

by Seth Phillips and Mark A. Gring

> *War is an ugly thing, but not the ugliest of things. The decayed and degraded state of moral and patriotic feeling which thinks that nothing is worth war is much worse. The person who has nothing for which he is willing to fight, nothing which is more important than his own personal safety, is a miserable creature, and has no chance of being free unless made or kept so by the exertions of better men than himself.*
>
> —John Stuart Mills (Lewis, 2004)

Such was the perceived plight of the British people in the years just before the election of Margaret Thatcher. It was the perceived plight Thatcher addressed when she assumed the role of prime minister on May 4, 1979. The economic conditions and ideological winds at the time were against this woman who would eventually become known as the

"Iron Lady," and who presaged and encouraged the Ronald Reagan economic and philosophical revolution in the United States.

In April 1979, Market & Opinion Research International Ltd (MORI) opinion polls showed that, among the British citizenry, only 26 percent of the population symbolically categorized the newly elected prime minister as *a capable leader* (Scammell, 1996). By May 1983, however, the MORI polls indicated that 62 percent of the citizenry interpreted Thatcher to be *a capable leader* (Scammell). While many political and military events transpired in the intervening years—failed trade union strikes, the Soviet Union's invasion of Afghanistan, the Iran-Iraq War, the Falklands War (Scammell)—by many accounts, Thatcher's (1980) dogged determination to "resist the blandishments of the faint hearts," "ignore the howls and threats of the extremists," and "stand together and do our duty" (p. 11) influenced the ideological landscape of Britain; won Thatcher the confidence of the British people; and brought a sweeping parliamentary victory for her party in 1983. The ideological road between these two markers was not easy. It involved a significant attention switch, which is the context for this analysis.

Seventeen months after her 1979 election, Thatcher faced what might be considered her darkest hour: the British public's perceived reality was not meeting their expectancies. The programs and policies the Tories had championed during the 1979 election were not having the rapid, pronounced results most of the British people expected (Films for the Humanities and Sciences, 1999). Unemployment and inflation had continued to increase, and the Thatcher government had raised tax rates much as the previous administration had done in 1972. Thatcher, perhaps anticipating a shift in political loyalties, warned in a 1979 address that "it will take time," specifically, "time to shake off the self-doubt induced by decades of *dependence on the state as master, not as servant*. It will take time and it will not be easy" (p. 3; emphasis added). Despite her call for patience, political pressure for change had set in, from the media and from her fellow Tories (Thatcher, 1980).

Thatcher's speech before the Conservative (i.e., Tory) Party Conference on October 10, 1980, not only needed to recast the vision for the Party, but also required her to address her critics' demands to initiate a U-turn in Conservative policies—back to Labour's government-spending policies, epitomized by the 1970–1974 central planning approach under Prime Minister Ted Heath. These critics advocated a need for a return to that approach to overcome the problems preventing Britain from achieving the ideological expectations of becoming a more prosperous and influential country. In response to this call,

Thatcher (1980) issued the lines that became the hallmark of the October address: "To those waiting with bated breath for that favourite media catchphrase, the U-turn, I have only one thing to say: You turn if you want to. The lady's not for turning!" (p. 8).

This essay examines Thatcher's October 10, 1980, speech as an example of how she sought to intervene in the British people's interpretation of Britain's economic situation at the time. Previously, the British people had viewed the economy as the complete responsibility of a centralized government, and the people as passive recipients of governmental solutions. Thatcher advocated a worldview that renamed the country's economic struggles as a *war* in which the people were active participants. The worldview also reorganized the power relationships between the citizens and the government by placing the future of this war in the hands of the people rather than the government. In addition, the worldview redefined the needs of the British people—from economic dependence on the government to economic self-determination. In all, Thatcher proposed an alternative worldview in which the citizens, rather than a centralized government, would create a more economically successful, prosperous, and influential Britain.

To highlight the rhetorical process of her social intervention, this paper analyzes Thatcher's October 10 speech through the lens of Brown's (1978) Rhetoric of Social Intervention (RSI) model. The model assumes that ideology arises out of and at the same time influences how we symbolically categorize our needs, relationships, and worldview—or what Brown calls need, power, and attention. These three concepts are considered holistic in that a shift in how we name ideas or relationships in one of the three subsystems results in corresponding shifts in the other two subsystems (Brown). Each subsystem serves as a potential starting point for analyzing the dynamics of a social system. The RSI model leads the rhetorical critic to attend to the rhetorical strategies, tactics, and maneuvers that interveners use to attempt to influence change through the symbolic construction of ideology.

Brown (1982) argues that attention switching is accomplished through the rhetorical strategies of anomaly-masking and anomaly-featuring communication. Anomaly-masking communication occurs when interveners background experiences that do not fit the expectancies of a worldview (often named *problems*) (Brown). Anomaly-featuring communication occurs when interveners highlight the aspects of experience that do not fit worldview expectancies (Brown). By foregrounding the problems, interveners attempt to promote an attention shift to an alternative interpretation of experience that makes sense of the problems.

From this understanding, the proposed shift in knowing, being, or valuing can be identified by the *name* given to the alternative world-view being proposed (Gring, 1998). Brown (1982) identifies these shifts in knowing, being, and valuing as the tactics of attention switching. The strategies and tactics of an attention switch are actualized in rhetorical maneuvers, such as the arguments, metaphors, imagery, and style within a speech such as Thatcher's address.

This essay first looks at the British social system prior to Thatcher's intervention. Then it examines the strategies, tactics, and maneuvers of her intervention to promote an attention shift in how the British public interpreted experience. This shift eventually resulted in the British people redefining economics, increasing the power share of the citizenry through a program of deregulation, and addressing the core human needs denied by years of socialist-style "handouts."

❖   THATCHER'S SOCIAL INTERVENTION

The RSI model leads the critic to consider how the social system symbolically categorized experience prior to the intervention, so this analysis begins with a summary of British experience into which Thatcher intervened.

Britain Before Thatcher

Prior to Thatcher's premiership, the Labour Party and pre-Thatcher Tory Party had symbolically categorized *economic centralization* and *effective government structuring* as the path to achieving market success and prosperity in Britain. This assumption came out of the system of international monetary management, which had been advocated at the Bretton Woods Conference in 1944 to address the need for post–World War II economic recovery. Under this interpretation of experience, the British government played the role of being solely responsible for control of the economy.

By 1979, however, Britain was being symbolically categorized as one of the *poorest performing economic systems* in Europe (Central Office of Information, 1979), clearly violating ideological expectancies associated with achieving success and prosperity. One attribute of experience that led to this categorization was Britain's high unemployment rate. During the 1970s, the unemployment rate had risen to its highest level in forty years (Central Office). Areas in the country hardest hit by unemployment were regions with heavy industry, such as shipbuilding, coal mining, heavy engineering, and metal manufacturing. In July 1978, the general unemployment rate ranged from 5.6 percent to 11.2 percent in areas such as Northern Ireland (Central Office).

Other attributes of experience that led to Britain's categorization as a poorly performing economic system included wages and purchasing power. Parliamentary action, such as The Trade Union and Labour Relations Acts of 1974 and 1976 and The Employment Protection Act of 1975, increased union power and the threat of strikes. These policies enabled unions to pursue higher wages for their members (Central Office, 1979). From 1973 to 1978, such measures resulted in an increase in nontaxed weekly earnings of 167 percent for men and 220 percent for women. However, those increases were undermined by a hyperinflationary rate of retail price increases (at 140 percent), with concurrent increases in both the national insurance and income tax rates (Central Office). Thus, despite huge increases in overall income earnings, by 1979 the pound sterling was valued lower and had less purchasing power, resulting in a take-home pay worth less than it had been five years prior (Central Office). Again, worldview expectancies about Britain as a dominant economic power were being violated.

The socialist policies put forward by the Labour Party in 1974 had created the expectancy of a Britain free of these economic woes, an expectancy that was not being met. Thatcher, who served as Leader of the Opposition from 1975 to 1979, had constantly criticized Labour's planned economics policies by foregrounding anomalies in the worldview it was promoting. In her campaign for prime minister, she offered an alternative view, one that would make sense of the anomalies and put Britain on a new path for achieving prosperity. Her election to prime minister suggested that the British public had chosen a future that ratified her approach.

Seventeen months into Thatcher's first term, though, the opposition, the British public, and even some members of her own Party were highlighting events that questioned the ability of the worldview she was advocating to return Britain to the economic power it once was. Thus, on October 10, 1980, Thatcher stood before the Conservative Party Conference and addressed these audiences through a speech that was designed to promote a renaming of Britain's economic experience, a redefining of the roles of the government and the citizens, and a reinterpretation of the British public's needs.

The Intervention

Thatcher's intervention, as exemplified in the October 10 address, was an attempt to encourage the social system—the opposition, her Party members, and the British public—to rename experience so that the overall ideology of achieving economic success, individual worth, and international influence could be maintained. Thatcher used her position as prime minister to promote an attention shift—from naming Britain as *a victim of uncontrollable circumstances* to renaming it as *a victim of socialist economics*. Thatcher (1995), greatly influenced by her small-business-owning father and the economic polices of Friedrich von Hayek, symbolically categorized property ownership and competitive free trade driven by market forces as the keys to economic growth. She interpreted these actions as necessary to end the economically venomous spirals of stagnation-inflation birthed from the policies of the 1970s. Thatcher argued that enacting private business ownership, market-driven free trade, and reduced government involvement would be the means for the British people to achieve economic prosperity and a better life.

To achieve this end, however, required a shift in how the British people named themselves and their place in world affairs. In the worldview previously promoted by the Labour Party, the British people were encouraged to view themselves as *economically dependent* on the government, which would enact socialist policies, which would create economic success and prosperity. However, in her speech, Thatcher (1980) featured anomalies in that interpretation of experience. She argued that government policies had reduced the ability of citizens to own their own homes, to earn competitive pay based on merit rather than a progressive Robin Hood–style tax system, and to freely run their own businesses. Thatcher interpreted such experiences, which violated ideological expectancies, as leading to a decrease in the *spirit* of the British people.

Thus, in her October 10 address, Thatcher (1980) focused not just on "economic recovery alone, but a new independence of spirit and zest for achievement" (p. 2). She advocated an overall shift *away from* the need for economic dependency *to* the need for economic self-determinism and empowerment. She proposed that such a need shift could be achieved only by willingly undergoing a pronounced period of economic penance for past mistakes—this would include some difficult months of economic readjustment. She named this penance as similar to what Britain endured during and after World War II, a time indelibly characterized by Sir Winston Churchill as Britain's "finest hour."

Strategies, Tactics, and Maneuvers

Thatcher's October 10 speech was a rhetorical maneuver to promote her interpretation of experience and to feature anomalies in the interpretations of her critics. She promoted her interpretation of *government-as-assisting-people-to-provide-for-themselves* rather than *government-as-economic-provider*, by equating inflation to an enemy to be fought through a *war on inflation* or as a *robber* to be apprehended. The British citizens would fight this war themselves rather than return micromanagement of the economy to government (the U-turn advocated by her critics). She also featured anomalies in the interpretation advocated by her opponents by contending that they presented arguments but never *did* anything.

In the speech, Thatcher advocated a redefinition of the attributes of inflation—*from* being a passive concept best left for economic theorists and Parliamentary intervention *to* an enemy to be fought and defeated through individual actions and self-sacrifice. The *war* name was powerful and had approach value; it was only thirty-five years removed from World War II and ever present in the ongoing *Cold War* name used to describe democratic, free market countries' relationships with Communist bloc countries. Thatcher emphasized this when she said, "Inflation destroys nations and societies as surely as invading armies do" (p. 3) and when she argued for a need to have a "conquest of inflation" (p. 4).

This *inflation-as-enemy* name implied that the Conservatives could not passively respond, but must systematically and actively target and eliminate this enemy with the right weapon through clear military-like objectives. This *inflation-as-war* name reminded the British people of the war against the Nazis and made the defeat of inflation a *cooperative* war effort that banded them together. By naming inflation, rather than people or the opposing political party, as *the enemy*, Thatcher implicitly redefined each man, woman, employer, and consumer from a *passive market casualty* to *active foot soldiers* in the economic war. Thatcher's government would lead the charge by providing fiscal restraint and anti-inflation ammunition to those fighting for Britain's economic campaign. Thus, as the role of the people was being redefined, so, too, was the role of the government. Government would now exercise self-restraint in its spending and reduce its involvement in the direct workings of the national economy.

Two metaphorical images framed the form of Thatcher's October 10 address. The overall organizing metaphor related to Thatcher's "U-turn" line (Thatcher, 1980). It shaped Thatcher's remarks and added impetus and urgency, especially on the foreign policy issues. Its positioning was strategic. The *U-turn* segment served as the transition between the domestic and foreign policy issues. It was used to crystal-lize British resolve and determination as the hallmarks of their domes-tic policy and to indicate the carrying over of these traits into the foreign policy realm. Just as the British people would now show indi-vidual resolve and fortitude through economic self-sacrifice and self-control to defeat inflation, so, too, would the government show equal resolve in handling interactions with foreign countries. This was not to be like Neville Chamberlain's negotiations with Adolf Hitler: This was to be more like Churchill standing defiantly against the Germans and uniting the British people.

Thatcher's (1980) use of the war metaphor became more significant in light of the U-turn analysis. In war, there is no turning back. The only option is victory or defeat, which was how she framed the "conquest" and "defeat of inflation" (p. 3). Unlike President Ronald Reagan's future orientation with his emphasis on the great "shining city on a hill," Thatcher argued for a past orientation where there was only the reality of war. However, Thatcher said she viewed challenge as "exhilarating" (p. 1). The only question, both for her and for Britain, was, "Has Britain the courage and resolve to sustain the discipline for long enough to break through to success?" (p. 4). Through measures such as increasing the conventional forces and acquiring the Trident missile system from the United States, Thatcher sought "a defensive policy which potential foes will respect" (p. 9). In her naming, she created expectancies about experience—they must fight until they defeated the enemy.

In light of Thatcher's (1980) use of the war rhetoric, her speech served to build particular expectancies about the problem and its solu-tion. She named the economic problem as *governmental policy that did not include the active participation of its citizens.* The *war* name shifted the focus from citizens as passive recipients of governmental solutions to citizens who are actively involved in solving their own problems through the marketplace. Rather than retreat to old government solu-tion paradigms in the face of economic struggle, she harnessed the boldness of Britain birthed during World War II—to "never give in" and "never surrender," as Churchill so eloquently put it (Churchill, 1940, 1941). The Labour Party's program of centralized economic control was a defensive policy. The Conservative plan was for offensive deregulation. Thatcher was "confident that they [the foreign and domestic problems] too will yield to the firm yet fair approach which has already proved much more effective than the previous govern-ment's five years of procrastination" (p. 10). The significance of this was the continuation or end of freedom: "If we were to fail, freedom could be imperiled" (p. 11).

Besides invoking the *inflation-as-enemy* naming, Thatcher (1980) also equated inflation with a robber. She described it as "the unseen robber of those who have saved" (p. 3). By labeling this economic phenomenon an *enemy to be fought* and *a robber to be apprehended*, she took a very obscure issue of macroeconomics, reified it into a concrete, living entity capable of being destroyed, and asked the public to get involved. This anomaly-featuring communication shifted the citizens' attention *away from* the passive expectancy of government intervention through socialist policies, *to* the expectancy of government as the catalyst for active change by means of individuals who employed a free-market approach and who would willingly shoulder any necessary hardship to achieve victory.

Response to Her Critics

Thatcher's critics, however, tried to feature anomalies in her proposed worldview to impede an attention switch. They symbolically categorized the new administration's programs as *overly revolutionary*. Thatcher (1980) addressed this criticism in her speech by reasoning that her policies should be named as *mainstream*, not revolutionary. To do this, Thatcher used anomaly-masking communication to portray her program as being *the same as* beneficial economic initiatives that were valued by European nations that could also be adopted by Britain. "But some people talk as if control of the money supply was a revolutionary policy. Yet it was an essential condition for the recovery of much of continental Europe" (p. 4). What she proposed was not new, she reasoned, but was simply the continuance of programs begun after World War II. She also supported her reasoning by referring to other experts who would agree with her name for experience. "[M]y fellow Heads of Government find our policies not strange, unusual or revolutionary, but normal, sound and honest. And that is what they are" (p. 4).

Besides foregrounding the similarities between her policies and the accepted policies of other nations, Thatcher (1980) also reasoned that her policies were different from those of her critics. More specifically, Thatcher differentiated her administration from previous administrations by co-opting the radical label for her administration's *implementation of the policy*. She explained, "This Government are [sic] determined to stay with the policy and see it through to its conclusion. That is what marks this administration as one of the truly radical ministries of post-war Britain" (p. 5). In making this argument, Thatcher promoted an axiological shift—*away from* valuing short-term solutions *to* implementing long-term policies to their conclusion. This government was *radical* because it would actually accomplish in the long run what it had promised.

Thatcher (1980) further promoted her worldview by featuring anomalies in the actions of her opposition. Thatcher labeled her opposition as having the ability only to make arguments, not to work for real solutions. To accomplish this strategic naming, Thatcher had to reason that her opposition did not enact the criterial attributes associated with *real work*. To do this, Thatcher invoked the rhetorical maneuvers of *ad rem* arguments and repetition based on an us-versus-them approach.

Ad rem, as defined by Schopenhauer (1962), is when a proposition is "not in accordance with the nature of things, i.e., with absolute, objective truth" (p. 341). Thatcher (1980) enacted this maneuver by pointing out all of the arguments she could use about unemployment, which Labour had used in the past, to account for growing economic woes. She looked at how "you can try to soften that [unemployment] figure a dozen ways" (p. 4). She then proceeded through a litany of statements beginning with how "you can try," "you can add," "you can stress," "you can emphasize," "you can recall," and "you can point out" all of the arguments why the economic situation is not as woeful as it may seem (pp. 4–5). "But when all that has been said the *fact* remains that the level of unemployment in our country today is a human tragedy" (p. 5; emphasis added). Thus, she contended that her accusers would try to talk the British people into accepting their economy as inevitable, but she continued to point to the *facts* that economic conditions had not changed for the better.

Thatcher (1980) then drew out this dichotomy through the rhetorical maneuver of contrasting images. She evoked the continuums of "dignity" versus "condemnation," "waste" versus that which is "precious," and "idleness" versus the innate "energy" of the British people (p. 5). Thatcher defined this contrast before shifting into further use of *ad rem* attacks in which she questioned her opposition as to whether there was the "smallest political gain" in allowing increased unemployment or whether her government's recent actions represented some "obscure economic religion" that required continued unemployment "as part of its grisly [added in Thatcher's verbal delivery] ritual" (p. 5). She asked rhetorically, "If I could press a button and *genuinely* solve the unemployment problem, do you think I would not press that button this instant?" (p. 5; emphasis added). In arguing from absurdity, Thatcher asked whether any of these attacks made much sense to her audience. In essence, the attacks begged the question about whom or what was more real: those positing these attacks, or the policies and problems posited by her government? This became an appearance versus reality argument in which Thatcher named her arguments as *reflecting reality* and her opposition's statements as *mere appearances*.

Through all of these attacks, Thatcher (1980) attempted to steal the ground away from her opposition by symbolically categorizing it as incapable of real work. She could have answered her critics with the successes of her government's policies. Instead, she went on the offensive. She attacked the grounds on which her critics' arguments stood and attempted to capture for her side the arguments of her opponents, within both Tory ranks and Labour ranks. She stole their impact by reframing the issue and, as a result, won the battle for the perspective on the economy and two more terms in office. In Thatcher's rhetoric, she named herself as the only one positing solutions. She was real and doing real work because her policies encouraged people to engage in entrepreneurial undertakings and to take responsibility for their economic futures. All her opponents did was raise questions and objections, a far simpler task. Through Thatcher's use of dichotomy, she named herself as being firmly established on the side of the real, while those across the aisle only had their arguments—clearly nothing of substance.

Power and Need Side Effects

The attention switch initiated in this social intervention also encouraged a shift in interpretation of power—from an economy fully controlled by unions and the government to one controlled by market forces and private investment. Thatcher (1980) attempted to alter power interdependencies by increasing the power shares of the citizenry to promote privatization of business and ownership of the economy by the people. "Our aim is to let people feel that they count for more and more. If we cannot trust the deepest instinct of our people we should not be in politics at all" (p. 7).

The attention intervention also created shifts in interpretations of world power. In the international arena, Thatcher's focus was on increasing the world's interdependence with Britain. She proposed "a defense policy which potential foes will respect" (p. 9) and "restoration of Britain's place in the world" (p. 10). She added, "We have no wish to seek a free ride at the expense of our Allies. We will play our full part" (p. 9). In her speech, she offered numerous other examples, such as Britain's procurement of the Trident missile system from the United

States and negotiations within the European Community under Britain's "firm yet fair approach" (p. 10). Clearly, Thatcher's goal of intervention included both shifting power shares between the British government and the British people so that the people felt less interdependence with the government, and simultaneously increasing Britain's power share on the world stage so that more of Europe and Latin America felt greater interdependence with Britain.

At the same time that Thatcher (1980) promoted an attention switch, she also rhetorically attributed and advocated the need for societal health. She linked inextricably the economy and the health of society. "Without a healthy economy we cannot have a healthy society. Without a healthy society the economy will not stay healthy for long" (p. 7). Thus, the need Thatcher addressed was economic liberation from socialism and the promotion of a healthy, free society driven by the instincts of its people. Thatcher's "diagnosis" and "treatment" for this condition were revealed through the policies she outlined throughout her speech and offered as the prescription for change. In her second term as prime minister, Thatcher's Cabinet even labeled these programs "Social Thatcherism" (Thatcher, 1995).

❖ CONCLUSION

Thatcher was not one to turn—she was fixed on pressing forward. Even in the light of calls for reversal and indicators of retreat, Thatcher did not yield. In proposing her view of the Conservative Party as the only position of substance, the only view ruled not by mere arguments but sound reasons and actions, the Prime Minister pressed forward her vision for Britain. She understood that there was no purpose in leading if no one would follow, especially if, as she outlined, the nation was to trust the basic instincts of its people. Therefore, Thatcher used an attention switch to redefine the ideology regarding her domestic and foreign policy views for Britain. By shifting the British public's worldview, Thatcher redefined the power and need interdependency between the people and the government so that the government became the servant of the people, and not vice versa. In light of this change, the people now had recognizable power shares in future choosing about inflation.

Thatcher's October 10 speech initiated the intervention sought by the Tory government by recasting the arguments in a way common citizens could understand their role in the new ideological enactment. After years of trying to find a solution to the economic equation of

Britain, Thatcher framed the issue in such a way that common people could join in the fight against inflation, socialism, individual insignificance, and international obscurity by rallying behind the banner of Thatcherism.

Thatcher showed that social intervention and change are not the province of a single person but the influence between a person and a critical mass necessary to accomplish the end goal. That end goal, however, is still something that must fit well into an ideological system that makes sense to audience members, that enables them to see how they will benefit from the end goal and, significantly, how they will participate in the future choosing of that very system. It is the vested individual interest along with the communal interdependency that allows the audience members to adopt a worldview as their own, and energizes them to enact the social change that brings about the future that they desire to share.

❖ REFERENCES

Brown, W. R. (1978). Ideology as communication process. *Quarterly Journal of Speech*, *64*(2), 123–140.

Brown, W. R. (1982). Attention and the rhetoric of social intervention. *Quarterly Journal of Speech*, *68*(1), 17–27.

Central Office of Information. (1979). *Britain 1979: An official handbook*. London: Her Majesty's Stationery Office.

Churchill, W. (1940, June 18). Speech to the House of Commons. *The Churchill Centre*. Retrieved May 17, 2008, from http://www.winstonchurchill.org/i4a/pages/index.cfm?pageid=418

Churchill, W. (1941, October 29). Speech to Harrow School. *The Churchill Centre*. Retrieved May 17, 2008, from http://www.winstonchurchill.org/i4a/pages/index.cfm?pageid=423

Films for the Humanities and Sciences (Producer). (1999). *Margaret Thatcher: The iron lady* [Motion Picture]. Princeton, NJ.

Gring, M. A. (1998). Attention, power, and need: The rhetoric of religion and revolution in Nicaragua. *World Communication*, *27*(4), 27–37.

Lewis, J. J. (2004). War quotes. *Wisdom Quotes: Quotations to Inspire and Challenge*. Retrieved December 4, 2005, from http://www.wisdomquotes.com/cat_war.html.

Scammell, M. (1996). The odd couple: Marketing and Maggie. *European Journal of Marketing*, *30*(10/11), 122–134.

Schopenhauer, A. (1962). The art of controversy. In R. Taylor (Ed.), *The will to live: Selected writings of Arthur Schopenhauer* (p. 341). New York: Anchor Books.

Thatcher, M. (1980, October 10). Speech to Conservative Party Conference. *Margaret Thatcher Foundation.* Retrieved October 18, 2005, from http://www.margaretthatcher.org/speeches/displaydocument.asp?docid=104431.

Thatcher, M. (1995). *The path to power.* New York: HarperCollins.

Reflections

Seth Phillips is the speech and debate coach at The Woodlands College Park High School in The Woodlands, TX.

This essay is based on a paper I wrote for professor Mark A. Gring's graduate course in Historical-Critical Research Methods at Texas Tech University and work I completed as part of my master's thesis there. I became interested in British public address and Margaret Thatcher as a result of my debate background and interest in international economics. I chose to use the RSI model for the paper and the thesis because it offered a more global perspective for analyzing an instance of political communication aimed specifically at social intervention. The RSI model approach helped to highlight Thatcher's use of war rhetoric along with the naming, need, and power changes stemming from the attention switch. Professor Mark A. Gring is listed as second author on the essay because he assisted in revising the published version.

1. Phillips analyzed Margaret Thatcher's October 10, 1980, speech as the primary symbolizing activity. What might be the strengths and limitations of focusing on one speech versus a variety of symbolizing activity to make sense of a social intervention?

2. How might Phillips's experience as a Thatcher admirer and a U.S. citizen influence his choice of materials to analyze and his interpretation of social naming pattern trends?

3. Phillips suggests that the British people saw themselves as economically subservient to government and unable to determine their own economic futures. How did using the RSI model enable him to reach this conclusion? How might this finding be relevant to other naming situations? What does it teach us about human symbolizing activity?

4. In what ways does or does not Phillips's essay fulfill expectancies associated with a critical essay?

The Butterflies' Rhetorical Challenge

The Choices of Social Interveners

Omolara Oyelakin

The thirty-one–year regime of President Rafael Trujillo (from 1930 to 1961) as the political leader of the Dominican Republic led to the loss of political freedom for the Dominicans (Alisky, 1973). As a result of the violence and cruelty that the Trujillo regime unleashed, underground groups formed to overthrow the dictatorship.

The Mirabal sisters—Patria, Minerva, Dedé, and María Teresa—were members of one such underground group (Alvarez, 1994). Their intervention was the acts they carried out as part of the group to challenge the social hierarchy. They intervened in a social system consisting of the citizens and government of the Dominican Republic. In response to their intervention, the Trujillo regime persecuted the sisters in an effort to halt them and eventually murdered three of them (Alvarez). To commemorate the courage of the Mirabal sisters, poems, stories, and museums have been dedicated to their memory. However, I chose to use the book *In The Time of the Butterflies* by Julia Alvarez, published in 1994, as the basis of my social intervention research.

Alvarez, whose family had to flee the Dominican Republic during Trujillo's reign, creates a narrative of the sisters' intervention based on historical accounts. She attempts to capture the "spirit" of what she considers the "real Mirabals" to engage readers in "an epoch in the life of the Dominican Republic" (Alvarez, 1994, p. 324). In addition, she considers the Mirabal sisters as "models for women fighting against injustices of all kinds" (p. 324). Thus, my paper analyzes the sisters' social intervention as portrayed in the Alvarez book, although Alvarez's book itself could be considered an intervention to influence how readers interpret the Mirabal sisters' actions.

The story of the Mirabal sisters represents an intervention based on real events that originated from the Mirabal sisters' support of an ideology that promotes freedom, equality, education, choice, and free will. It makes an interesting study because what they fought for is closely related to the American dream—the ideology that we can make the world a more nearly perfect place (Brown, 1970). Alvarez's account highlights the interactions among power shareholders as they act as interveners to promote or impede social change.

I use the Rhetoric of Social Intervention (RSI) model to explore the communication patterns underlying the Mirabal sisters' attempt to intervene and transform the Dominican Republic into their idea of a better place. Although I treat the sisters as the primary interveners, the essay shows that other power shareholders, such as Trujillo, also acted as interveners. I examine the intervention described in the book from the starting point of power because the power holder, President Trujillo, is shown as taking the stance of "'do this because I say so' with the sanction of 'or else'" (Brown, 1986, p. 183). However, I also reference shifts in attention and need that are interconnected with shifts in interpretations of interdependency.

I discuss life in the Dominican Republic before the Mirabal sisters' intervention, during the intervention, and after the intervention, based on Alvarez's (1994) narrative. I describe what the sisters believed in and what they hoped their intervention would accomplish. This paper follows the narrative of the sisters' lives from childhood to their deaths, examining how they shifted and promoted a social shift *away from* cooperating with *to* challenging the social hierarchy to bring about change.

❖ APPEARANCE OF PERFECTION:
   LIFE BEFORE THE INTERVENTION

She remembers a clear moonlit night before the future began. They are sitting in the cool darkness under the anacahuita tree in the front yard, in the rockers, telling stories, drinking guanábana juice. Good for the nerves, Mama always says. (Alvarez, 1994, p. 8)

Alvarez (1994) attributes the above description of life before the intervention to Dedé. At this point in the narrative, the sisters were all young, with the oldest in her midteens and the youngest a child. The words in the description—cool darkness, anacahuita tree, front yard, rockers, story telling, and guanábana juice—convey a serene, almost perfect setting. But this was "before the future began," before the sisters' lives underwent drastic changes (Alvarez).

During this period, the sisters cooperated with the rules and roles of the social hierarchy promoted by the Trujillo regime. They lived a day-to-day life that went with the flow. The book suggests that they were unaware of abnormalities in the social system's constitution. The experiences they would later fight against (e.g., government spies, inadequate education, inadequate freedom, etc.) were not seen as anomalies because they backgrounded these experiences in their discourse. Instead, they foregrounded experiences such as family, love, and education (Alvarez, 1994). But this would change as the sisters gradually shifted their role in the social system away from *cooperative citizens* to *interveners*.

❖   AWARENESS OF IMPERFECTION:
THE SHIFT FROM COOPERATIVE CITIZEN TO CRITICS

Before the sisters became attentive to the anomalies in the hierarchy promoted by the Trujillo regime, the goal-mediating roles in the Dominican Republic social system could be described as follows: The president was a representation of God who could not be questioned, and the people were his subjects (Alvarez, 1994). Citizens were expected to place the president's picture in their houses as a sign of respect and subservience (Alvarez; Brown, 1999). In turn, citizens expected the Trujillo regime to create a country in which their needs—such as freedom, safety, and long life—would be met. The interdependency between the Dominicans and President Trujillo was cooperative, but, over time, the motive that organized this interdependency became one of threat (Brown, 1986; Brown, 1999). The people became aware that they would be subjected to varying levels of sanctions if they challenged the social hierarchy promoted by Trujillo.

The book describes the sisters' early life as comprising fulfilled expectancies (Alvarez, 1994). That is, everything they expected to have seemed to be within their grasp. They appeared to be satisfied with their lives and had everything they thought was imperative to living— love, family, education, and a family business (Alvarez). Yet Minerva became increasingly aware that something was missing, an unmet need—her need for freedom (Alvarez).

Alvarez (1994) begins the narrative of the sisters with the interventions that changed Minerva's interpretation of social hierarchy, and I shall do the same in this paper. Minerva was considered "the most educated sister and the most overtly political" of the four (Rich, 2002, p. 167). Alvarez suggests that the sisters' shift to their role as interveners started with her.

The book names Minerva's greatest problem—what she tagged as the greatest anomaly in her life experiences—as her lack of *freedom*. By age 12, Minerva already had an expectancy of *freedom*, which she defined as women having the opportunity to be fully educated and to be involved in politics (Alvarez, 1994).

Minerva advocated her need for freedom by complaining that she and her sisters had to ask permission before doing anything (Alvarez, 1994). She compared her home life to rabbits locked in a cage. Hence, when she was sent to convent school, she thought she would gain her freedom. But Minerva eventually realized that she had succeeded only in leaving "a small cage to go into a bigger one, the size of our whole country" (Alvarez, p. 13).

Despite her apparent need for freedom, Alvarez (1994) suggests that Minerva backgrounded her discontentment until she began encountering people who criticized the Trujillo regime. Alvarez captures these experiences in the character of Sinita, whom Minerva befriended at the convent. Sinita had lost all the males in her family. The regime killed them for challenging Trujillo's authority. The men had become dissenters when they realized that Trujillo was responsible for actions such as killing his opponents (Alvarez).

As a result of such events, Sinita interpreted the Trujillo regime as violating the societal expectancy of building a better Dominican Republic (Alvarez, 1994). Sinita named these incidents *Trujillo's secret*. She tried to intervene and reason with Minerva that Trujillo was not the saint she believed him to be by giving examples of his actions that did not fit the name *saint* (Alvarez).

But to Minerva, Trujillo was all that was good (Alvarez, 1994). Alvarez suggests that Minerva could not imagine that he would commit such hideous crimes. "'Trujillo was doing bad things?' It was as if I had just heard Jesus had slapped a baby or Our Blessed Mother had not conceived Him the immaculate conception way. 'That can't be true'" (p. 17). Minerva named the events described by Sinita as "a terrible mistake that wouldn't happen again" (p. 20). She masked the anomalies that Sinita attempted to highlight, thus impeding a possible attention shift.

Sinita did not give up. In another instance, Trujillo visited the convent and started courting one of Minerva's upper-class friends, Lina, even though he was married (Alvarez, 1994). Trujillo impregnated Lina, then moved her to a private residence (Alvarez). After Minerva and Sinita heard about this incident, they tried to negotiate a name for the president. Sinita symbolically categorized him as *a devil*, and Minerva categorized him as *a man* (Alvarez).

Minerva used rhetorical maneuvers to reason that Trujillo was *not a devil*. For example, she named him *the same as* other men who make mistakes: "But I was thinking, No, he is a Man. And in spite of all I'd heard, I felt sorry for him. ¡*Pobrecito!* At night, he probably had nightmare after nightmare like I did, just thinking about what he'd done" (Alvarez, 1994, p. 24).

Eventually though, after several more similar occurrences involving Trujillo, Minerva's way of interpreting experience—*a man who makes mistakes*—no longer made sense. Gradually, the name advocated by Sinita—*a devil*—seemed to better fit and explain the events that Minerva witnessed. Alvarez (1994) shows Minerva's shift in how she talked about the president. She too began symbolically categorizing the president as *evil*. She now named him as *a threat that needed to be removed* (Alvarez). As a result, Minerva became an intervener. Her renaming of Trujillo led her to start challenging the social hierarchy by joining others in an underground group.

In the case of Patria, Alvarez (1994) describes her world as seeming as perfect as it could be. She married at sixteen and was the model of a good Catholic wife and mother who believed women should be seen and not heard (Alvarez). Patria is characterized as firmly believing in Jesus and the leadership of President Trujillo. She placed their pictures side by side and paid reverence to both (Alvarez). As far as Patria was concerned, Trujillo was not a saint, but he was "building churches and schools" (Alvarez, p. 53). Hence, she saw no reason to challenge the social hierarchy. Despite all she heard, she backgrounded the people's "cries of desolation" and did not recognize any abnormality in her life or in her country until after bearing a stillborn baby (Alvarez, p. 53).

Alvarez (1994) uses Patria's loss of her child to illustrate Patria's shift in how she named experience. After Patria lost her baby, she felt hurt by Jesus, whom she interpreted as violating the expectancy of a better life. She explained the senselessness of her baby's death by accusing Jesus of not meeting her need for a child (Alvarez). At this point, she began sympathizing with people who had been hurt by the Trujillo regime because she named the event of Trujillo taking loved ones away from their families to be *the same as* Jesus taking away her baby (Alvarez).

Along with renaming the Trujillo regime, Patria began attributing needs that she now interpreted Trujillo as not fulfilling (Alvarez, 1994). She renamed the government from being *needs-meeting* to being *non-needs-meeting*. Patria slowly shifted from being a *cooperative citizen* in supporting the social hierarchy to becoming a *critic* and later an *intervener*. She started pointing out anomalies and renamed President Trujillo away from *representative of God* to *murderer* (Alvarez).

In Alvarez's (1994) story, the next sister to step back and start analyzing the social hierarchy was Dedé. Dedé never attended to any anomalies until she met Virgilio Morales (Leo), whom Trujillo categorized as a *communist* and an *enemy of the state* (Alvarez, 1994). After reading a newspaper article that named Leo *a terrorist*, Dedé reasoned that if Leo was *an enemy of the state* because of what he advocated, then Minerva was also *an enemy of the state* because she shared the same beliefs as Leo—that the Trujillo regime should be stopped (Alvarez).

As a result of the article, Dedé started paying more attention to newspapers and reflecting on what she read (Alvarez, 1994). Dedé concluded that by rounding up people and killing them and by creating rules such as dress codes, the Trujillo regime was not meeting the country's needs (Alvarez). Leo's run-in with the Trujillo regime, which in turn led to the published articles, helped Dedé to see how the government was not meeting symbolically created expectancies such as freedom, safety, and education. Hence, in the book, Leo's actions served as an intervention that led Dedé to rename the president from *leader* to *dictator* (Alvarez).

Alvarez (1994) portrays the intervention that shifted the fourth sister's interpretation of interdependency as beginning with a discussion in which María Teresa questioned Minerva about her involvement with *communists*. Minerva explained that she joined the underground group because she wanted María Teresa to grow up in a free country (Alvarez). She attributed to María Teresa and to the citizens of the country the need for *freedom*, which she interpreted to be an imperative (Alvarez). As a result of Minerva's intervention, María Teresa began attending to anomalies in the social system. Even though she was not yet an intervener, María Teresa had gone from cooperating with to critiquing the social hierarchy.

In Alvarez's (1994) narrative, the four sisters took different paths to become *critics* and eventually *interveners* (Rich, 2002). The sisters' ideology, as described in Alvarez's book, created the expectancy that their country could be made a more nearly perfect place to live through freedom, equality, and education. Initially they cooperated with the social system that treated the Trujillo regime as if it would create a better Dominican Republic, but as they increasingly attended to events that did not make sense in this interpretation of experience, they began advocating for a shift in attention to account for the anomalies.

In their revised interpretation of events, they named Trujillo's role in the social system as *a dictator* who would make paradise unachievable. They began to challenge the social hierarchy, with plans to remove Trujillo. They began advocating the need to eliminate Trujillo to the citizens of the Dominican Republic and featuring attention to the corruption of the Trujillo government to encourage the citizens to shift their interpretation of interdependency and overthrow the government. They would work together to achieve the ideology of creating a more nearly perfect country.

❖ CHALLENGES TO PERFECTION:
    THE SHIFT FROM *CRITIC* TO *INTERVENER*

> You know, everyone says our problems started after Minerva had her run-in with Trujillo at the Discovery Day Dance. But the truth is Minerva was already courting trouble two or three years before that. . . . You might have heard of Virgilio Morales?—*Dedé* (Alvarez, 1994, p. 66)

Even though Minerva had become a critic as a result of what she abstracted from her experiences, she did not begin enacting the role of intervener until she also met Leo. Alvarez (1994) shows Leo continuously featuring attention to the shortcomings of the government. Leo reasoned that it did not meet the symbolically created expectancies of giving people freedom, free speech, and life, because the president killed all who opposed him (Alvarez). Leo named *killing Trujillo* as the best way to meet the collectivity-stressing needs for *political freedom* and *equality* (Alvarez).

In the book, the sisters' shift to becoming *interveners* started after Minerva met Leo (Alvarez, 1994). Leo later met the other Mirabal sisters, but he was not in their lives for long. He soon fled the country to avoid being captured by Trujillo's secret police (Alvarez). Trujillo named Leo as *a threat* that needed to be eliminated. After Leo's disappearance, the sisters paid more attention to the regime (Alvarez). The sisters began renaming the law as benefiting government officials rather than the citizens and keeping the power holder at the top of the hierarchy. The sisters concluded that the government was denying the people the symbolically created needs of *peace, education, equality, free speech,* and, above all, the *right to live* (Alvarez). For this reason, the sisters gradually created a social intervention to take power away from the power holder, Trujillo.

Alvarez (1994) provides numerous examples of how Trujillo's power code violations continued to reinforce the sisters' belief that the social hierarchy needed to change. For instance, to show support for Trujillo and the established social hierarchy, government officials held parties in honor of Trujillo. The Mirabal family was invited to a party that commemorated Christopher Columbus's landing on the island of the Dominican Republic (Rich, 2002).

Minerva received a special invitation to come as Trujillo's guest (Alvarez, 1994). Minerva was invited because she had grown into a beautiful woman. The president loved beautiful women and had numerous girlfriends around the country (Alvarez). The dictator named women as *property* and used them as such (Brown, 1999). During this party, Alvarez portrays Minerva as initiating "what was to become the demise of her family's life" (Brown, p. 106). Trujillo fondled Minerva while dancing with her, and she slapped him. This violated the power holder–power subject power code, which said that power subjects should not show public disregard of a power holder.

Minerva's actions had dire consequences. The president jailed the sisters' father, who died a few weeks after his release (Alvarez, 1994). When Minerva was graduated from law school, Trujillo seized her diploma and forbade her to practice law (Alvarez). These incidents and more reinforced the sisters' interpretation that something had to be done to take power away from Trujillo.

How did the sisters plan to achieve their dream of overthrowing Trujillo to enact their ideology of freedom, free speech, equality, and education? Interveners can use a variety of rhetorical maneuvers to challenge social hierarchy and promote their ideology, including protests, writing complaint letters, or appealing to international authorities (Brown, 1986). The sisters became part of an underground group. They chose this maneuver because of the unspoken power code that governed the *president/subject* relationship. The sisters knew that Trujillo could use violence as a punishment for their resistance if they chose more flamboyant ways to make their discontent known (Rich, 2002).

At this point in Alvarez's (1994) narrative, the sisters were adults. Minerva had married, and María Teresa lived with Minerva and her husband. Minerva and her husband joined a national underground group whose overall aim was to bring down the Trujillo regime by killing Trujillo (Alvarez). In Alvarez's account, María Teresa did not become involved in this intervention until she met one of Minerva's handsome comrades who delivered a package to the house. Curiosity led María Teresa to check the package, and she discovered ammunition (Alvarez). After this incident, she demanded to join Minerva's underground group and she later married the comrade who had delivered the package that day.

In the book, Patria joined the underground group after she witnessed the killing of a young soldier during one of her pilgrimages (Alvarez, 1994). Dedé married a family friend, but opted not to enact the role of intervener because her husband was against it. The sisters and their husbands, except Dedé and her husband Jaimito, had become what Trujillo named *politicals* (Alvarez). However, the RSI model would call them *interveners*.

An underground group called the Fourteenth of June Movement was created to communicate the intervention of challenging social hierarchy (Alvarez 1994). An underground group meant that the sisters had to create interdependencies with others to accomplish their goals. In the book, Alvarez shows the sisters discussing Trujillo's impending death. Dedé asks, "You're going to do it yourselves?" María Teresa replies, "Heavens, no. . . . The action group does the actual justice" (p. 178). As part of the action group, the sisters worked with other people who had been encouraged to challenge the social hierarchy.

Within the group, the sisters enacted the role of delivery agents in Alvarez's (1994) narrative. Their houses were used as distribution points for ammunition and other necessary material. The sisters were also responsible for making bombs, polishing guns, providing safe meeting points, and storing supplies (Alvarez). Overall, the interdependent underground group portrayed in the book was organized around the need to assassinate the president and his cohorts as a means to achieve a more nearly perfect country. As the sisters enacted their tasks to meet this need, they were aware that they placed their lives and their families in danger (Alvarez). Nevertheless, they still carried out their roles, signifying the importance they placed on this power intervention.

Trujillo attempted to mask attention to the sisters' actions, which pointed out anomalies in the social system, and tried to maintain his status as power holder (Alvarez, 1994). He began enacting sanctions for challenging the power code. The first sanction he issued was a roundup of the men involved in the underground system, including the husbands of María Teresa, Minerva, and Patria (Alvarez). This was closely followed by the arrests of María Teresa and Minerva.

Up until this point in Alvarez's (1994) story, Dedé had been a critic who refused to act as an intervener to challenge the social hierarchy. The arrest of her sisters and their husbands encouraged Dedé and her husband to start serving in the underground group to save her sisters (Alvarez). As Dedé's needs shifted (to the need to save her family members), so did her interdependencies.

In Alvarez's (1994) account, the Dominican people heard about the sisters' struggles to eliminate the power holder, and the sisters became local heroes. The public began calling the sisters *the butterflies*. This rhetorical maneuver emphasized the expectancy of freedom advocated by the sisters. A butterfly represents freedom as it flies from one point to another without any worries or hindrances. The citizens believed that regardless of having been locked in a prison, the sisters would eventually fly free like butterflies and help bring a better life to the Dominican Republic. Hence, the reluctant power subjects of Trujillo— the citizens of the Dominican Republic—interpreted what the sisters were doing as *inspirational*.

Because the sisters were challenging the symbolically constructed social hierarchy and the people were supporting the sisters' actions, Trujillo became even more adamant in preventing their power intervention (Alvarez, 1994). He thought that he could mask the sisters' intervention by a threat of non-needs-meeting behavior. In Alvarez's story, he began punishing the sisters by withdrawing the fulfillment of their needs. Some of these punishments included the loss of property, imprisonment of family members, and deaths (Alvarez). Trujillo used these punishments to communicate to the citizens that his regime would not tolerate those who dared to challenge hierarchy. He attempted to force cooperation by threat. Thus, more people were killed, tortured, jailed, and abducted.

However, President Trujillo seemed to forget that a power holder has an interdependent relationship with the power subjects (Brown, 1986). According to the RSI model, the more people Trujillo killed, the more power he lost because, as a power holder, he has no power unless he has subjects to rule (Brown, 1986). A power holder needs power subjects to cooperate to build complementary relationships such as *president/citizens* (Brown). The more Trujillo had to enact sanctions to maintain his power holder position, the less his needs and the needs of the people were being met. The communication patterns in the system became what the RSI model calls *deviance amplifying* (Brown).

❖ ALTERNATIVE FUTURES TO PERFECTION: LIFE AFTER THE INTERVENTION

[Power] depends upon shared interpretations that during future choosing, power holders and power subjects must mediate each other's goals in order to make real those futures. (Brown, 1986, p. 185)

The Dominican Republic power shareholders appeared to hold different interpretations of their complementary interdependency (Alvarez, 1994). President Trujillo believed he had ultimate power as the power holder and the right to control the people's lives. He expected the people to be grateful for his leadership, to worship him, and to obey him (Brown, 1999). The sisters, on the other hand, saw Trujillo's actions as "power over consciousness" (Brown, 1986, p. 1). The sisters firmly believed in the ideology of freedom, free speech, equality, and education. All these were needs that the Trujillo regime refused to meet long before Minerva and María Teresa were arrested. By not meeting these needs, the social hierarchy promoted by the regime violated ideological expectancies.

Trujillo attempted to mask attention to the anomalies by killing other interveners who worked with the sisters (Alvarez, 1994). However, the citizens already knew of the sisters' challenge of social hierarchy. As related in the book, the people deemed the sisters *saints* and named the Mirabal sisters' actions as *courageous* because they challenged the social hierarchy in the attempt to make the country a better place (Alvarez). Even though the sisters were in prison for six months, their intervention was already encouraging more and more people to begin criticizing the government.

Although many people named the sisters *courageous*, Trujillo symbolically categorized them as *a threat* (Alvarez, 1994). He had numerous opportunities to kill the sisters while they were in prison, but did not do so. Trujillo apparently did not enact that sanction because he wanted them to suffer for daring to challenge hierarchy (Alvarez). Also, he was aware that people had been naming the sisters *heroes* and *admirable* (Alvarez). Thus, he enacted sanctions such as imprisonment, assuming that if he could make the sisters abandon their interpretation of interdependency and ratify him as a power holder, then the rest of the people would also accept this interpretation. Despite Trujillo's threats, the sisters refused to abandon their interpretation of experience (Alvarez). They even refused to leave prison when the president granted them a pardon because they wanted to set a good example for the people (Alvarez).

Trujillo eventually released the sisters after inquiries by a peace organization that investigated human rights abuses (Alvarez, 1994). After their release, Trujillo expected the sisters to reduce their anomaly-featuring communication because he had given them a first-hand experience of the consequences of disobedience (Alvarez). After the sisters' release, they became even more admired by the people of the Dominican Republic because they now were named as the ones who *challenged the dictator and lived to tell the story* (Alvarez).

In Alvarez's (1994) narrative, the sisters' intervention shaped how others saw their role in the social system. More people began realizing that they could exchange the life they had for the sisters' interpretation of achieving a better country through peace, freedom, equality, education, and so on. People stopped the sisters in the streets, churches, and shops to wish them well and to thank them for challenging hierarchy (Alvarez). As a result of the support the sisters received and their apparent refusal to quit challenging the social hierarchy, Trujillo found more ways to sanction the sisters, such as seizing their lands, cars, and houses (Alvarez). Trujillo tried to maintain his position at the top of the social hierarchy by threatening those who dared to challenge his power.

Trujillo also refused to release the sister's husbands from prison and allowed the sisters to visit only a few times a month (Alvarez, 1994). It was on one such visit that Trujillo carried out his most extreme sanction to reinforce his position as power holder. On November 25, 1960, Minerva, María Teresa, and Patria were murdered on their way back from visiting their husbands in prison (Alvarez). Hence, Trujillo carried out his own intervention by eliminating the threat.

By carrying out the ultimate sanction, Trujillo attempted to remind the power-subject citizens that those who challenged the hierarchy would suffer grave consequences. However, Trujillo apparently did not consider how the people would make sense of his actions, according to Alvarez (1994). They renamed the sisters *martyrs*, and their heroic actions would propel more people to intervene and challenge social hierarchy (Alvarez).

After the sisters' intervention and death, more underground groups arose that challenged the social hierarchy. Eventually, in 1961, Trujillo was assassinated. Trujillo's death ultimately led to free elections, free zones, and equal education (Alvarez, 1994). In Alvarez's account, the Dominican Republic became "the playground of the Caribbean" (p. 318). Hence, the sisters' attempted power shift eventually became a reality, even if it was only one sister, Dedé, who lived to see it. It is through her eyes and voice that Alvarez tells the story of the Mirabal sisters and their intervention to challenge the hierarchy promoted by President Rafael Trujillo.

❖ CONCLUSION

By viewing Alvarez's narrative through the lens of the RSI model, the communication patterns that develop in non-needs-meeting systems are revealed. Interveners, such as the Mirabal sisters, begin creating social disorder to challenge social hierarchy when they become aware that the system's interdependencies no longer met their needs. The RSI model also highlights the communication patterns that arise when those opposed to change take steps to prevent change. Interveners, such as Trujillo, attempted to stop the shift by enacting sanctions.

Alvarez (1994) ends the story with Dedé, the remaining sister, reflecting on the sisters' work and choices. With the realization of the sisters' dreams, Dedé could be expected to admire the sisters' accomplishments, but Alvarez portrays her otherwise. "Was it for this, the sacrifice of the butterflies?" Dedé asks (p. 318). Was the loss of the Mirabal sisters' lives to promote their ideology of a better world worth it? This question is significant because, as human beings, we sometimes forget that ideas such as *freedom, free will, education*, and *success* are not laws set in stone. The American dream and the dream of the Mirabal sisters are symbolically constructed ideas that a social system has deemed important and vital to its survival—they are not our birthright.

If the social hierarchy prevents us from enacting these ideas that we take for granted, the RSI model suggests that we will find ways to change power holders, but it is left to us to decide what method we will use to challenge the hierarchy. If, like the Mirabal sisters, we choose to risk our lives while seeking to make the world a better place, it is best that we look deep within ourselves and ask these questions: Is my ideology worth losing my life? Will all the sacrifices be worth it? Do we have to suffer so much simply to have freedom, education, success, and equality? The example of the Mirabal sisters' intervention, as described by Alvarez (1994), reveals the extent to which human beings will sometimes go to in order to achieve their ideology of making the world a more nearly perfect place.

❖ REFERENCES

Alisky, M. (1973). Book notes: Era of Trujillo: Dominican dictator. *Western Political Quarterly, 26*(2), 376. Retrieved June 1, 2007, from JSTOR database.

Alvarez, J. (1994). *In the time of the butterflies*. Chapel Hill, NC: Algonquin Books.

Brown, I. Z. (1999). Historiographic metafiction in "In the Time of the Butterflies." *South Atlantic Review, 64*(2), 98–112. Retrieved June 1, 2007, from JSTOR database.

Brown, W. R. (1970). *Imagemaker: Will Rogers and the American dream*. Columbia: University of Missouri Press.

Brown, W. R. (1986). Power and the rhetoric of social intervention. *Communication Monographs, 53*(2), 180–199. Retrieved June 1, 2007, from Communication and Mass Media Complete database.

Rich, C. (2002). Talking back to El Jefe: Genre, polyphony, and dialogic resistance in Julia Alvarez's "In the Time of the Butterflies." *Melus, 27*(4), 165–182. Retrieved June 1, 2007, from JSTOR database.

Reflections

*Omolara Oyelakin wrote this paper for
an undergraduate course at Salem College, Winston-Salem, NC.*

I became interested in the Mirabal sisters' intervention because their dream to make the Dominican Republic a better place is closely related to my dream of helping my home country of Nigeria to become a better place. From studying the sisters' intervention, I have learned that ideologies such as the American dream, which is constituted from freedom, education, success, and equal rights, were not born with us. These are simply ideas that we have deemed important to our survival. If social hierarchy prevents us from enacting these ideals, it is left to us to find ways to challenge hierarchy, while intervening and showing others the merits of our ideology.

I like that the RSI model teaches that, regardless of our ideology, we need to build interdependent relationships with others to accomplish it—no person is an island. We must get cooperation from others for our interventions and our ideology to have any chance whatsoever.

1. Oyelakin drew on a secondary source—a book based on historical accounts about the intervention—rather than a primary source such as the recorded discourse of the interveners themselves. What might be the limitations of using a secondary source for critiquing the original experience? How is the secondary source itself an intervention?

2. Could Oyelakin have created this essay without the language of the RSI model? What are the advantages and disadvantages of using RSI model terminology when writing an analysis?

3. What kinds of intervener choices does Oyelakin's essay highlight? How might these choices relate to a system's ethical and moral expectancies?

4. In what ways does Oyelakin's essay meet or not meet the criterial attributes of a critical essay?

ESSAY 4

Born to Power

*Influence in the Rhetoric of
the Posse Comitatus*

Lee Snyder

The two great wonders of humanity are how alike everyone is and how different everyone is. To study an extremist group, such as the Posse Comitatus (the Posse), is to experience these two wonders alternatively. First, the student is struck by the bizarreness of the worldview owned by the group. Further research, though, causes the student to see with uncomfortable clarity how some of those bizarre beliefs can seem to make perfect sense.

Why should communication students study groups whose worldviews may be repugnant to them? First, little is known about such extremist groups. Instead of studying them, scholars tend to dismiss them as merely symbolic asylums for the disaffected, people fortunately exiled to the Northwest or Midwest United States where they can spin their secret plots and do little public harm. Second, relevant communication publications about such groups are few and are limited to Kay (1987), Baker and Bode (1990), Rendahl (1989, 1990, 1991), and Riley, Hollihan, and Klumpp (1998). This is unfortunate, because the communication discipline, especially rhetorical theory, offers the best tools for understanding people with radically divergent worldviews.

This essay uses William Brown's (1978) Rhetoric of Social Intervention (RSI) model as a tool for investigating how the extremist group Posse Comitatus attempted to shift the public's perceived relationship with the U.S. government to attract followers to its divergent worldview. Brown suggests three possible ways groups can act as change agents in their audience's worldview. Interveners may encourage *attention* to alternative worldviews, changed perceptions of *needs*, or fresh interpretations of interrelated responsibility—that is, of *power* (Brown, 1986). Most RSI critiques (including those written by Brown) focus on whichever one of these interventions seems most important. In this case, the author was able to answer his research question by attending only to the Posse's power interventions. (See the section Reflections at the end of this essay.)

Accordingly, this essay highlights the Posse's attempt to shift the symbolically constructed social hierarchy, a power intervention that has yet to materialize in the form imagined by Posse members. First, the essay provides background on the Posse, data collection, and method. Then, it examines the Posse's rhetoric as a message of power creation. Next, it considers power itself as a communication medium for the Posse's intervention into the social system. It concludes with observations about the Posse's future.

❖ BACKGROUND OF THE POSSE INTERVENTION

Henry Beach started the Posse Comitatus (which translates as the "power of the county") in 1969, in Portland, Oregon (Zeskind, 1985). The group derives its name from the Posse Comitatus Act of 1878. This act forbade the use of federal troops to enforce U.S. law. Instead, the sheriff could create a local *posse* to help enforce laws in an emergency.

During the early 1970s, the Posse Comitatus grew as the public interpreted it to be primarily *a tax-protesting organization* (Zeskind, 1985). This characterization was accurate, if incomplete: Its members did not believe in paying income or property taxes, and they taught others how to safely avoid paying such taxes. People suffering from financial stress welcomed such messages, especially farmers and ranchers, who during prosperous times incurred large debts for new equipment or land, but who now faced foreclosures and sheriffs' sales.

In the late 1970s, James Wickstrom was the Posse's most visible leader. He claimed that the Posse had 2 million adherents in chapters in every state except Hawaii (Wickstrom, 1983). However, *The Kansas City Star* reported that the Posse numbered about ten thousand, and that they were primarily in Missouri, Kansas, Iowa, and Nebraska (Singer & Moore, 1982). The Posse attracted increased public attention in 1983 when one member, Gordon Kahl, killed two federal marshals near Medina, North Dakota (Zeskind, 1985). He was later killed in a shootout with law enforcement agents in Arkansas.

Gathering data on this group was challenging. Members were not eager to talk about their movement. Their reasons included the ongoing possibility of being investigated by law enforcement agencies, the unpopularity of their beliefs, and the fact that their worldview posits that the establishment (including state universities) is determined to destroy them. Thus, this essay relies on secondary sources, such as the Jewish Anti-Defamation League and law enforcement reports. Neither group is disinterested.

Some information came from individuals willing to talk to the author, who must keep their names confidential. (They are cited in this paper as "Informant.") Much of the printed material used is ephemeral—newsletters, tracts, and pamphlets—without an official publisher. Thus, all information has been corroborated from more than one source.

Also challenging is the fact that white supremacist organizations are loosely affiliated with each other. Both information and members flow easily in and out of each group. Members may belong to, sympathize with, and read material from other organizations, without necessarily approving all that the other groups teach (Barker, 1986).

This essay highlights symbolic power, not physical coercion. Power is defined here as the ability to choose the future, to influence others, to shape destiny without absolutely controlling it (Brown, 1986). It is rhetorically created and symbolically grounded. It does not exist in society as an attribute carried around by a credible individual: rather, it must be mutually negotiated among various people who hold power shares (Brown). These power shareholders mutually perceive that they need the others to help them mediate their own goals.

A researcher using the RSI model, then, must study the communication within a group and between the group and other power shareholders to discover the significant power shares in the whole system. What roles do the system's members enact? Power, after all, is attributed not only to individuals, but also to roles and to those who occupy them. For example, in the U.S. social system, some roles imply behaviors of legislation and administration; others, of training and education; still others, of production; and others, of preservation of the order.

As people work out their roles with the help of others, they develop three kinds of interdependency: a *cooperative* one (in which the hierarchy is accepted and affirmed), a *competitive* one (in which the hierarchy is challenged), and a *mixed* one (in which "a hierarchy is both affirmed and challenged" [Brown, 1986, p. 194]). A change agent, then, may strategically intervene by encouraging the system members to change their interpretations of other power shareholders from one of these relationships to another one. To achieve such an intervention, a change agent is likely to pursue one of three tactics: inviting people to perceive their power shares as based on *threat* ("If you don't stop driving through my flower-bed, I'll slash your tires"), on *exchange* ("You will unstop my sink, and I will give you money"), or on a policy of *integry* ("You will do this math homework because I am a teacher and you are a student") (Brown).

A change agent enacts strategies and tactics through rhetorical maneuvers, which include all of the basic means of persuasion—building credibility, staging a hunger strike, or playing martial music. Because maneuvers are easier to see than tactics and strategies, the essay begins by discussing the Posse's maneuvers for intervening to create a share of power for its members and to negotiate its power share within a social system consisting of the U.S. public, U.S. institutions, and the U.S. government.

❖ THE CREATION OF POWER THROUGH COMMUNICATION

The first question at issue is, "How may power be attributed to those who believe they have none, such as the farmers and ranchers who were losing their properties?" This essay discusses five prominent maneuvers used by the Posse that actualize the tactics and strategies of its attempted power intervention: questioning of the mystery, objectification of the foe, identification through creating a mystery, organizing of the worldview, and action corollaries.

Questioning the Mystery

A social order depends on maintaining a certain *mystery*. Mystery is an assumption that cannot be proved yet that allows a society to function. For example, how could an educational system survive if most students did not trust that the teacher has the right to instruct them? How could transportation work if people assumed no need to follow traffic regulations? Rights, obligations, hierarchy, glamour, piety—all are based on mystery (Duncan, 1968). To question the mystery at the root of a social order is to delegitimize it by attacking it at its weakest point, the point where people must simply have faith.

The Posse Comitatus attempts to create power by demystifying the present U.S. social order. Although its members revere the Constitution and pursue the American dream, they construct their own reality out of those raw materials. For example, they question the legitimacy of banks to seize property if a debtor does not make the scheduled payments, a right that is essential to capitalism's functioning. To the Posse, the banking institutions are not a part of the American way. Rather, banks are tools of an international conspiracy to enrich themselves at the expense of hard-working Americans.

The average citizen often sees the U.S. legal system as a complex system that may be understood only by professionals. People might either ignore it or hire a professional to cope with it. To the Posse, though, authentic law is simple. It is rooted in the Constitution. Ultimate authority rests in the hands of "We the people," as one Posse handbook explains:

> The Constitution is a simple document. It says what it means and means what it says. It means today what it meant when it was written. . . . The Federal government is a servant of the States and the people, not their master. (Posse by Law of Posse Comitatus, n.d., pp. 3–4)

The Posse communicates to its prospective members that they have no reason to trust the current U.S. social system—it is just as ridiculous as they always suspected. The system is rigged against the common person whose only real chance for survival is to opt out. By a deliberate act of will, a citizen can recapture stolen rights and help transform the U.S. system into what it should be.

The Posse suggests that among the instruments available to the common person for deconstructing the social system is citizen's arrest. It is, ironically, a part of that very system:

> Citizens' Arrest [sic] is your God-given, natural and unalienable right (see Declaration of Independence) AND it's your responsibility to support and defend this country—that includes securing the peace.
>
> For example; trespassing includes anyone (that includes ALL government employees, judges, legislators, FBI, IRS, Building and

Zoning personnel, etc.) that trespasses against your person, property or rights without a U.S. constitutional warrant. They should be ARRESTED (they are committing a crime, see Title 18, sec. 241, 242 in this book). American citizens are bound by law to arrest that felon or felons (right on the spot, in the very act of committing the crime) and if they kill him, or them, provided he or they cannot be taken otherwise, it is "justifiable." (Cunningham, n.d., p. 119; emphasis in original)

The Posse emphasizes that citizens are not helpless unless they choose to be, for the established social system, which keeps its people in ignorant bondage, is not the rational and proper order. It was designed by a conspiracy. This conspiracy cannot keep in bondage the informed citizen who refuses to capitulate.

Objectification of the Foe

A second maneuver of the Posse to create power is to name the enemy so that it may be hated efficiently. Political and religious advocates have used terms such as "right-wing extremists," "tree-huggers," or "secular humanists" to name their opponents. Smith (1969) called this technique *objectification* because it involves treating human beings as objects.

To the Posse, as to other white supremacist groups, the major opponent is the Jew. However, the Posse (especially in its earlier years) subsumes a wide spectrum of members. It has no central authority to ensure conformity to any creed, and the nature of the movement encourages individual and autonomous activity. Some members emphasize the racial elements of the Posse's beliefs more than others, while others are more concerned with helping farmers in crisis or resisting an intrusive federal government.

Although some members of the Posse reject bigotry, comments by Wickstrom (1983) confirm that the Posse, as a whole, is anti-Semitic. To eliminate some of the sting of being anti-Semitic, the Posse disassociates itself from Hitler's version of anti-Semitism. Some members deny that the Holocaust happened. They separate themselves from the charge of bigotry by naming themselves *the true Israel* and contemporary Jews as *imposters*. By objectifying its foe, the Posse makes it much easier to fight them. As Wickstrom said during his appearance on *Phil Donahue*, "Citizens have the power and the right to overthrow their oppressors."

Besides objectifying Jews, the Posse also objectifies members of the establishment. For example, in 1983, in Grand Island, Nebraska, Arthur Kirk, a Posse sympathizer, spoke to law enforcement officials by telephone. He referred to the officers on his property as "a bunch of damn striped yellow varmints" and "God damn critters," among other terms. He described his enemies as "the fucking Bank and the Jews," a "slimy . . . bar member," and the Jews who run the banks, nuclear power plants, and have all the power (Kirk, 1983). While the enemy wears many masks, there is one face behind the mask. With his words, though, Kirk killed that foe symbolically even before raising a weapon. A few hours after the conversation, he was killed in a shootout with the "varmints."

Identification Through Creating a Mystery

A third maneuver used by the Posse to constitute power enables it to create internal identification and to bolster its own authority—the creation of its own mystery. The Posse and other extremist groups that use this maneuver are described as *identity* groups (Kay, 1987). Zeskind (1985) explains the identity faith:

> [T]he Ten Lost Tribes of Israel migrated through the centuries and became the peoples of Northern Europe. These Northern Europeans are the people with whom the Lord is supposed to have a Covenant. They believe that Biblical prophecy is being revealed through the history of the Northern Europeans, God's "chosen people," and that America is the land of God's promise. . . . Jews are literally the Children of the Devil and that people of color are "pre-adamic," that is false starts before God made a perfect Adam and Eve. (p. 28)

Thus, by rewriting its past to give its members a sacred heritage, the Posse designs its future (Brown, 1986). This particular history gives the Posse a name—the highest imaginable name—in which to act. It also legitimizes acts of defiance, including murder. Many of the Posse's converts are self-proclaimed conservative Christians who revere the Bible; they know its promises to the Jews and its curses against the enemies of the Jews. The identity story, then, identifies each member with the Jewish heritage, with all its hopes and promises.

Their identity as the true Israel is mingled with a revered secular identity, that of the "true American." The Founding Fathers are their saints, and the Constitution is as sacred as the Bible (Wickstrom, 1983). They name the law of the United States to be *the same as* the law of the Bible. Wickstrom claims that the Constitution and the Bill of Rights are directly from the Bible, and God is the king of the United States. Thus, the Posse transforms the United States into a theocracy in the minds of its members. God's laws are their laws. They will be blessed by following the biblical principles embodied in the Constitution and the Bill of Rights. Consequently, the Posse promotes both religion and patriotism.

Organizing of the Worldview

A fourth maneuver for creating power is the careful organizing of the Posse's ideology, so that its fabric is thick and warm. The survival of a worldview depends on its perceived consistency and comprehensiveness; otherwise, anomalies abound (Brown, 1978). When the comprehensiveness of an ideology is increased, its effectiveness also increases. The Posse's ideology is developed so that it comprehensively accounts for all the evils that trouble its members. One Posse handbook uses the International Jewish Conspiracy to explain busing, Equal Employment Opportunity regulations, minimum wage laws, organized crime, divorce, pornography, degenerate music, abortion, and the military draft (Cunningham, n.d.). Wickstrom (1983) also connects the conspiracy with conflicts in Korea and Vietnam, which he calls "illegal wars for the mineral rights of the Jews."

The Posse presents a network of plausibility that has a place for each element of this chaotic world, bringing some order out of it. Such a worldview is especially attractive to the people the Posse targets—not liberals or minorities, but people who are dissatisfied with a world that is moving too fast, who "don't really want to move into the twenty-first century" (Informant).

Action Corollaries

A fifth maneuver for creating power is the acting out of appropriate behavior that confirms the Posse's beliefs and solidifies its members' commitment to their beliefs. The behavior that follows from taking on a role is what Brown (1970) labels an *action corollary*. Appropriate actions for members include attending meetings and seminars where they purchase religious tracts and tapes, other propaganda, survivalist equipment, and weapons (both legally and illegally) (Informant). Members also march and engage in protests, which demonstrate the numerical power of the members. Other behaviors involve acting out their belief that they alone have the truth; therefore, they emphasize reading to discover more truth. There must be constant growth in "opening your eyes to see what's going on" (Informant).

One prominent belief is the immanency of a cataclysmic confrontation, one that will be precipitated either by divine intervention or by nuclear war. Members respond to this potential crisis by stockpiling food and weapons. When one woman objected to a Posse writer that Christians should let Jesus solve the world's problems, the writer replied, "But folks, we can't solve it that way. Jesus helps those who help themselves" (Cunningham, n.d., p. 90).

Another action corollary flows from the belief that the county sheriff is the highest legal authority. Wickstrom (1983) explains, "The sheriff is the chief executive law enforcement officer of the country." This authority comes from the fact the sheriff is elected directly by the people, rather than appointed to office. The sheriff's responsibilities include serving the people and protecting them from bank foreclosures. In 1986, the Posse sent letters to local sheriffs with the following exhortation:

> The sheriff is duty-bound to preserve and protect *private rights* of the county residents against tyranny of *public wrongs* by public administrators.
> Please consider the above, and put a STOP in your county to the plunder of your county residents by allowing the county attorney (public attorney) to use you and your office for plunder, plunder. (Committee of the states in Congress assembled, 1986, p. 1; emphasis in original)

As an action corollary, then, the Posse's members call on the local sheriff to protect his or her people. Any sheriff who fails to stand up for them against bankers foreclosing on farm property should be removed from office. As a betrayer of the people, the sheriff should be hanged in town at high noon. Some sheriffs have received polite invitations to their own hangings, which, so far, have been only *pro forma*, since the key participant has never shown up (Informant). Nevertheless, perhaps to show respect for the office, perhaps to win some cooperation, sheriffs' departments are on the Posse's mailing list.

Tactics and Strategy

These five prominent maneuvers used by the Posse actualize one of the Posse's tactics: encouraging its audience, the U.S. public, to interpret one or more of three kinds of relationships between power shareholders: relations of *integry*, *exchange*, and *threat*. The shared fear of outsiders and the justifiable threat of infiltration, and the communal joy of sharing an in-joke encourage the members to feel a strong identity with each other, or *integry*. Such conceptions of shared power help cement them together in spite of the strongly individualistic bent among members. They are the elite, the cognoscenti. When Wickstrom (1983) and others try to explain their ideas to interested listeners or potential converts, they frequently use phrases such as, "You have to know," "If you'll look it up," and "Most people are illiterate."

A second tactic is to encourage perceptions of *exchange* between the Posse and the undecided public. The power code of the Posse entails that they reveal "what is going on" to nonmembers and that nonmembers heed their words. In exchange, nonmembers ought to study and then act on what they learn. Posse members believe that many of the public are not evil, but are asleep and need to be awakened.

A third tactic is to encourage perceptions of *threat* from any outsiders who wish to oppress or destroy them. This is one reason Posse members reject the Social Security system, refuse to pay income tax, and drive without a state driver's license. (As law-abiding people, though, they make their own driver's licenses as well as their own notes to replace the money issued by the Federal Reserve Banks.) Another reason to reject the income tax and the Social Security card is that such records make it easy for their persecutors to trace them.

These tactics actualize a grand strategy of encouraging perceived *competitive* relationships between the Jewish conspiracy (including U.S. institutions and government) and "We the people," whether the people are Posse members or are still asleep. This strategy simultaneously fosters perceived *cooperative* relations between the Posse and the public it tries to awaken. When the public refuses to listen, though, and when the pressure from the conspiracy threatens, the public also becomes *competitive* with the Posse. The only recourse for the members facing hostile opposition from a closed-minded public is to quit, engage in violence, or go underground. The next part of this article examines how this actually worked out.

❖   POWER AS A MEDIUM OF COMMUNICATION

The first part of this essay highlighted the symbolic creation and attribution of power through the communication of the group. Power was treated as the *content* of communication. The second part considers the use of power as a *medium* of communication, particularly communication about roles and relationships. The power code symbolically constituted by the Posse now can be seen as prompting decisions without engaging in deliberations in the usual sense. It regulates relations among three major power shareholders—the Posse Comitatus, the Zionist Occupational Government (ZOG), and the "sleeping" public.

First, there is the Posse itself. Its share of power shapes the members' social role. They act out their roles in various ways. For example, by harassing minorities they communicate their view of racial *hierarchy*. These acts of reprisal communicate their justified *indignation*. The non-sensed relationship of threat between the Posse and ZOG becomes sensible in the members' stockpiling of arms and food.

By calling on sheriffs to fulfill their responsibilities and by ignoring or despising other law enforcement agents, they communicate their sense of *order*. By avoiding income taxes, they communicate a rejection of the establishment. By sharing written handouts with the public and by interpersonal proselytizing, they communicate their *sincerity* and the transparent value of their cause.

The second role in the perceived social system is that of the establishment or, as it is called by some in the Posse, ZOG. Posse members are shut out from this establishment both by their own choice and by that of their opponents. Members of the establishment are deceptive, greedy, and satanic.

Through guile, however, the Posse can use the oppressors' methods against them. For example, even though media treatment is usually unsympathetic and hostile, the Posse may stage media events in such a way that they cannot be ignored. In addition, because the court system and the lawyers obfuscate the law, the Posse clogs up the courts by initiating frivolous lawsuits—more than 100 cases in one week in Wisconsin, for example. The "jailhouse-lawyer" expertise of some members, they believe, gives them exceptional advantages in court. One informant says he drives at any speed he wishes on the interstate because "the Highway Patrol is afraid to stop me" (Informant).

The third power share belongs to the "sleeping public," or white citizens. Although born of a superior race, they have been brainwashed by the establishment and so are ignorant of their identity and power. These citizens have a glorious potential because of their racial heritage and their constitutional rights. They need only to be instructed and motivated in order to act properly. The Posse's power code reduces the complexity of being white at the end of the twentieth century. By joining hands with the Posse, these citizens demonstrate heroism.

The history of the Posse Comitatus may be summarized as a story of changing power messages. In the early 1980s, the movement, centered in the Midwest, grew without interference. There was little threat from either law enforcement or intelligence agencies, because the suspicion and sensitivity of the Watergate Era had a chilling effect (Singer & Moore, 1982). The farm crisis provided a need for the Posse to address. Low interest rates in the 1970s encouraged farmers to borrow more than was prudent. However, the overproduction of the early 1980s, as well as tightening of foreign markets, brought disaster. The result was that, by 1984, "farming households earned only about 80 percent as much as the national average, compared with their historic high in 1973 when they earned almost 50 percent more than the national average" (Harrington & Carlin, 1987, p. 4).

The Posse realized its opportunity. "The Posse," says Wickstrom (1983), "is the result of people being out of work and rising crime and the increase in illegal aliens." The public seemed more open to the message of the Posse, especially when its populist theme was highlighted and its racism backgrounded (Singer & Moore, 1982). Wickstrom and other leaders traveled around the country, holding seminars that were more or less open to the public. Wickstrom appeared on *Phil Donahue* and on *The Larry King Show*. The movement also enjoyed some success— it stopped a farm foreclosure through an armed but peaceful protest in Macon, Georgia. Members expected the sheriff's department to provide security at a 1986 conference held in Kearney, Nebraska. There appeared to be increasingly cooperative relations between the Posse and the public. By the time of the convention, however, the convention motel reneged, and the sheriff refused to cooperate and provide security.

The role of the Posse, though, entailed more than good pubic relations. Its beliefs impelled members to engage in more vigorous activism. Several shoot-outs and fugitive hunts invited frightening and negative publicity from the media. The Anti-Defamation League, sensitive to the movement's anti-Semitism, poured out reports on the bigotry of the Posse and its allies. Law enforcement agencies paid more serious attention to the Posse, perceiving that the movement might expand its base of operation by winning public approval and even public office. One speaker at the Kearney convention, Everett Sileven, ran for governor of Nebraska (Levitas, 2002).

Surveillance of the Posse increased. Income tax protestors were arrested. Shortly before the meeting in Kearney, Arthur Kirk was killed. Pressure from Jewish and other protestors against the Posse encouraged the Holiday Inn to cancel its contract to host the convention. Hostile media coverage continued, and academic researchers began to study the Posse (Baker & Bode, 1990; Kay, 1987; Rendahl, 1989, 1990, 1991; Snyder, 1989).

In short, the establishment brought serious sanctions to bear on the Posse when it attempted to challenge the social order. Such behavior disconfirmed the legitimacy of the Posse in the eyes of the public. Among its members, though, persecution confirmed their suspicions of a conspiracy, and many of them gloried in it, now that they had their own martyrs. Still, the membership was affected. One informant says that after the FBI closed the encampment of The Covenant, Sword, and Arm of the Lord on the Arkansas-Missouri border, "The Posse began to die down right then" (Informant).

The public had been open to the Posse's messages about injustices perpetrated against farmers and about illegal taxes and government intrusion, such as gun control. However, as the labels of *racist* and *violent* seemed to fit the Posse, many audience members turned away from the group. Given the worldview of most of its listeners, such names created uncomfortable gaps. The public became less open to the Posse than when it seemed to be a *farming support movement*. Many sympathizers now found the Posse too radical, so they tried to solve their own problems informally, sometimes by starting new organizations, such as the informal yet effectively organized Pro Se Movement, which helped people in trouble defend themselves in the courts. In such a movement, practical political action is featured and, if any members cherish a racist ideology, it is backgrounded. Thus, the relationship between the Posse and the public came to be a *competitive* one.

This is where the Posse stands as of the writing of this essay. Pruned of its moderate members, the radical members have gone underground (Informants). They have solidified and seem to be situated largely in isolated encampments, more insulated than ever from the hostile establishment and the suspicious public. They pass their time training themselves and their young, storing provisions and weapons, perhaps engaging in criminal actions such as growing marijuana to raise money, and waiting for the holocaust (Informant). They have been confirmed in their insular beliefs by the bloody installation of several members in their pantheon of martyrs and by the actions of government agents against them.

The less radical and militant members may change their names, perhaps joining other organizations, such as the short-lived Montana Freemen or Save Our Land in Washington state. They can start their work anew without the stigma attached to the name of the Posse, but the message will no doubt be the same (Informant). As one member says, "The system tries to destroy our family, but we're building a new one right under their noses" (Informant).

Overall, the Posse appealed to rural Americans, reaching with surprising success people who were traditionally individualistic and self-sufficient—and unlikely to join such a group. Its appeal was based on its ability to create power relationships through its communication. Primarily, the Posse encouraged audience members to perceive themselves as in competition with the forces that oppress them, specifically a Jewish conspiracy embodied in the banking system and in the Zionist Occupational Government (the federal government). At the same time, people were encouraged to see the Posse as an organization that cooperated with rural white Americans to help them with their problems. The Posse then used the power attributed to it by its listeners to communicate about the relationships it had posited, including how people should act according to their roles. The RSI model has highlighted these strategies and provided a viewpoint from which to construct a history of the movement's rise, collapse, and continued survival.

❖ CONCLUDING OBSERVATIONS

If Posse members change their name in order to continue their activity or find some new need for which they have a solution (as the Aryan Nations did by offering a strong heroic identity to skinhead computer hackers), or both, they may again intervene in the U.S. social system and carve out some share of power for themselves. But it will not be in the same place and in the same way again. Today, corporations more than banks threaten to take over family farms. To meet the needs of rural folk for legal assistance, other organizations have arisen, such as the Prairie Fire Rural Action, which offers help within the system through sympathetic and skilled lawyers, deliberately offering an alternative to conspiracy theorists.

On October 17, 2006, Public Law 109–364 effectively did away with the provisions of the Posse Comitatus law. Nevertheless, in 2007, the Posse still exists, though it is much less public than it was in the 1980s. There are rumors that the Posse and similar groups, such as the Aryan Nations, are in sympathy with al-Qaeda, all united in their hatred of Israel and of the U.S. federal government (Michael, 2003). Even though the Posse may be underground at the moment, its attempted interventions in the 1970s and 1980s had effects. Levitas (2002) notes that the Posse and allied tax-protest groups influenced the public's attitudes about the IRS enough to lead to the congressional overhaul of the IRS in 1995 and 1997, which "cost as much as $300 billion in lost tax revenues" (Levitas, pp. 327–328). Another effect of the tax protests is that a federal jury found not guilty an attorney who had not paid income taxes for more than ten years. It unanimously agreed that the IRS had not proved its right to collect income taxes on personal labor (Wilson, 2007).

By using the RSI model, this essay has shown how a group may obtain symbolic power by giving it to others. This power may be used both to reallocate power shares of various actors in a system and to redefine relationships among these power shareholders. Such interventions offer justice, influence, and independence, certainly parts of the American Dream. They may fail, though, if achieving those goals requires their audience members to give up other elements of the dream, such as tolerance, equality, and nonviolence.

❖ REFERENCES

Baker, G. A., & Bode, R. A. (1990). The survivalist right's rhetorical justification of violence. *North Dakota Journal of Speech and Theatre, 3*(1), 45–56.

Barker, W. E. (1986). *The Aryan Nations: A linkage profile.* Unpublished manuscript.

Brown, W. R. (1970). *Imagemaker: Will Rogers and the American dream.* Columbia: University of Missouri Press.

Brown, W. R. (1978). Ideology as communication process. *Quarterly Journal of Speech, 64,* 123–140.

Brown, W. R. (1986). Power and the rhetoric of social intervention. *Communication Monographs, 53,* 180–199.

Cunningham, D. (n.d.). *U.S. citizen's handbook for justice.* Unpublished manuscript.

Committee of the states in Congress assembled. (1986, March). Letter and notices sent to a Nebraska sheriff's office, from Lodi, CA.

Duncan, H. D. (1968). *Symbols in society.* London: Oxford University Press.

Harrington, D., & Carlin, T. A. (1987). The U.S. farm sector: How is it weathering the 1980's? *Agriculture Information Bulletin No. 506.* Washington, DC: U.S. Government Printing Office. (ERIC Document Reproduction Service No. ED280998).

Kay, J. (1987). Arguing for and against a white homeland: The Aryan World Congress versus the Kootenai County Task Force of Human Relations. In J. Wenzel (Ed.), *Argumentation and critical practices: Proceedings of the fifth SCA/AFA Conference of Argumentation* (pp. 533–540). Annandale, VA: Speech Communication Association.

Kirk, A. (1983). Telephone conversation. Tape recording provided by Informant.

Levitas, D. (2002). *The terrorist next door: The militia movement and the radical right.* New York: Thomas Dunne Books.

Michael, G. (2003). *Confronting right-wing extremism and terrorism in the USA.* New York: Routledge.

Posse by law of Posse Comitatus. (n.d). Unpublished manuscript. Tigerton, WI.

Rendahl, S. (1989). Gordon Kahl's demonic rhetoric. *North Dakota Journal of Speech and Theatre, 2,* 4–10.

Rendahl, S. (1990). The rhetoric of Oklahoma Fest: White supremacist attacks on society. *North Dakota Journal of Speech and Theatre, 3,* 26–33.

Rendahl, S. (1991). White Aryan resistance: A radical communication system. *North Dakota Journal of Speech and Theatre, 4,* 44–52.

Riley, P., Hollihan, T., & Klumpp, J. F. (1998). The dark side of community and democracy: Militias, patriots, and angry white guys. In. J. F. Klumpp (Ed.), *Argument in a time of change: Definitions, theories, and critiques* (pp. 202–207). Annandale, VA: National Communication Association.

Singer, D., & Moore, R. (1982, July 25). Of families, "supremacy," and survival. *Kansas City Star,* pp. 1, 12, 13.

Smith, A. (1969). *Rhetoric of Black revolution.* Boston: Allyn & Bacon.

Snyder, L. (1989). Born to power: The rhetoric of the Posse Comitatus. Paper presented at the Central States Speech Convention. Kansas City, MO.

Wickstrom, J. (Guest). (1983, February 23). *The Phil Donahue Show* [Television broadcast, Donahue Transcript #02233]. Chicago, IL: WBBM-TV.

Wilson, L. (2007, July 13). Local attorney acquitted on federal income tax charges. *The Shreveport Times.* Retrieved July 13, 2007, from http://www.shreveport times.com/apps/pbcs.dll/article?AID=2007707130321.

Zeskind, L. (1985). The far right. *Shmate, 11–12,* 25–32.

Reflections

Dr. Lee Snyder (1949–2008) was a professor of Communication at the University of Nebraska at Kearney.

I first heard of the Posse Comitatus on the way back to Nebraska from the 1986 National Communication Association Convention. The *Chicago Tribune* had run a full-page report covering the trial of white-supremacist cult members, who were accused of torturing and killing an adult male and a five-year-old boy. Back home, colleagues told me of the Posse Comitatus conference that had convened in Kearney in January 1986. Later, a farmer told me that the Posse frequently distributed tracts and handbills at farm auctions. Finally, a nontraditional student who had unusual access to primary sources wrote a paper on an incident involving a Posse member.

These events inspired my rhetorical study of the Posse. I hoped to understand the riddle of the attraction and influence of the cult, beyond the sociological folk wisdom that states that troubled times encourage bizarre behavior. Specifically, I wondered how an organization could achieve a great deal of success in enlisting farmers and ranchers, not known for joining organizations. I presented an early version of this essay at the 1989 Central States Speech convention.

1. Snyder conducted interviews with Posse informants and collected information written by Posse associates. What might be the strengths and limitations of relying on this type of symbolizing activity to interpret an organization's intervention?

2. How does the use of the RSI model enable Snyder to identify communication patterns that might attract people to the Posse who otherwise might find its worldview repugnant?

3. Snyder suggests that if the Posse constitutes a new need that it can meet, it might again intervene and regain some share of power. What contemporary needs potentially could promote this shift? How might the RSI model be used to track changes in an organization's power share?

4. How does Snyder's essay meet or fail to meet expectancies associated with a critical essay?

Glossary

abstract: to attend to some aspects of experience to form sensory and symbolic categories

advocacy: a needs-intervention tactic that involves communicating needs to persons or groups that might be able to satisfy those needs

American dream: an example of a U.S. ideology in which participants assume a more nearly perfect and ideal world can be achieved

anomaly: an apparent difference between symbolically constituted expectancies about experience and lived experience

anomaly-featuring communication: an attention-intervention strategy that directs attention to or emphasizes apparent anomalies in naming patterns

anomaly-masking communication: an attention-intervention strategy that directs attention away from or de-emphasizes apparent anomalies in naming patterns

attention: to create an interpretation of experience by foregrounding and backgrounding aspects of experience

attention intervention: an attempt rhetorically to encourage or discourage the adoption of an alternative interpretation of the events and actions of daily experience

attention shift: *See* attention switch

attention switch: to shift from one interpretation for experience to another interpretation that compensates for apparent anomalies

attribute: a feature or a characteristic of experience that is interpreted as varying from experience to experience

attribution: a needs-intervention tactic that involves communicating to others what they do and do not need

background: to direct attention away from aspects of experience

being: an attention-intervention tactic that involves communicating about ontological assumptions about experience

biosocial needs: biological and social givens that must be fulfilled for growth and survival

category: a range of different experiences that are treated as if they were the same

closed-channel behavior: a needs-intervention tactic that involves reduced communication toward potential needs-meeters or the lack of response from potential needs-meeters

code switching: the symbolic-to-reality transformation in which an internal symbolic category is treated as if it has external existence and an external experience as if it were a symbolic category

collectivity-stressing: a needs-intervention strategy that emphasizes group-oriented needs

competition: a power-intervention strategy that involves challenging a symbolically constituted social hierarchy by offering a competing interpretation of interdependency or power code

complementary: a relationship that is constituted by emphasizing the differences in social identity between self and other

complex name: a symbolic category created by relating together several symbolic categories

cooperation: a power-intervention strategy that involves maintaining a symbolically constituted social hierarchy by enacting the accepted interpretation of interdependency or power code

criterial attribute: an attribute that makes a difference in how experience is symbolically categorized

deviance: the difference between a name-generated expectancy about experience and lived experience

deviance amplifying: symbolizing activity that increases attention to anomalies in naming patterns

deviance compensating: symbolizing activity that reduces attention to anomalies in naming patterns

exchange: a power-intervention tactic that involves constituting an interdependency that is motivated by the expectancy of "I will do this for you if you will do this for me"

foreground: to direct attention to aspects of experience

future choosing: making decisions and selecting futures on the basis of power code

holographic: to reflect the characteristics of a hologram in which the parts contain the whole and the whole contains the parts

holistic: to be interconnected, interdependent, and interrelated

ideological system: a superordinate system of comprehensive meaning that emerges from the interaction of the need, power, and attention subsystems

ideology: an ultimate, superordinate name for comprehensive experience that is generated from and shapes the symbolic categorization of experience

individuality-stressing: a needs-intervention strategy that emphasizes individual needs

integry: a power-intervention tactic that involves constituting an interdependency that is motivated by the expectancy of "I will do this because of who or what I am, and because of who or what you are"

intervener: a person or group that enacts interventions

intervention: a communicative act that attempts to promote or prevent change in a social system's interpretations of needs, interdependencies, and the events and actions of experience

knowing: an attention-intervention tactic that involves communicating about epistemological assumptions about experience

language tutor: a person who teaches the language community's symbols and its way of symbolically categorizing experience

maneuver: an intervener's specific actions and messages that enact the tactics and strategies of an intervention

mixed: an interdependency that entails both cooperative and competitive behaviors

naming: the process of transforming sensed and non-sensed experience into symbols, such as words and stories

need intervention: an attempt rhetorically to encourage or discourage the adoption of an alternative interpretation of needs

needs-meeters: individuals and groups that are interpreted to have the potential to satisfy needs

negotiate: to discuss and agree on the organization of experience into symbolic categories and the symbols to use to represent those categories

open-channel behavior: a needs-intervention tactic that involves increased communication toward potential needs-meeters or a response from potential needs-meeters

power: the degree to which a person or group feels interdependent with others in the system for meeting needs and choosing futures

power code: the behavioral expectancies associated with a particular interdependency that influence choices when choosing futures

power intervention: an attempt rhetorically to encourage or discourage the adoption of an alternative interpretation of power-sharing interdependency or power code

power share: the share or responsibility in the choosing of futures attributed to individuals or groups in the system

ratify: to recognize and agree to enact the expectancies associated with a naming pattern

reciprocal: a relationship that is constituted by emphasizing the shared social identity between self and other

reify: to make real, to act as if a symbolically constructed interpretation of experience exists

rhetoric: the creation and study of meaningful symbols that symbolically constitute reality

rhetoric of social intervention: communication that creates, maintains, and changes a social system's symbolic reality

rhetorical artifacts: written, spoken, and/or visual symbolizing activity that communicates an intervener's strategy, tactics, and maneuvers

rhetorical criticism: a systematic method for investigating the patterns of symbolizing activity

rhetorical reasoning: to advocate a proposed name for experience by explaining the criterial attributes that support the appropriateness of the proposed name for experience

sanction: power-holder action that attempts to force compliance with the power code

sensory categorization: the process of attending to and selecting sensory experience and organizing that sensory data into shape and form categories

social system: a structure of human interconnections that appears to have order and pattern

strategy: the overarching communication pattern of an intervention, which is actualized in tactics and maneuvers

subsystem: a system component that is itself a system

superordinate: to be superior to or more abstract than, to encompass less-abstract categories

symbol: a word that a social system agrees stands for or represents a particular categorization of experience

symbolic categorization: the process of abstracting details from sensed and non-sensed experience and transforming those details into symbolic categories

symbolic reality: a symbolically created interpretation of experience

symbolically categorize: to name or transform sensed and non-sensed experience into symbols

symbolically created needs: needs that are created in communication with one another

symbolizing activity: written, spoken, or visual communication

system: a structure and process of interconnections that appear to exhibit order and pattern

tactic: an intervener's plan for increasing or decreasing the system's attention to anomalies and disorder when promoting or impeding need, power, and attention shifts

threat: a power-intervention tactic that involves constituting an inter-dependency that is motivated by the expectancy of "If you don't do this for me, then I will do this to you"

trend reversal: to rhetorically reverse or halt the tendency toward deviance-amplifying communication patterns

valuing: an attention-intervention tactic that involves communicating about axiological assumptions about experience

vicious circle: a pattern in which system components interact with each another in a way that amplifies system deviance and can lead to system breakdown

Additional Readings

RSI-Related Works by William R. Brown

Brown, W. R. (1970). *Imagemaker: Will Rogers and the American dream*. Columbia: University of Missouri Press.

Brown, W. R. (1978). Ideology as communication process. *Quarterly Journal of Speech*, *64*(2), 123–140.

Brown, W. R. (1982). Attention and the rhetoric of social intervention. *Quarterly Journal of Speech*, *68*(1), 17–27.

Brown, W. R. (1983). The televised Watergate hearings: A case study in information overload. In J. L. Golden, G. F. Berquist, & W. E. Coleman (Eds.), *The rhetoric of western thought* (pp. 229–238). Dubuque, IA: Kendall/Hunt.

Brown, W. R. (1985). Mass media and society: The development of critical perspectives. In T. Benson (Ed.), *Speech communication in the twentieth century* (pp. 196–220). Carbondale: Southern Illinois University Press.

Brown, W. R. (1985, January). Publish what? *Journal of the Association for Communication Administration*, *51*, 30–34.

Brown, W. R. (1986). Power and the rhetoric of social intervention. *Communication Monographs*, *53*(2), 180–199.

Brown, W. R. (1987). The holographic view of argument. *Argumentation*, *1*, 89–102.

Brown, W. R. (1990). Classical argument, dialectics, and trialectics. In R. Trapp & J. Schuetz (Eds.), *Perspectives on argumentation: Essays in honor of Wayne Brockriede* (pp. 190–206). Prospect Heights, IL: Waveland.

Claussen, E. N., & Brown, W. R. (1974). Making present the past: Public address history. *Quarterly Journal of Speech*, *60*(2), 237–240.

Makay, J., & Brown, W. (1972). *The rhetorical dialogue: Contemporary concepts and cases*. Dubuque, IA: Wm. C. Brown.

Works Using the RSI Model: Books and Book Chapters

Huang, S. (1996). *To rebel is justified: A rhetorical study of China's cultural revolution movement, 1966–1969*. Lanham, MD: University Press of America.

Opt, S. K. (2003). Organizational change: An attention-switching view. In J. Biberman & A. Alkhafaji (Eds.), *Business research yearbook: Global business perspectives* (pp. 773–777). Saline, MI: McNaughton & Gunn.

Opt, S. K. (2008). Public relations and the rhetoric of social intervention. In T. L. Hansen-Horn & B. Dostal Neff (Eds.), *Public relations: From theory to practice* (pp. 227–241). Boston: Pearson Education.

Snyder, L. (2004). The church in the post-post-modern world: Communicating the holographic faith. In E. Johnson (Ed.), *Selected proceedings of the 2004 conference of faith and communication* (pp. 94–100). Buies Creek, NC: Campbell University.

Snyder, L. (2004). The rhetoric of transcendence in the book of Revelation. In J. D. Hester & J. D. Hester (Eds.), *Rhetorics and hermeneutics: Wilhelm Wuellner and his influence, Emory studies in early Christianity* (pp. 193–217). New York: T & T Clark International.

Works Using the RSI Model: Journal Articles

Gonzalez, A. (1989, Fall). "Participation" at WMEX-FM: Interventional rhetoric of Ohio Mexican Americans. *Western Journal of Speech Communication, 53,* 398–410.

Gring, M. A. (1998). Attention, power, and need: The rhetoric of religion and revolution in Nicaragua. *World Communication Journal, 27*(4), 27–37.

Keith, S. (2006). Abigail Scott Duniway: The rhetoric of intervention and the new northwest. *Texas Speech Communication Journal, 30*(2), 146–157.

Leroux, N. (1991, Spring). Frederick Douglass and the attention-shift. *Rhetoric Society Quarterly, 21,* 36–46.

Opt, S. K. (1988). Continuity and change in storytelling about artificial intelligence: Extending the narrative paradigm. *Communication Quarterly, 36*(4), 298–310.

Opt, S. K. (1996). American frontier myth and the flight of Apollo 13: From news event to feature film. *Film and History Journal, 26*(1–4), 40–51.

Opt, S. K. (1997). The Earth Summit: Maintaining cultural myth. *Journal of the Northwest Communication Association, 25,* 1–22.

Opt, S. K. (1998). Confirming and disconfirming American myth: Stories in and about the suggestion box. *Communication Quarterly, 46*(1), 75–87.

Opt, S. K. (1999). Early computer advertising: Resolving mythic tensions. *Journal of the Northwest Communication Association, 27,* 1–20.

Opt, S. K. (2001). The search for paradise: Rise and fall of the Houston Astrodome. *Texas Speech Communication Journal, XXVI,* 13–22.

Snyder, L. (1999, September). Apologetics before and after postmodernism. *Journal of Communication and Religion, 22,* 237–271.

Snyder, L. (2000). Invitation to transcendence: The *book of Revelation. Quarterly Journal of Speech, 86*(4), 402–416.

Snyder, L. (2005, Fall). Argument as intervention in the Revelation of John: A rhetorical analysis. *Stone-Campbell Journal, 8,* 245–259.

Stoner, M. R. (1989). Understanding social movement rhetoric as social intervention. *Speech Communication Annual, 3,* 27–43.

Works Using the RSI Model: Dissertations

Anderson, R. E. (1983). The symbolic processing of continuity and change using the case of Carl F. H. Henry. (Doctoral dissertation, The Ohio State University, 1983). *Dissertation Abstracts International, 44* (09A), 2620.

Baker, J. W. (1991). The hope of intervention: A rhetorical analysis of the English translations of the writings of Jacques Ellul. (Doctoral dissertation, The Ohio State University, 1991). *Dissertation Abstracts International, 52* (11A), 3766.

Corley, J. R. (1983). A communication study of Arthur F. Holmes as a worldview advocate. (Doctoral dissertation, The Ohio State University, 1983). *Dissertation Abstracts International, 44* (11A), 3204.

Grindstaff, R. A. (1990). The institutionalization of Aimee Semple McPherson: A study in the rhetoric of social intervention. (Doctoral dissertation, The Ohio State University, 1990). *Dissertation Abstracts International, 51* (07A), 2190.

Gring, M. A. (1993). Rhetoric and ideology: An analysis of interaction among epistemology, praxis, and power. (Doctoral dissertation, The Ohio State University, 1993). *Dissertation Abstracts International, 54* (12A), 4305.

Huang, S. (1994). To rebel is justified: A rhetorical study of China's cultural revolution movement, 1966–1969. (Doctoral dissertation, Bowling Green State University, 1994). *Dissertation Abstracts International, 56* (04A), 1183.

Lopez, J. M. (1985). Rhetoric of national development policy making: The "ideology of national development" and administration of President Juscelino Kubitschek of Brazil during 1956–1958. (Doctoral dissertation, The Ohio State University, 1985). *Dissertation Absracts International, 46* (03A), 0546.

Martycz, V. K. (1991). Identification as process: A rhetorical study of three televangelists as social intervenors. (Doctoral dissertation, The Ohio State University, 1991). *Dissertation Abstracts International, 52* (05A), 1573.

Opt, S. K. (1987). Popular discourse on expert systems: Communication patterns in the acculturation of an artificial intelligence innovation. (Doctoral dissertation, The Ohio State University, 1987). *Dissertation Abstracts International, 48* (09A), 2194.

Pondozzi, J. (1988). The case for identity creation: Reproductive technology and the rhetoric of social intervention. (Doctoral dissertation, The Ohio State University, 1988). *Dissertation Abstracts International, 49* (04A), 0659.

Simon, A. M. (1986). The upward way: The rhetoric of transcendence in the Unity School of Christianity. (Doctoral dissertation, The Ohio State University, 1986). *Dissertation Abstracts International, 47* (03A), 0711.

Snyder, L. L. (1987). Alexander Campbell as a change-agent in the Stone-Campbell movement from 1830–1840. (Doctoral dissertation, The Ohio State University, 1987). *Dissertation Abstracts International, 48* (05A), 1057.

Stoner, M. R. (1987). The free speech movement: A case study in the rhetoric of social intervention. (Doctoral dissertation, The Ohio State University, 1987). *Dissertation Abstracts International, 49* (02A), 0167.

References

Aristotle. (2007). *Aristotle on rhetoric: A theory of civic discourse* (G. A. Kennedy, Trans.). New York: Oxford University Press.

Banner, D. (1994). *Designing effective organizations: Traditional and transformational views*. Thousand Oaks, CA: Sage.

Beebe, S. A., & Beebe, S. J. (2006). *Public speaking: An audience-centered approach*. Boston: Allyn & Bacon.

Bekenstein, J. D. (2003, August). Information in the holographic universe. *Scientific American, 289*(2), 58–76.

Berger, P. L., & Luckmann, T. (1966). *The social construction of reality: A treatise in the sociology of knowledge*. Garden City, NY: Anchor Books.

Bergquist, W. (1993). *The postmodern organization: Mastering the art of irreversible change*. San Francisco: Jossey-Bass.

Bishop, R. L., & Kilburn, J. (1971). Penny whistle or public's advocate? *Public Relations Quarterly, 16*(4), 7–9.

Bohm, D. (2002). *Wholeness and implicate order*. New York: Routledge Classics.

Bormann, E. (1985). *The forces of fantasy*. Carbondale: Southern Illinois University Press.

Boulding, K. (1978). *Ecodynamics: A new theory of societal evolution*. Beverly Hills, CA: Sage.

Boulding, K. (1985). *The world as a total system*. Beverly Hills, CA: Sage.

Brown, R. (1958). *Words and things*. New York, NY: Free Press.

Brown, W. R. (1970). *Imagemaker: Will Rogers and the American dream*. Columbia: University of Missouri Press.

Brown, W. R. (1978). Ideology as communication process. *Quarterly Journal of Speech, 64*(2), 123–140.

Brown, W. R. (1982). Attention and the rhetoric of social intervention. *Quarterly Journal of Speech, 68*(1), 17–27.

Brown, W. R. (1986). Power and the rhetoric of social intervention. *Communication Monographs, 53*(2), 180–199.

Brown, W. R. (1987). Need and the rhetoric of social intervention. Unpublished manuscript, The Ohio State University.

Brummett, B. (2006). *Rhetoric in popular culture*. Thousand Oaks, CA: Sage.

Bruner, J. S., Goodnow, J. J., & Austin, G. A. (1965). *A study of thinking*. New York: John Wiley & Sons, Inc.

Burke, K. (1966). *Language as symbolic action*. Berkeley: University of California Press.

Cherwitz, R. A., & Hikins, J. W. (1986). *Communication and knowledge: An investigation in rhetorical epistemology*. Columbia: University of South Carolina Press.

Corley, J. R. (1983). A communication study of Arthur F. Holmes as a worldview advocate. (Doctoral dissertation, The Ohio State University, 1983). *Dissertation Abstracts International, 44* (11A), 3204.

de Toledano, R. (1975). *Hit & run: The rise–and fall?–of Ralph Nader*. New Rochelle, NY: Arlington House.

Dyson, M. E. (2005, September 23). *Some of us are in first class, but the plane is in trouble*. Speech presented at the 2005 Unvarnished Truth Awards in Washington, DC. Transcript retrieved February 4, 2007, from http://www.democracy now.org/article.pl?sid=05/10/14/1353201.

Eisenberg, E., & Goodall, Jr., H. L. (1997). *Organizational communication: Balancing contraint and creativity*. New York: St. Martin's Press.

Foss, S. K. (2004). *Rhetorical criticism: Exploration and practice*. Long Grove, IL: Waveland Press.

Gring, M. A. (1993). Rhetoric and ideology: An analysis of interaction among epistemology, praxis, and power. (Doctoral dissertation, The Ohio State University, 1993). *Dissertation Abstracts International, 54* (12A), 4305.

Gring, M. A. (1998). Attention, power, and need: The rhetoric of religion and revolution in Nicaragua. *World Communication Journal, 27*(4), 27–37.

Gring, M. A. (2006). Epistemic and pedagogical assumptions in informative and persuasive speaking: Disinterring the dichotomy. *Argumentation and Advocacy: The Journal of the American Forensic Association, 43*, 41–49.

Hanson, B. G. (1995). *General systems theory: Beginning with wholes*. Washington, DC: Taylor & Francis.

Holtzhausen, D. (2000). Postmodern values in public relations. *Journal of Public Relations Research, 12*(1), 93–114.

Johnson, W. (1946). *People in quandaries*. New York: Harper & Brothers.

Johnston, S. F. (2006). *Holographic visions: A history of new science*. New York: Oxford University Press.

Keil, F. C. (2005). The cradle of categorization: Supporting fragile internal knowledge through commerce with culture and the world. In W.K. Ahn, R. Goldstone, B. Love, A. Markman, & P. Wolff (Eds.), *Categorization inside and outside the laboratory: Essays in honor of Douglas L. Medin* (pp. 289–302). Washington, DC: American Psychological Association.

Kochan, T. A. (2006). *Restoring the American dream: A working families' agenda for America*. Cambridge: MIT Press.

Kövecses, Z. (2006). *Language, mind, and culture: A practical introduction*. New York: Oxford University Press.

Kuhn, T. (1996). *The structure of scientific revolution*. Chicago: University of Chicago Press.

Langer, S. (1980). *Philosophy in a new key: A study in the symbolism of reason, rite, and art*. Cambridge, MA: Harvard University Press.

Laszlo, E. (1972). *The systems view of the world*. New York: George Braziller.

Leach, E. (1976). *Culture and communication: The logic by which symbols are connected*. Cambridge: Cambridge University Press.

Luhmann, N. (1979). *Trust and power*. Chichester, England: John Wiley & Sons.

Makay, J., & Brown, W. (1972). *The rhetorical dialogue: Contemporary concepts and cases*. Dubuque, IA: Wm. C. Brown.

Martin, J. (2002). *Nader: Crusader, spoiler, icon*. Cambridge, MA: Perseus.

Maslow, A. H. (1998). *Toward a psychology of being*. New York: John Wiley & Sons.

McCarry, C. (1972). *Citizen Nader*. New York: Saturday Review Press.

Nadel, M. (1971). *The politics of consumer protection*. Indianapolis: Bobbs-Merrill.

Nader, R. (1965). *Unsafe at any speed: The designed-in dangers of the American automobile*. New York: Grossman.

Nickerson, D., & Newhall, S. M. (1943). A psychological color solid. *Journal of the Optical Society of America, 33*(7), 419–422.

Nimmo, D., & Combs, J. (1980). *Subliminal politics*. Englewood Cliffs, NJ: Prentice-Hall.

Obama, B. (2006). *The audacity of hope: Thoughts on reclaiming the American dream*. New York: Crown.

Opt, S. K. (1997). The Earth Summit: Maintaining cultural myth. *Journal of the Northwest Communication Association, 25*, 1–22.

Opt, S. K. (1998). Confirming and disconfirming American myth: Stories in and about the suggestion box. *Communication Quarterly, 46*(1), 75–87.

Opt, S. K. (2003). Organizational change: An attention-switching view. In J. Biberman & A. Alkhafaji (Eds.), *Business research yearbook: Global business perspectives* (pp. 773–777). Saline, MI: McNaughton & Gunn.

Opt, S. K. (2008). Public relations and the rhetoric of social intervention. In T. L. Hansen-Horn & B. Dostal Neff (Eds.), *Public relations: From theory to practice* (pp. 227–241). Boston: Pearson Education.

Pinker, S. (2007). *The stuff of thought: Language as a window into human nature*. New York: Viking.

Pondozzi, J. (1988). The case for identity creation: Reproductive technology and the rhetoric of social intervention. (Doctoral dissertation, The Ohio State University, 1988). *Dissertation Abstracts International, 49* (04A), 0659.

Pribram, K. (1971). *Languages of the brain*. New York: Prentice-Hall.

Robertson, J. O. (1980). *American myth, American reality*. New York: Hill & Wang.

Rosenhan, D. L. (1984). On being sane in insane places. In P. Watzlawick (Ed.), *The invented reality* (pp. 117–144). New York: W.W. Norton.

Scheidel, T. M. (1976). *Speech communication and human interaction*. Glenview, IL: Scott, Foresman.

Sillars, M., & Gronbeck, B. (2001). *Communication criticism: Rhetoric, social codes, cultural studies*. Prospect Heights, IL: Waveland.

Skyttner, L. (1996). *General systems theory: An introduction*. London: Macmillan.

Stein, H. H. (1990). American muckraking of technology since 1900. *Journalism Quarterly, 67*(2), 401–409.

Susskind, L., & Lindesay, J. (2005). *An introduction to black holes, information and the string theory revolution: The holographic universe*. Singapore: World Scientific Publishing.

Swanson, D. (1977a). The reflective view of the epistemology of critical inquiry. *Communication Monographs, 44*(3), 207–219.

Swanson, D. (1977b). The requirements of critical justifications. *Communication Monographs, 44*(4), 306–320.

Talbot, M. (1992). *The holographic universe*. New York: HarperPerennial.

Tomasello, M. (2003). The key is social cognition. In D. Gentner & S. Goldin-Meadow (Eds.), *Language in the mind: Advances in the study of language and thought* (pp. 47–57). Cambridge: MIT Press.

Wagner, R. (2001). *An anthropology of the subject: Holographic worldview in New Guinea and its meaning and significance for the world of anthropology*. Berkeley: University of California Press.

Watzlawick, P. (1990). *Münchhausen's pigtail: Or psychotherapy & "reality" essays and lectures*. New York: W.W. Norton.

Wilbur, K. (1982). *The holographic paradigm and other paradoxes*. Boston: Shambhala.

Woodward, A. L. (2004). Infants' use of action knowledge to get a grasp on words. In D. G. Hall & S. R. Waxman (Eds.), *Weaving a lexicon* (pp. 149–172). Cambridge: MIT Press.

Index

About the Authors

Susan Opt (Ph.D. & M.A., The Ohio State University; B.F.A., Wright State University) is chair and associate professor in the Communication Department at Salem College, in Winston-Salem, North Carolina. She has experience teaching a wide variety of undergraduate and graduate courses including communication theory, communication research, intercultural communication, public relations, public speaking, organizational communication, journalism, and special topics such as the rhetoric of social intervention. Opt has three main areas of research: social/cultural change from a rhetorical perspective, college students' perceptions of HIV/AIDS, and the relationship of Myers-Briggs personality types to communication variables. Her work has been published in journals such as *Communication Quarterly*, *Journal of Radio Studies*, *Journal of Psychology*, and the *New Jersey Journal of Communication*. She has also authored or co-authored four book chapters. Prior to becoming a full-time academic, Opt worked in the publishing industry as a journalist, typesetter, and book production editor.

Mark A. Gring (Ph.D., The Ohio State University; M.A. & B.S., University of Texas at Austin) is an associate professor of communication studies at Texas Tech University, in Lubbock, Texas. He has taught courses in rhetorical theory, rhetorical criticism, persuasion, communication theory, argumentation and debate, and communication pedagogy at the graduate and undergraduate levels. His research foci include the analysis of religious discourse that brings about sociopolitical change (in the United States and in Latin America), the epistemic nature of rhetorical activity, the application of ideological assumptions to the mass media, and the pedagogy of public speaking. His most recent work has been an analysis of post-9/11 sermons and their response to terrorism and war. His work has appeared in journals such as *Rhetoric and Public Affairs, World Communication Journal, Journalism History, Basic Course Annual,* and *Journal of Communication and Religion.*